EARLY BUDDHISM AND INDIAN THOUGHTS

EARLY BUDDHISM AND INDIAN THOUGHTS

P Pathak

MD PUBLICATIONS PVT LTD
NEW DELHI
www.mdppl.com

Published by :

MD Publications Pvt Ltd
"MD House", 11, Darya Ganj,
New Delhi - 110 002
Phone : +91-11-45355555
E-mail : contact@mdppl.com
Website: www.mdppl.com

ISBN: 978-81-7533-358-1

Published and Printed by Mr. Pranav Gupta on behalf of **MD Publications Pvt Ltd** at Times Press, Delhi.

PREFACE

Buddhism is a world religion, which arose in and around ancient Magadha, India (modern Bihar), and is based on the teachings of Siddhartha Gautama, who is known as the Buddha (literally the Enlightened One or Awakened One). It spread outside of Magadha starting in the Buddha's lifetime, and with the reign of the Buddhist Mauryan Emperor Ashoka, spread across India and became the dominant religion. Followers of Buddhism, called Buddhists in English, referred to themselves as Sakyan-s or Sakyabhiksu in ancient India.

Buddhism has spread outside of India through two main traditions; Theravada which extended south and east and now has widespread following in Southeast Asia, and Mahayana, which diffused first west, then north and later east throughout East Asia. Both traditions have since spread throughout the world, mainly in North America. Buddhism in India began with the life of Siddhartha Gautama (ca. 563-483 B.C.), a prince from the small Shakya Kingdom located in the foothills of the Himalayas in Nepal. Brought up in luxury, the prince abandoned his home and wandered forth as a religious beggar, searching for the meaning of existence.

Several hundreds of years after the advent of Mahayana Buddhism (in the fifth century CE), the early Buddhist schools entered a period of decline in India, while Mahayana Buddhism became stronger. The seventh century Chinese pilgirm Xuanzang reports, however, that non-Mahayana Buddhists continued to comprise a substantial majority of Buddhists in India at that time, and it is likely that this was the case right up to the end of Buddhism in India altogether.

The practice of Buddhism as a distinct and organized religion declined from the land of its origin in around 13th century, but not without leaving a significant impact. Hindus continued to absorb Buddhist practices and teachings, such as meditation and the renunciation of the material world. Buddhist practice is most common in Himalayan areas like Ladakh, Arunachal Pradesh and Sikkim. Buddhism has reemerged as a major faith in India in the past century, thanks to its adoption by many Indian intellectuals, the migration of Tibetan Buddhists displaced by the Chinese invasion, and the mass conversion of hundreds of thousands of Hindu untouchables. Breaking through the final barriers, he achieved the knowledge that he later expressed as the Four Noble Truths: all of life is suffering; the cause of suffering is desire; the end of desire leads to the end of suffering; and the means to end desire is a path of discipline and meditation. Gautama was now the Buddha, or the awakened one, and he spent the remainder of his life traveling about northeast India converting large numbers of disciples. At the age of eighty, the Buddha achieved his final passing away (parinirvana) and died, leaving a thriving monastic order and a dedicated lay community to continue his work.

I am very grateful to Mr. Pranav Gupta, Director of MD Publications Pvt Ltd, New Delhi, for his kind cooperation and support for this book.

P Pathak

CONTENTS

1

Early Buddhism and Indian Thoughts

An Introduction

The Buddhists, who believe that Gotama, the Buddha of the sixth century before Christ, was the twenty-fifth in a line of Buddhas commencing from Dipankara (or the 29th, commencing from Tanhankara), have no difficulty in explaining that the Buddha's reference was to the doctrines of the earlier Buddhas. The Buddhist commentators from very early times accepted this explanation.

In fact, one of them, Buddhaghosa, the most illustrious translator of Sinhala commentaries in the fifth century CE, went further and suggested that the Vedas themselves were only a degenerated version of the teachings of Buddha Kassapa, the immediate predecessor of Gotama, the Buddha. But in the absence of reliable historical data, one does not readily accept this Buddhist tradition. So there has been an attempt to review the statement of the Buddha in the light of what is known for certain of Indian philosophy.

ASSUMPTIONS OR THEORIES OF EARLY SCHOLARS

There are a number of generalised statements by scholars whose genuine quest for the truth is not disputed. They are –

1. That the Buddha restated what was already current among the Brahmanical thinkers of the Indian subcontinent;

2. That the Buddha based his teachings on the teachings of the Upanishads;
3. That the Buddha was a follower of the Yoga system of Patañjali; and
4. That the Buddha's doctrine derives its inspiration from the Samkhya Philosophy.

Each of these statements has been made presumably after careful examination of whatever data were available and, therefore, should be examined with due care.

It was Professor T. W. Rhys Davids who stated most emphatically that the Buddha was in every respect a product of the Brahmanical environment. He says, "Gautama was born and brought up and lived and died a Hindu. Such originality as Gautama possessed lay in the way in which he adopted, enlarged, ennobled and systematised that which had already been well-said by others; in the way in which he carried out to their logical conclusion, principles of equity and justice already acknowledged by some of the most prominent Hindu thinkers. The difference between him and other teachers lay chiefly in his deep earnestness and in his broad public spirit of philanthropy."

Professor Herman Oldenberg in his pioneering work, Buddha, too, was of the same opinion when he said, "It is certain that Buddhism has acquired as an inheritance from Brahmanism not merely a series of its most important dogmas but what is not less significant to the historian, the bent of its religious thought and feeling, which is more easily comprehended than expressed in words."

Much later, Dr. Sarvapalli Radhakrishnan had been the most ardent supporter of these views. In a foreword written in 1956 to the Government of India publication, "2500 years of Buddhism" (ed. P. V. Bapat), he says, "The Buddha did not feel that he was announcing a new religion. He was born, grew up and died a Hindu. ... Buddhism was an offshoot of the more ancient faith of Hindus, perhaps a schism or a heresy."

Dr. Radhakrishnan's assessment of the relationship between Buddhism and Brahmanism has undergone a gradual change. In his magnificent work Indian Philosophy in two volumes published in London in 1927 he began the chapter on Buddhism with the statement, "There is no question that the system of early Buddhism is one of the most original which the history of philosophy presents."

This is followed by the comment, "Early Buddhism is not an absolutely original doctrine. It is not a freak in the evolution of Indian thought. Buddha did not break away completely from the spiritual ideas of his age and country. To be in open revolt against the conventional and legalistic religion of the time is one thing; to abandon the living spirit behind it is another."

THREE PRELIMINARY CONSIDERATIONS

There are a number of points, which should be clarified before we proceed to discuss these views:

The foremost among them is the question of chronology. As far as Buddhism is concerned, chronology presents little difficulty. According to the tradition preserved in Southern Buddhist countries, the demise of the Buddha took place in 544-43 BCE and this date has been fairly satisfactorily established with historical evidence. Even otherwise, the date as accepted by most modern scholars on the basis of Chinese records and Greek and Latin sources is 483 BCE. In a country where events have to be dated vaguely as falling within centuries or even millennia, a difference of sixty years is negligible.

While the date of Buddhism is known with a greater degree of certainty even after considering the recent dates suggested by Western scholars like Heinz Bechert and Richard Gombrich, other philosophical systems have to be dated purely on speculation. But the antiquity of Brahmanism is not disputed even though the actual dates are in dispute. (I have excluded from this discussion the dates as proposed by the publications of Akhil Bharatiya Itihasa Sankalan like Rajendra Singh Kushwaha's Glimpses of Bharatiya History or the prolific writings of David Frawley which call for in-depth scrutiny. In refuting the theory of an Aryan Invasion, these works place the Vedas in the fifth millennium BCE and the Buddha in 1800 BCE).

The Rgveda, which on linguistic and cultural evidence is dated not later than 1500 BCE, is, no doubt, the oldest document of the Aryans, which reflects the growth as well as the consolidation of those religious and philosophical views that ultimately formed the basis of Brahmanism. It is also agreed that the later Samhitas, namely the Smaveda and the Yajurveda, came into existence in their present form at a date not later than 1000 BCE, while the development of the Brahmana literature on sacrificial rites and ceremonies is assumed to have taken place between 1000 BCE and 800 BCE. By this time, two of the fundamental aspects of Brahmanism were well established: namely, the concept and technique of sacrifice and the caste system. Thus, if the Buddha, who lived in the sixth century BCE, was really a follower of the Brahmanical way of life, he should have subscribed to the doctrines relating to these matters even during the earlier phase of his life.

The second problem, which has to be settled as a preliminary step in our discussion is the question of geography. Whether as invaders or as peaceful migrants, the Rgvedic Aryans appear to have come to the Indian subcontinent via the passes in the North-western Frontier Region. The early hymns of the Rgveda refer to geographical features of this region. The ancient settlement of the Aryans in the Indian subcontinent was known as "Sapta-sindhava," that is, "the land of seven rivers."

Though there had been several interpretations of this term by Max Muller, Ludwig, Lassen and Whitney, the most reasonable view appears to be that the seven rivers were the Indus, the five rivers of Punjab and the Sarasvati. The gradual widening of the geographical horizon is reflected in the Rgveda itself. Thus in a later hymn, reference is made to such rivers as Gang and Yamun, which lay further towards the East. In commenting on this hymn, Max Muller said, "It shows us the widest geographical horizon of the Vedic poets, confined by the snowy mountains in the North, the Indus or the sea, in the South and the valley of the Jumna and Ganges in the East. Beyond that, the world, though open, was unknown to the Vedic poets."

The geographical data in the later Samhitas and the Brahmanas merely reveal a drift to the east, but there is no definite evidence either to indicate the route or to mark the eastern-most boundary. If Revottaras in Satapatha-Brahmana is a variation of Reva, the southern boundary of the areas known to Aryans of the Brahmanas might have been the river Narmad. The names of the two cities Kausambi and Kampila in the same Brahmana help to establish the eastern limit with a certain amount of accuracy. But it is presumed that the Aryans had moved further east at the time of the Brahmanas; however, the evidence on which a definite conclusion can be drawn is somewhat vague.

The problem is related to the identification of the river Sadnra mentioned in Satapatha-Brahmana as the boundary between the Kosalas and the Videhas. The mention of Videha is of special significance, as it occurs in a story, which deals with the spread of Aryan culture. Videgha Mathava, with his priest Gotama Rahuga, is said to have carried the sacrificial fire from river Sarasvati to the land across river Sadnara, where the kingdom of Videha was established. This is clearly an indication of the manner in which Brahmanism spread eastwards. It was very unlikely that the Aryans as a hoard invaded or migrated en masse into this region. Only a few adventurers could have gone eastwards to seek their fortune and incidentally to spread their culture.

The accounts found in the epic Ramayana about the Aryanization of the Southern parts of the Indian subcontinent also give us an idea of the role which Ris and Brahmans might have played. They might have spread into the eastern region, too, in a similar manner and established hermitages, which might have served as pockets of Brahmanical culture. This is an important aspect to be borne in mind when the extent to which Brahmanism was known in the east is to be gauged.

There is a third problem, which is closely related to that of the geographical horizon. Were the Aryans the only people who contributed towards the cultural evolution of ancient Indian subcontinent? Only a very few scholars had so far devoted adequate attention to this question. The majority were apparently satisfied with the theory that Aryans, a branch of the Indo-European family, entered the Indian subcontinent through the passes in the North-western Frontier and moved steadily towards the east and the south widening their range of settlements in the shape of a mighty wedge and that their religious and philosophical views evolved gradually from animism to polytheism, and from polytheism to pantheism and monism, while their religious practices ranged from elaborate sacrificial rites to asceticism and pure philosophical speculation.

This, indeed, is a very simple explanation of the cultural processes of ancient Indian subcontinent; but its simplicity is the result of two factors:

Firstly, the pioneering scholars were over-impressed by the volume as well as the character of the ancient Indian literature. Rgveda, the later Samhitas, the Brahmanas, the Aranayakas and the Upanishads, in addition to Vedangas and the later works showed a development in Indian thought which appeared so logical, regular, and sequential. It was, therefore, difficult for them to visualize any other influences, which in their own way could have been adequately formidable as to leave an indelible mark in the cultural pattern of the Indian subcontinent.

Secondly, the real serious work in this field was undertaken and completed long before the discovery of the Indus Valley Civilization, which was a significant eye-opener. It was enough evidence to refute the argument that Aryans met in the Indian subcontinent only aboriginal tribes with no cultural Attainments. The Aryans, in fact, could have come in contact with a superior civilization or mingled with an existing civilization to enrich it further. To imagine that the Indus Valley people merely succumbed to the "Aryan invaders" is idle. What was most likely was a cultural synthesis. What evidence is there to disprove that the culture reflected in the Rgveda and the later Vedic works is not the result of an admixture of the Aryan and Indus Valley cultures? To my mind, the differences, which exist between the Avestan Aryans of Iran and the Rgvedic Aryans of the Indian subcontinent, were brought about by this synthesis. If this was possible, there is nothing to prevent one from concluding that similar cultural contacts were possible in other parts of the Indian subcontinent. It should also be noted here that the general conception has been that various peoples entered the Indian subcontinent through her passes in the North-west.

Were there no other migrations to the Indian subcontinent? Could not some tribes find a way by her passes in the North-east? In fact, the Aryan migrants themselves could have moved into the North-eastern region of the Indian subcontinent and settled down long before the Rgvedic Aryans came. Who were the Vrtyas? There were also other possibilities. The Chinese, too, were active in very early times. They had evolved a highly developed culture and were in a position to influence these parts of the Indian subcontinent culturally and by physical presence. One would, however, call for evidence. It should be admitted that there are no documents whatsoever to support this contention. But there is one very important piece of evidence.

There are two references in Buddhist literature and the Ramayana to kings of North-eastern Indian subcontinent, who were playing a leading role in the agricultural life of the people. In the Buddhist works, we meet King Suddhodana of Kapilavatthu participating in ceremonial ploughing. The king is said to have been at the head of the train of people who ploughed their fields on this ceremonial occasion. Similarly, the Ramayana narrates how King Janaka found Sita on the occasion of ceremonial ploughing. This custom finds no reference in the Vedic literature.

The only parallel, which one aware of, is from Chinese culture. As far back as the Shang Period (1760 -1122 BCE) the

Chinese had evolved the concept of the farmer-emperor and had maintained the traditional rite of the emperor ploughing a field at the Temple of Earth at the beginning of each year until the fall of the Manchu dynasty two centuries ago.

BUDDHISM AND BRAHMANISM

The issues are so complicated that one cannot afford to be too confident, as both Professor Rhys Davids and Dr. Radhakrishnan had been in summarily stating that the Buddha was born, grew up and died a Hindu. Let us take the data at our disposal. As the Vedic texts do not give us any definite material to establish.the relationship between Brahmanism and Buddhism, we should search for evidence in Buddhist literature. From the Pali Canon, whose authenticity is the least in dispute, we find that Buddhist circles of the Indian subcontinent in the east were familiar with the Vedas and the principles of Brahmanism. The early texts of the Buddhist Canon speak of the Three Vedas, the Devayna, Rgvedic gods, the Svitr hymn of twenty-four syllables, some of the Vedic Sikhas such as Addhariya, Tittiriya, Chandoka, Chandava, and Brahmacariya, and a list of Vedic seers which recurs a number of times as the ancient Risi, composers of the Mantras.

They were also quite conversant with the subject-matter of the Brahmanas. The fire sacrifice and also Asavamedha, Puruamedha and Vajapeya are referred to. Analysing the Brahmanadhammika Sutta of the Suttanipta, it will be seen that the contemporary religious practices were identical with those of the Brahmanas. Sacrifices attended by bloodshed were the normal procedure and the Buddha vehemently opposed them. The Brahmanadhammika Sutta is an unambiguous exposition of the Buddha's attitude to both Brahmans and their ritual; he traces a gradual degeneration of the Brahmans from selfless seekers after truth to money-grabbing sacrificers who kill cattle and persuade kings to perform sacrifices, saying, and "Much indeed is your wealth".

Increase it by the performance of sacrifice." The Buddha states that even Indra and other deities discard these

Brahmans. Similar, and even more severe, Attacks on the ancient Brahmana institution of sacrifice are found in abundance in the Buddhist Canon. Not only-were sacrificial rites the target of the Buddha's Attacks; the caste system of the Brahmans too was severely criticised. The standpoint of the Buddha is, however, too well known to be discussed in detail. It will, nevertheless, suffice me to state that the Buddha was opposed to the caste system from both the spiritual and the social point of view. As a teacher of a lofty code of ethics, he revolted against the unfair discrimination against humans on grounds of birth.

Further, as a Kshatriya he treated the Brahmans with little respect. It is interesting to note how the Buddha winds up an argument on caste in the Ambahasutta of the Dighanikya by reciting an ancient stanza to the effect that the Kshatriyas are the best of men. There should be no doubt from these data that the Buddha was not prepared to accept either of the two fundamental principles of Brahmanism. Dr. Radhakrishnan, of course, is unable to refute it. But he considers that the open revolt against these does not constitute a complete breakaway from the spiritual ideas of his age and country.

This is no doubt true, provided it is conceded that Brahmanism, alone, did not constitute the spiritual ideas of the Buddha's age and the part of the country in which he lived and taught. The need for such a proviso is based on the fact that even the metaphysics and ethics, which the Buddha preached, had developed with no direct connection with Brahmanism. For instance, Brahmanism places very little emphasis on ethics. It is impossible even to imagine that the inspiration for such codes of ethics as one meets in Buddhism and Jainism came from the Vedic literature.

Buddhist ethics are closely related to the ascetic ideal of life it upholds. But one does not find that aspect of religious life in any Vedic texts of the pre-Buddhist times. The evidence in both Buddhism and Jainism leads most poignantly to a conclusion that the religious values of the Northeastern region of the Indian subcontinent were more ethical and that they were connected with the doctrines of Karma and Rebirth, which were specifically non-Brahmanical in origin.

The ascetic ideal developed with the aid of such doctrines. Dr. E. J. Thomas was correct when he said in A History of Buddhist Thought, that "probably pre-Aryan influences were at work"; presumably what he meant by 'pre-Aryan' is really the non-Brahmanical Sramana Cult, whose origins seem to extend to the Indus Valley Civilization. The doctrines of Karma and Rebirth are neither Vedic nor Brahmanical. They find no reference in the early Vedic literature. The Chandogya Upanishad, in fact, gives some valuable data to establish the contention that Brahmans knew nothing about these doctrines. It says,

"As to what you have told me, O! Gautama, this knowledge has never yet come to Brahmans before you and therefore in all the world has the rule belonged to the Kshatriya only."

In the seventh Chapter of Chandogya Upanishad, we come across another interesting statement: Narada, apparently the revered Risi of the Brahmanas, comes to Sanatkumra, saying, 'Teach me, Sir." Sanatkumra teaches him the doctrines of soul and karma. It is not so much the doctrines, which draw our attention as the name, Sanatkumra. We meet him so often in the Buddhist literature; the Buddha himself refers to him as a Kshatriya teacher.

Even though not marshalled enough data to warrant a definite conclusion, one may yet venture to hazard the opinion that even the fundamental Upanishadic teachings arose in the East and their propagation was particularly sponsored by the kings of Videha and Kasi among whom Janaka and Ajatasatru find specific mention in the Bhadrayaka Upanishad.

These data will no doubt show that Buddhism can in no way be called a restatement of Brahmanical teachings.

BUDDHISM AND THE TEACHINGS OF THE UPANISHADS

Let us now examine the second statement that the Buddha based his system on the teachings of the Upanishads. The earlier scholars were not emphatic in associating Buddhism with the Upanishads. For instance, Professor Max Muller merely stated, "In that fifth century B.C. took place the rise of Buddhism, a religion built up on the ruins of the Vedic religion, and founded, so to say, on the denial of the divine authority ascribed to the Veda by all orthodox Brahmans."

It was George Grimm, who in 1926 in his The Doctrine of the Buddha, hinted at a possible connection between the two systems. He said, "Thus the Buddha has not become untrue to Indian thinking; rather is his doctrine the flower of Indian thought. He is 'the true Brahmana,' who has completely realized the ideal of the Upanishads. And precisely because this is so, India will again greet him as her greatest son, as soon as she again shall have recognized this."

The Indian subcontinent was not so late in recognizing this, for in the very next year, Dr. Radhakrishnan in his Indian Philosophy advanced the theory that the Buddha was not so much creating a new dharma as rediscovering an old norm. It was presented most cautiously as a conjecture. He said, "Early Buddhism, we venture to hazard a conjecture, is only a restatement of the thought of the Upanishads from a new standpoint."

He also explained the manner in which the doctrines of the Upanishads were adapted by the Buddha:

"To develop his theory Buddha had only to rid the Upanishads of their inconsistent compromises with Vedic polytheism and religion, set aside the transcendental aspect as being indemonstrable to thought and unnecessary to morals and emphasize the ethical universalism of the Upanishads."

Further in his discussion of early Buddhism he admittedly assumed that the spirit of the Upanishads is the life-spring of Buddhism. Let us examine these views in the light of what is revealed by the Buddhist Canon. First and foremost, the absence of any reference to the Upanishads should be noted. There is, however, a Pali word upanis which some have attempted to explain as meaning the Upanishads. In verse 75 of the *Dhammapada*, this word occurs in the following form:

"Ann lbhpanis aññ nibbagmi". In *Majjhimanikya* II, it occurs in a compound as "*Samadhi* saupanisa." In both contexts the only permissible meaning is that of upanisaraya (cause or means).

BRAHMANA, ATMAN AND BRAHMASAHAVYAT

The two main terms of the Upanishads, Brahmana and *Atman* are, however, profusely used in the Suttas. At first sight the shades of meaning and the philosophical import of these terms seem to reveal an actual relationship between the Upanishads and Buddhism. But a more careful examination reveals entirely different results. The term Brahma, which is always used in the masculine sense in Buddhist texts, refers to the personal God. The Upanishadic notion of a neuter principle is not found in the Buddhist Canon.

Here Brahma is described in the Brahmajalasutta as the great Brahma, the conqueror, the unconquered, the all-seeing, the controller, the lord, the maker, the creator, the greatest, the mover, the powerful and the father of all past and future beings. In the Kevasutta he is not even omniscient. The epithets used for Brahma elsewhere in the Canon, too, have no relation to the Upanishadic principle. Here the Brahma is said to be celibate, free of hatred, malice and stain and very powerful, while the Upanishadic Brahman can only be described in negative terms as imperishable, infinite, unqualified and neti neti (not this only, not that only).

There is in the Tevijjsutta an important term. The Buddha, in discussing the religious practices of Brahmans, states that the goal of such rites is "Brahmasahavyat" (the company of Brahma). Dr. I. G. Jennings believes that this reference is to the neuter Brahma of the Vedanta and in his The Vedantic Buddhism of the Buddha, interprets "Sahavyat" as complete absorption. It is rather difficult to assume that the Upanishadic concept of a universal soul into which individual souls were re-absorbed is what is expressed in this Sutta. On the other hand, one can discern a more ancient and primitive concept behind this term. "Brahmasahavyat" appears in all likelihood to be a synonym of "Brahmasalokat"; that is, being in the same realm as the personal god Brahma. The path for the Attainment of this state is given in the Tevijjsutta.

It is plainly the Vedic karma-marga - the path of sacrifice. The preachers of this path are listed and we do not find the names of Upanishadic teachers of repute such as Yajñavalkya, Uddalaka, Sakalya or Gargi. Instead, we meet Ahaka, Vamaka, Vamadeva, Vessmitta, Yamataggi, Angrasa, Bharadvja, Vaseha, Kassapa and Bhagu. These were really the composers of Rgvedic hymns. How it was that Buddhist literature shows no knowledge of the great Upanishadic thinkers? My contention, therefore, is that the fundamental doctrine of a universal soul from which the individual souls emanated and into which they should ultimately return was also unknown in the Buddhist circles. The trends of Indian philosophy with which they were familiar belonged to an earlier era than that of the Upanishads.

Let us examine the philosophical import of the other Upanishadic term so frequently used in the Buddhist Canon. "*Atman*" occurs in the Suttas in both a positive form, *Atta* and a negative formulation, *Anatta*. *Atta*, in addition to being a reflexive pronoun, means the "soul." In this sense it finds no place in Buddhist philosophy, but occurs always in the criticisms and enunciations of rival teachings. Thus we hear of sixteen ways how *Atta* is conscious after death, eight ways how it is unconscious and not subject to decay and seven ways how it is annihilated. As such, we have here an opportunity of investigating the traces, if any, of the Upanishadic concept of *Atman* in the theories of *Atta* known to the Buddha.

Atta as identical with the body was a concept well-known in Buddhist circles. Pohapada speaks of a material (*Olarika*) *Atta*, having a form composed of the four elements and enjoying food (rupi, catumahbhtika, Kabalinkhrabhakkha). Also, the Buddha is reported to have said, "It would be better if an uninstructed person should consider as his *Atta* this body composed of the four elements, rather than the mind." There are a few places in the Canon, where the *Atta* and the form (*rupa*) are treated as identical: "My form is the *Atta*" (*Rupa me Atta*):" Commentarial literature explains it as "He looks upon the form and *Atta* as indivisible."

This conception of *Atta* evinces some resemblance to certain views found in the old Upanishads. The Bhadrayaka Upanishad states, "His body (*Atman*) indeed is his work, for with his body he performs work." Taittirya I, 4 further remarks "This indeed, is its bodily self." But the *Atman* as Sarra marks only a very primitive stage of the Upanishadic speculations and is turned down as an imperfect understanding, which satisfies only the Asuras. Furthermore, it can be questioned whether a material *Atta* as described by Pohapda refers to the Upanishadic or the Caravka materialistic teachings of *Atman*.

A second *Atta* is mind-made (Manomaya), comprising all major and minor limbs and not devoid of sense-organs (Sabbanga-paccangim ahnindriya).' The notion of *Atman* as the mind, the receptacle of sense-perceptions, no doubt, represents also a stage, though a passing one, in the gradual development of the Upanishadic *Atman* concept. If the rather ambiguous statement in *Anguttaranikya*, "Att te purisa ajnti sacca va yadi va mus" can be explained as "Your *Atman*, 0 men, knows if it is true or false," we can surmise that the *Atman* as the subject of sense perception was a notion familiar to the early Buddhists.

The third *Atta* enunciated by Pohapada, is formless and made of *Sanna* (consciousness). The old Upanishads, however, refer to a formless *Atman* made of *Sanna*. But we may consider that this notion has its prototype in the old Upanisadic prajñâmaya-*Atman*.

A fourth theory postulates an *Atman*, which is eternal (Sassato) and having form and consciousness. These four theories of *Atman* can be connected only with certain stages in the development of the Upanishadic *Atman* concept as observed by Betty Heimann in her Studien Zur Eigenart Indischen Denkens. But the fully developed Upanishadic *Atman* as the imperishable, unperceived all-functioner, the inner controller, that is immanent in all beings and things of the Universe and is identical with the super-personal creative, underlying and re-absorbing principle of Brahmana, is neither here nor anywhere in the Buddhist Canon expounded.

On the other hand, the *Atta* which is denied in Buddhism is more a psychological illusion of Ahakra (I-ness) and Mamatva (My-ness). Hence the formulation of the Buddha's refutation of *Atta* runs as "Na eta mama. Na eso aha asmi. Na me eso *Atta*." The Anattalakkhasutta emphatically states that there is no *Atta* - or rather room for *Atta* - for one cannot determine for one's self how one's *rupa, Vedana, sanna,* etc., should be. Physical change from growth to decay in bodily existence is a natural law beyond human control. This teaching of *Anatta,* as far as the Suttas go, compares only with the Nirmamatva and the Nirtmakatvam of later Upanishads like the Maitryana Upanishad, which had been strongly influenced by the teachings of Yogic system and even quite likely by Buddhism.

While the Buddha stresses man's incapacity to control the course of natural evolution and stops at a negation, the Upanishads postulate an inner controller (Antar-ymin) in the form of the *Atman,* who is identical with the Brahmana or the Paramatman. Brahmana, again, it is taught, transcends the relativity, the impermanence and the imperfection of the single *Atman.*

NAMARUPA, SAMSARA AND NIRVANA

We shall also consider, now, the apparently common notions of *Namarupa, Samsara* and Nirvana. *Namarupa* in the Upanishads is a term suggesting two concrete and empirical factors, viz., the name or designation and the form. Every embodied *Atman* has a *Nama* and a *Rupa*. In Buddhism the term *Namarupa* is given a new and wider interpretation. The five aggregates or the component parts (*khandhas*), which constitute a being, are divided into the two categories of *Nama* and *Rupa,* where *Nama* represents the four psychological phenomena of *Vedana, Sanna,* Sakhra and *Vinnana*. The belief in *Samsara* was common to all sects of the Indian subcontinent other than the Carvakas since the times of the Brahmanas and hence it can be regarded as belonging to the religious and philosophical public property of the Indian subcontinent. The direct influence of the Upanisads, therefore, is not necessarily to be surmised here.

With regard to the concept of Nirvana, we have to apply a slightly different method. It is true that the word "Nirvana" occurs, not in the old and the middle Upanishads, but only in the Bhagavada Gita and later Upanishads, such as Aruneya Upanishad and Nirvana Upanisad, which are later than Buddhism. Even if we could assume that Buddhism here has influenced Hindu thought, the contents of the Upanishadic Nirvana or the Brahma-Nirvana concept develop not on Buddhist lines, but under the influence of pre-Buddhist Upanishadic notions. In Buddhism, Nirvana, whether it is complete cessation of existence or a state of ending all suffering is a form of liberation Attained through psychological development. It is a Yogic Attainment. The Upanishadic Nirvana or Brahmanairvana, on the other hand, is the re-absorption into the universal source of Brahmana, caused by the realization of the true knowledge that the *Atman* is essentially the same as Brahmana.

With this survey we may arrive at the conclusion that the Buddha and his disciples, whose speeches and discourses are recorded in the Canon, knew for certain the Vedas and the Brahmanas; they were quite conversant with the Brahmanic ritual. But their knowledge of the Upanishads was not complete in so far as they did not take into consideration the climax of Upanishadic teachings: namely, the cosmic doctrines of Brahmana and *Atman*, which are united in a primary and final, pre- and post-empirical, stage. The Buddhist circles knew Brahmana as a personal deity - Brahma, and *Atman* as a psychological and merely individual factor. In the Tripitaka, as a whole, a characteristic vagueness pervades all that is akin to the Upanishadic teachings.

It is very doubtful whether one can still hold the view that the Upanishadic teachings were the life-spring of Buddhism. The absurdity of the claim made by some writers that the Buddha's contribution to Indian thought was made in the role of a popularizer of Upanishadic doctrines should be abundantly clear from the foregoing discussion of actual literary data. A comparison of the essential doctrines of the two systems will throw further light.

2

The Basic Difference Between Buddhism and the Upanishadic Philosophy

ORIGIN AND NATURE OF THE UNIVERSE

The basic difference between Buddhism and the Upanishadic philosophy relates to their notions of the origin and the nature of the Universe. It is true that the Buddha was not inclined to discuss the question of the Universe seriously, simply because he pragmatically considered that such knowledge, though of academic interest, did not contribute towards the salvation of humankind. His attitude was vividly expressed by means of the parable of the wounded man. "When a man is shot at with an arrow and a doctor comes to attend on him, the primary concern of the wounded man should be to have the arrow removed and the wound attended to. Instead, if he were to inquire as to whom shot the arrow, what his caste or complexion or stature was, he would, long before the answers are found, succumb to the injury."

Thus from the Buddha's point of view, the search was meaningless and hence to be abandoned in preference to the path that leads one to complete deliverance. But, on the other hand, the Upanishadic philosophy has no foundation if its teachings relating to the origin of the universe are not there. The neuter principle of Brahmana, the active as well as the material cause of the Universe, is an essential concept. The Universe comes into existence when all phenomena including individual souls emanate from it and the end of suffering (and hence the final bliss) lies in the reabsorption into it. By its very nature, it has to be permanent and static.

Unborn, imperishable, immutable and eternal, the Brahmana is the very antithesis of change. Such a view is repugnant to the Buddhist concept of the nature of the Universe. According to the Buddha, impermanence is the very nature of all existence. There is nothing that escapes this universal law. An eternal phenomenon even as the first principle is unimaginable. This doctrine of impermanence goes hand in hand with that of Dependent Causation or Origination.

There is no cause, which is uncaused. Existence is the result of an ever-continuing chain of actions and reactions; one thing leads to another and that to a further thing. This doctrine of Dependent Causation or Origination, called the *Paticca-samuppada* (Walpola Rahula p. 53ff) is the most salient contribution made by the Buddha to Indian thought. With this the Buddha shattered the very foundation of the Upanishadic philosophy. Neither the Brahmana nor the *Atman*s can retain their Upanishadic character when viewed from the point of view of *Paticca-samuppada*. Therefore, can one continue to recognize in the Buddha's mission a direct or even an indirect attempt to propagate or popularise Upanishadic teachings?

BUDDHISM AND PATAÑJALI YOGA

Let us now examine the third statement, namely, that the Buddha was a follower of the Yoga system of Patañjali. On purely chronological grounds this contention stands disproved. Though the orthodox Hindus claim a hoary antiquity for Patañjali, there is no evidence to date him earlier than 300 BCE. In fact the general consensus of opinion is that the date of Patanjali's Yoga Stra falls between 300 and.100 BCE. But the Yoga system is very old; perhaps, it is even older than Rgveda.

In several seals discovered in the Indus Valley, there is a figure seated in a conventional yogic posture. Yoga, however, is not referred to in any early Vedic texts. The earliest references are in the later Upanisads such as the Kaha, Taittirya and the Maitryani. These works are more or less contemporaneous with the Buddha, if not later. But they do not give us any definite or detailed information of the Yogic system. On the other hand, the Buddhist texts evince a greater familiarity with Yogic practices. The Buddha was not only conversant with this system but also ready to adapt it to his path of deliverance. From the accounts of the Buddha's quest for deliverance, it is clear that the teachers, Alra Kalama and Uddaka Ramaputta, to whom he went for instruction, were masters of Yoga, and the spiritual attainments which he experienced under their guidance, were Yogic in character.

The term "Yoga" occurs in the Pali Canon, though not in the sense of a particular system of spiritual training. In most contexts, it means:

1. Application, endeavour, undertaking, effort
2. Magic power or spells and
3. Bondage, tie, Attachment.

The term "Yogi" occurs in older verses and here it is used as a synonym for "muni." A Bhikkhu, devoted to meditation and spiritual exercises is called a "Yogavacara" which need not strictly mean "one who is at home in Yoga" because the first part of the compound can also mean simply 'endeavour'. Thus "Yogavacara" can mean a bhikkhu who is dedicated to spiritual endeavour. Similarly the frequent epithet to Nibban, "Yogakkhema" does not necessarily mean "safety gained through Yoga", as the general interpretation as "peace from bondage" appears justifiable.

Again, in a statement like "savna khayya yogo karayo" in the Dutiya Samadhisutta of *Anguttaranikya*, the term "Yoga" is used more as a common noun meaning "endeavour or effort" than as a proper noun denoting a philosophical system. Likewise, the two Buddhist texts, which are called Yogasuttas in the Samyutta and *Anguttaranikya*, refer to fourfold bond of sensual desire, becoming, wrong view and ignorance. While a doubt thus exists as to the term "Yoga," the terminology of the Yogic system is frequently confronted in the Buddhist Canon. *Samadhi, Jhana (Dhyana), Sampatti, Sayama,* etc. occur in identical meanings in both Buddhist and Yogic systems.

Besides the terminological similarities, which are not unusual as all religious and philosophical systems of the Indian subcontinent used a common vocabulary, there are many resemblances in practices, which establish the dependence of Buddhism on early Yogic teachings. With the paramount importance assigned by the Buddha to the purification of the mind as an essential part of a person's spiritual training, meditation and the control of the mind are fundamental to the Buddhist path of deliverance.

The mind, which according to Buddhism is the sixth sense organ, is fickle and subject to constant change; it has to be brought under one's control. For this purpose, many forms of mental culture are recommended by the Buddha. The development of mindfulness by pondering over subjects of meditation is stated to be the surest way to control one's mind and thereby attain the goal of spiritual pursuit. In a very early text, the Mahsatipahnasutta of both Dighanikya and *Majjhimanikya,* embodying a sermon which the Buddha had preached on his own accord, four subjects of meditation, namely, the human body, sensations, thoughts and mind-objects were described as the "Foundations of Mindfulness."

The preparation for meditation outlined in this text is not only reminiscent of Yoga but also adumbrates a system, which the Yoga Sutras had subsequently elaborated. Here the "Yogavacara" is enjoined to find a quiet place, free from disturbances, such as a forest, the foot of a tree or an empty house. He should sit cross-legged with his body erect and then he should proceed to mindful breathing (*anapanasati*), by which he is expected to breathe in and out consciously and with awareness.

The subjects of meditation are taken up when the mind is calmed and brought to a point of concentration through this meditation. This process, though only briefly presented in the Buddhist text, includes the salient elements of the eight-fold method of Yoga advocated by the Yoga Sutras, which is as follows:-

- *Yama* -abstension (equivalent to *sila* or moral purity of Buddhism).
- *Niyama* -observance of internal and external purification (also included in Buddhist sila).
- *Sana* -posture, which has to be easy, comfortable and steady (which corresponds to the requirement in Buddhism that the meditator should sit cross-legged with the body erect).
- *Pranayama* - regulation of breath (comparable to the Buddhist concept of "Mindfulness in regard to breathing" though not quite correctly. The Buddhist *anapanasati* calls for only awareness or mindfulness of the process of breathing e.g. whether the breathing is brisk or slow etc. But the Yogic Pranayama is a deliberate regulation of the breath according to set patterns which should be mastered with conscious effort, guidance and practice.).
- *Pratyhara*- withdrawal of the senses.
- *Dhyana* -fixed attention or trance.
- *Dhra* -contemplation, and
- *Samadhi* -concentration.

The similarity which exists between the four dhynas of Buddhism and four states of conscious concentration in Yoga as well as their common emphasis on faith, energy, thought, concentration and wisdom are also noteworthy.

The striking point of divergence between the Buddhist concept and the Yogic system is the importance attached to the state of *Samadhi*. In the Yoga Sutras, *Samadhi* is the ultimate goal and from it precede other attainments such as suspended animation, levitation, knowledge of past births and others' minds and also the mastery over the first cause which results in absolute independence (*kaivalya*). But in Buddhism, *Samadhi* is only an intermediary step in spiritual training, Sila or moral purity being the first and *Paññâ* or insight (i.e. the realization of the true nature of life as embodied in the Four Noble Truths etc.) being the final stages. Such an extension of the Yogic concept of the ultimate goal is understandable in Buddhism because the Buddha reportedly rejected the teachings of his Yogic teachers on the ground that they did not go far enough.

Another significant factor, which should be noticed in comparing Buddhism with Yoga, is the acceptance by the Buddha of higher mental Attainments of Yoga as not only possible and desirable but also as conducive to one's spiritual perfection. But these, in Buddhist texts, are not claimed to be intrinsically Buddhist for many an ascetic is said to have possessed Yogic powers even before the appearance of the Buddha. Besides, the use of Yogic powers of levitation, knowledge of others' thoughts etc. for purposes of worldly gain and renown has been strongly criticized by the Buddha.

The above facts very clearly show that the Buddha, besides knowing the Yoga as an ancient system of spiritual training, accepted its fundamental doctrines and, in evolving his system of mental culture, went beyond what the Yoga laid down. The elaborate system of meditation, which the Buddha formulated with as many as forty subjects of meditation, thirteen vows of physical restraint, and many aids for concentration, had an effect on the development of classical Yoga, while the developed Yoga techniques subsequently influenced the evolution of the Yogcra Buddhist school.

BUDDHISM AND SAMKHYA PHILOSOPHY

The last of the statements, which discuss, necessitates a reference to Dr. Radhakrishnan. He says in his Indian Philosophy, "The relation of Samkhya to early Buddhism has given rise to much speculation as to mutual borrowing. Though Samkhya works, which have come down to us, are later than the origin of Buddhism, and may have been influenced by Buddhist theories, the Samkhya ideas themselves preceded Buddha and it is impossible to regard Buddhism as the source of the Samkhya If the Buddhist chain of causation resembles in some respects, the Samkhya theory of evolution, it is because both of them have for their common source the Upanishads."

Further on, he says,

"It seems to be very probable that the earliest form of the Samkhya was a sort of realistic theism, approaching the Vicœiadvaita view of the Upanishads. While this type of Samkhya may be regarded as a legitimate development of the teaching of Upanishads, the dualistic Samkhya, which insists on the plurality of Puruas and the independence of Prakti and drops all account of the Absolute can hardly be said to be in line with the teachings of the Upanishads. The question is how did it happen that the Samkhya rejected the idea of the Absolute, which alone could make the system satisfactory? The Samkhya did not become a well-co-ordinated system until after the rise of Buddhism. When Buddhism offered a challenge to realism, the Samkhya accepted the challenge and argued on strictly rational grounds for the reality of selves and objects. When it developed on a purely rationalistic soil, it was obliged to concede that there was no proof for the existence of God."

The relationship between the Samkhya system and Buddhism cannot be traced with any degree of certainty. The dissimilarities between them are as strong as the similarities. If Dr. Radhakrishnan is correct in his view that the Samkhya was theistic at the beginning and that its theory of God was abandoned as a result of Buddhist influence, it is the Samkhya system that is indebted to Buddhism. If the Samkhya did drop one of its fundamental principles in deference to Buddhism, it is most likely that other aspects of the system were also influenced by Buddhism.

The non-acceptance of the theistic principle, which characterizes both Buddhism and the Samkhya system, is the most conspicuous similarity between the two systems and has naturally raised the question of possible borrowings and influence in either direction. Dr. Arthur Berridale Keith in A History of Samkhya Philosophy dismissed the possibility of the development of the Samkhya system out of Buddhism. He says, "It is true that Samkhya abandons the idea of existence of the Absolute, but it is, on the other hand, careful to retain the idea of spirit and nature; the doctrine of Buddhism, on the other hand, has in effect abandoned these two conceptions, and has left itself with only the fleeting series of mental states as a quasi reality, from which the development of the doctrine of the void is a natural enough step. It is impossible to prove, and certainly not plausible to believe, that from so developed a doctrine as that of Buddhism there could have grown the Samkhya, which is indeed not a believer in the Absolute, but as little a believer in the view that the only existing principle is the law of movement, which in essence is the view of Buddhism."

With regard to the view that Buddhism could have been influenced by Samkhya concepts, Dr. Keith, like most other scholars who attempted to examine this issue, confronted the difficulty caused by the fact that the works on classical Samkhya were of a much later origin than Buddhism. He felt that the Samkhya as found in the Epics might be compared with Buddhism. Here, too, his conclusion was speculative:

"It seems best, therefore, to draw the conclusion that Buddhism did not draw its inspiration from the Samkhya in the form in which it appears even in the epic, for there the doctrine of the isolation of spirit and nature and of the three Gunas is fully and completely evolved."

But no less than twelve points of similarity are traceable between the two systems, viz.

i. Negation of or indifference to theism.
ii. The belief in constant evolution (*parinamanityatva*.)
iii. The denunciation of Vedic sacrifices and ascetic extravagances as well as the open hostility to caste system or the laxity with regard to Brahmanical restrictions.
iv. The acceptance of suffering or misery as the nature of life.
v. The role played by saskra (impressions) and vsans (tendencies) of past lives in determining the conditions of present and future lives.
vi. The renunciation of the concept of self, expressed in

Buddhism as "Ne'ta mama; N'eso'ham asmi; Na m'eso att ' (This does not belong to me; this am I not; this is not my Self) and in the Samkhya as "Nasmi, na me, naham" (I am not; naught is mine; the ego exists not), as fundamental to deliverance.

vii. The stress on the concept of causality or the law of cause and effect.

viii. The correspondence between the four noble truths of Buddhism with the Samkhya view of the disease (that from which release is to be sought), health (final release), the cause of disease (the cause of that from which release is to be sought) and healing (the means of Attaining release).

ix. The adoption of yogic approach of meditation, (*dhyana*) as the path of release in both systems.

x. The emphasis laid on ignorance as the cause of bondage and suffering.

xi. The postulation of deliverance as the end of existence through knowledge by the elimination of avijja in Buddhism and aviveka in Sankhya and;

xii. The correspondence between the Buddhist doctrine of Sopadisesa and Anupadisesa Nibbana with the Samkhya concept of Jivanmukta and Videhakaivalya.

These similarities, however, fail to establish any lines of influence from Samkhya to Buddhism or vice versa because these broad points of agreement lose their significance when fundamental details are examined. While the approach to causality is common to the two systems, the theory of causation of one system differs from the other so vastly that each has to be stretched to its utmost to admit a semblance of what the other teaches. This is what Dr. Hermann Jacobi did not realize when he came to the conclusion that the mere correspondence between the twelve principles of the Buddhist doctrine of Dependent Causation (Paticcasamuppda) and the evolution series of the Samkhya proved the dependence of the Buddha on the Samkhya teachings.

The significant difference, which existed in the order of

evolution and in the stress laid on the evolution were glossed over by him altogether. Firstly, the Sankhya system begins with the postulation of a permanent entity, Purua; secondly, the Samkhya Chain of Causation explains the evolution of the material aspect of the universe. In both respects the Buddhist *Paticca-samuppada* is different. While no permanent entity is recognised here, it explains the evolution of the individual.

An examination of the literary data may also prove useful. Dr. Heinrich Zimmer in his Philosophies of India says,

"Sankhya is referred to in the Buddhist Pali Canon and Buddhist legends mention Kapila as one of the predecessors of the Buddha."

Apparently Dr. Zimmer was depending on Dr. Rajendra Lal Mitra's statement quoted in Dr. Radhakrishnan's Indian Philosophy,

"There is abundant evidence, both in Hindu and Buddhist works, of unquestionable antiquity and authenticity of the Samkhya and Yoga systems having been current before the time of Buddha".

Both Dr. Radhakrishnan and Dr. Zimmer refer to the Brahmajlasutta of the Dghanikya, wherein, among the sixty-two heretical teachings the Buddha describes a system of philosophy comparable to the Sankhya;

"There are, 0, Bhikkhus, some recluses and Brahmans who are eternalists, and who on four grounds proclaim that both the soul and the world are eternal. They are addicted to logic and reasoning and give utterance to the following conclusions of their own, beaten out by their argumentation and based on their sophistry. 'Eternal is the soul; and the world is steadfast as a mountain peak, as a pillar firmly fixed; and these living creatures, though they pass from birth to birth, fall from one existence and spring up in another; yet they are for ever and ever."

But the Samkhya system is not referred to by name in the Buddhist Pali Canon. While several Brahmans by the name of Kapila are mentioned in the Canon, only one, who may resemble the founder of the Samkhya system, is referred to in the *Udana* Commentary as an ancient teacher who taught that soul was limitless (na antav).

A very interesting word occurs often in the Pali Canon as an epithet to the higher life of renunciation and religious training: Sankha-likhhitam Brahmacariyam. The meaning of this expression is obscure and the commentaries explain it as "likhitasankha-sadisa, dhota-sankha-sappaibhga" - pure, bright or perfect like the polished, inscribed or washed mother-of-pearl". This interpretation is not only far-fetched but also too figurative to be used in otherwise prosaic contexts as a frequent qualification for the life of religious training.

One may, therefore, wonder whether the expression "Sankha-likhita" bears any reference to a form of religious life, which had been associated with the Samkhya system. Patrick Olivelle's study of Yatidharmasamuccaya in his Rules and Regulations of Brahmanical Asceticism has thrown much light on the identification of Sankha and Likhita as two ancient and duly recognized authorities on asceticism. Amidst such authorities as Saunaka, Yajnavalkya, Jabali, Gargi and others, these two are referred to individually and, quite frequently, jointly as exponents of certain specific aspects of ascetic life. Whether Sankha has anything to do with Samkhya is nowhere suggested.

Asavaghosa, in circa 100 CE gave a clue which may be usefully pursued in our attempt to trace the connection between Buddhism and the Samkhya system. In his poem on the life of the Buddha, Buddhacarita, Alara (i. e. Alra Kalama) is said to have held Samkhya views in a theistic setting. To what extent Aœvaghoa relied on a now-lost tradition, we cannot be sure; but the association of Samkhya beliefs with a theistic element therein is not altogether untenable. Yoga has been very closely related to the Samkhya system from very early times and Yoga was founded on a theistic footing.

There is every reason to believe that a teacher of the calibre of Alara Kalama could be an exponent of the combined teachings of Samkhya and Yoga. Whatever similarities, exist between Buddhism and the Samkhya, can be explained as a reflection of the Buddha's philosophical training under Alara Kalama. The Buddha and his disciples were not only aware but familiar with the teachings of Samkhya. Hence Dr. E. J. Thomas in A History of Buddhist Thought asks the question, "Did Buddhism get its notions of Samkhya through the Yoga philosophy?

The data so far presented seem to permit the conclusion that the Buddha treated the Samkhya teachings in identically the same manner as he dealt with the Yogic teachings. He used them in the formulation of his system of philosophy but went beyond their scope rejecting what was inapplicable. But the Samkhya, he knew, was not the developed system of the classical age. The classical Samkhya, on the other hand, can be shown to owe much of its development to Buddhism.

This brief survey of the place of Buddhism in Indian thought has brought to light a number of significant facts:

Firstly, the inadequacy of the current theories about the cultural evolution of the Indian subcontinent was strongly felt. There is a need to re-examine the data available with a view to assessing the pre-Aryan and other influences on Indian thought.

Secondly, the question of the relationship between Upanishadic philosophy and Buddhism is not so simple as to be dismissed with the generalized statement that Buddhism is another version of the Upanishads. The issues involved are so complicated that one should go deeper into details; it is idle to talk in terms of the spirit behind the Upanishads and general impressions, which unfortunately tend to be highly subjective. Literary data, alone, can give a full picture and with the evidence, which could be collected from the Pali Texts, there was adequate proof that the most popular theory on the subject is unacceptable. And this applies not only to the Upanishadic problem but also to that of the Samkhya system.

Lastly, the contributions to Indian thought made by the Buddha should be carefully borne in mind. It was no doubt the Buddha's admirable sense of humility, which led to his statement that he was not an original thinker. His theory of Dependent Causation or Origination was the most remarkable contribution to Indian thought. It is unique in the history of philosophy.

The eminent scholar of Indian philosophy, Professor S. N. Dasgupta, observes, for example: "Hindu philosophy in later times seems to have been influenced by the later off-shoots of the different schools of Buddhism, but it does not appear that Pali Buddhism had any share in it." A serious challenge to traditional Indian thought that the need was at once felt to put its house in order and meet the challenge by readjusting and remodeling its views in the light of the new developments. Such an attempt seems to be made in the Bhaqauadqita which tries to shake off some crude elements of the traditional orthodoxy like animal sacrifice and external ceremonialism, reduces the rigor of caste, opens the gate of holy life to all without distinction, recognizes the equality of all professions, and compromises with the changing order of things while sharply reacting at the same time against renunciation or abandonment of worldly duties, atheism, and *Anatta*.

One may object, however, that these trends of the *Gita* cannot adequately establish the impact of early Buddhism on it unless (1) the *Gita* is chronologically shown to be later than early Buddhism, and (2) the former's acquaintance with the latter is established through some other evidence. Regarding the first point modern scholarship does not seem to be unfavorable. But the second point does not find favor with scholars. They feel that the *Gita* even if later in origin, has developed its views without being aware of the Buddhist viewpoint.

The date of the Buddha is reasonably well settled. According to tradition he was born in 624 B.C., although the consensus of historians is in favor of assigning 563 B.C. as the year of his birth. In any case, it is a difference of only about 60 years and there can be little doubt that the Buddha (who attain ed enlightenment at the age of 35) was vigorously engaged in preaching and propagating his doctrines in the last quarter of the sixth century B.C. According to the later date, he died in 483 B.C., that is, the first quarter of the fifth century B.C., by which time the fundamental tenets of Buddhism appear to have been well propounded and established.

The chronology of the *Gita* is not so well settled. The earliest date assigned by Western scholars to the composition of the *Gita* is 200 B.C. But Indian scholars, with some plausible evidence in their suppport, argue for its greater antiquity. K. T. Telang thinks that "the latest date at which the *Gita* can have been composed must be earlier than the 3rd century B.C."R. G. Bhandarkar feels that it is at least as old as the fourth century B.C. B. G. Tilak, through his lengthy arguments, pleads in support of 500 B.C., and S. Radhakrishnan, largely agreeing with him, says that "its date may be assigned to the 5th century B.C., though the text may have received many alterations in Subsequent times." Thus, scholarly opinion appears to favor regarding it as a post-Buddhist composition, and evidence is weighty in support of this view.

But none of these scholars is inclined to see any Buddhist influence on the *Gita*. Telang and Bhandarkar both regard the *Gita* as representing the thought of the pre-Buddhist era. In the words of Bhandarkar, "The *Bhagavad Gita* is the result of development of the religious and philosophic speculation that prevailed before the rise of Buddhism." Tilak quite unambiguously asserts that "the elements of the *Gita* are not borrowed from the Buddhist religion." Radhakrishnan also does not notice "any borrowing from Buddhism."

It is no doubt true that the *Gita* does not contain any direct and clear allusion to the Buddha or Buddhism, yet it contains some ideas, words, and expressions which are strikingly suggestive of Buddhism. They are conspicuous by their absence in any of the pre-Buddhist literature, including the Upanisads, which the *Gita* freely draws upon for its material. Again, some pointed statements are made in the *Gita* which seem to be intended to counter those of early Buddhism.

Besides, an indirect allusion to the views of Buddhism seems to be made by the *Gita* when, in the course of its denunciation of the adherents of faulty doctrines, it refers not only to materialists who regard this world as a place of sensual enjoyment but also to the followers of a system of thought according to which the world is unsubstantial, unreal, without God, and caused by desire. Though the materialists, like Buddhists, also denounce God, they never, unlike the latter, regard this world as unsubstantial or unreal. Rather, they consider it to be the only solid reality. Nor do they regard this world as caused by desires.

We cannot expect the *Gita* to make direct mention of the names of all such thinkers or their schools, especially in view of a not uncommon habit in ancient Indian literature to make indirect reference to various doctrines. The *Gita*, in the same way, is interested more in presenting or combating thoughts rather than thinkers. This alone explains why there is no mention of either the Upanisads or the Carvakas in the whole of the *Gita*, though their views are obviously referred to in its text.

Coming to the important words, ideas, and passages of the *Gita* which indicate its familiarity with Buddhism, we may first draw attention to the word nirvana, which occurs repeatedly in the *Gita* and which is nowhere to be met with in any of the pre-Buddhist Upanishads. It seems to have been used for the first time in its technical sense in Buddhism. Again, virtues like nirvana, dvesa, karuna, and maitri also are striking peculiarities of the *Gita* and Buddhism, and these words do not occur in the Upanishads. Similarly, raga and dvesa occur in compounds in the *Gita* just as in Buddhism.

The way in which they are used in *Gita* and *Dhammapada*, as well as in *Gita* and *Dhammapada*, is similar. The epithets used for a muni in the *Gita*-like aniketa, nirmama, nirasi, nirasraya, nirahara; naiskarmya, sama dukkha-sukha, tulya, ninda, stuti, tulya manapamana, etc. are exactly the same as the corresponding Pali words of early Buddhism.

None of these words is traceable in the pre-Buddhist Upanishads. Then the vices, krodha, mada, dambha, atimanita enumerated in the *Gita* are strikingly similar to those listed in the Amaqandha Sutta (Kodho, mada, thambho... usuyya... manatimano) and people having such vices are alike called naradhama: Again, just as the Buddha regards to be the best of all sacrifices, so also the *Gita* speaks of the *jana, yajna* as the best. Similarly, the teachings of samacariya in Buddhism are well reflected in the teachings of samatua in *Gita.*

Gita while describing the practice of yoga. The gradual psychological stages in the process of concentration as described in Buddhism-pamujjam, piti, passaddhi, and sukha are similar to prasadam, prasannata 'Santi and sukha referred to in the *Gita*. Then, life has been characterized as suffering in typical Buddhist style. Furthermore, there are a number of passages betraying similarity or close affinity between the *Gita* and the Nikayas. We list here some of the important ones for illustration:

Gita	Early Buddhism
I.46: yauan artha udapane saruatah samplutodake	Ud 79: Kim kayira udapanena apa ce sabbada siyum
I. 1., 28: auyaktadini bhuutani.... avyaktanidhanany eua tatra ka parideuana. Ubhayor api drsto 'ntah.	Sn 110: yassa maqqa.m na janasi aqatassa qatassa ua, ubho ante asampassam nirattham parideuasi
VI. 5: uddhared *Atman*a 'tmanam ...	Dh 379: Attana codaya' ttanam . . .
VI.32: atmaupamyena saruatra....	Dh 129-130; Sn 137: Attanam upamam Katua na haneyya na qhataye
I.58: yada samharate ca 'yam kurmo 'anqani 'ua saria`sah	S I. 7: kummo ua anqani sake kapale
I. 11: a`sppuam anua`socas tua.m... qatasuum aqatasuums ca na 'nu`socanti panditah	S I.5: atitam nanusocanti nappauappanti naqatam anaqatappajappaya atitassanusocana etena bala sussanti....
I. 56: duhkhesu anuduiqNamanah sukhesu uiqatasprhah	S IV.71: phassena phuttho na sukhena majje dukkhena phuttho pi na sampauedhe
VI. 3: manusuya nam sahasresu ka`scid yatati siddhaye	S V.24: appaka te manussesu, ye jana Paraqamino
XI. 8: na tu mam `sakyase drastum anenaiua suacaksusa diuyam dadami te caksuh	D I.329: na kho rajan na euam pare loko datthabbo yatha tuam mannasi mamsacakkhuna.... te dibbena cakkhuna....passanti
XVI. 19, 16: tan aham duisatah ... naradhaman prasaktah kamabhoqesu patanti narake '`sucau.	Sn43: naradhama ye' dha karonti kibbisam.... patanti sAtta nirayam aua.msira

These similarities of expressions and ideas are ample indication that the *Gita* has assimilated all those Buddhistic elements which fit conveniently into its scheme. But in other matters, like renunciation, atheism, and the doctrine of *Anatta* (soullessness), it sharply reacts against the Buddhist approach. If we examine, for example, the mode, tone, and words of the dialogue of Krsna and Arjuna with that of Asurendra Vepacitti and Surendra 'Sakra (which is almost the same as that of Matali and 'Sakra), it becomes evident that the arguments of Asurendra Vepacitti (or of Matali), are utilized by Krsna to win over Arjuna, who uses arguments similar to those of 'Sakra.

A battle is said to have been fought between gods and demons in which the latter are defeated and their chief, Vepacitti, is caught and brought by the gods before their king, 'Sakra. Vepacitti, though a captive, abuses 'Sakra off and on in his very presence. At this Matali tells 'Sakra that it would be weakness and fear on his part to tolerate Vepacitti's abuses, but 'Sakra replies that it would be unbecoming of an enlightened being like him to care about such fools. Matali tells him that not to fight and control evil is to give it encouragement, but 'Sakra replies emphatically that to remain awakened and silent at the anger of others is alone the best way to control it.

Matali further argues that by so doing he will not only be betraying his fear and weakness, but will also earn ill fame, to which 'Sakra replies that fame or ill fame, praise or slander are immaterial to the really enlightened one. To resist force with force is only brutal and is really an indication of weakness. For the enlightened one, tolerance and forgiveness matter most. To fall victim to anger is a sin. The real victory lies in victory over anger.

One who does not give way to anger does well both to himself and to others. Now one can find a clear echo of these ideas when Arjuna places his point before Krsna, saying that he at least, who is sensible enough to realize the inherent sin and evil of the brutal act of fighting, should not behave like his opponents, who are stupid and deluded by greed. But Krsna, using Matali's arguments, asks Arjuna to stick to his svadharma and not to betray futile weakness of heart and fear.

It is remarkable that the very same words, "bhaya" and "daurbalya," are used by Krsna in relation to Arjuna (*Gita* I. 3 and 35) which were used by Matali in relation to `Sakra (bhaya nu maqhaua sakka dubbalya no titikkhasi-S I.221). Krsna further reminds Arjuna of the evil consequences of ill fame and slander, as Matali had done. But in the light of the Buddhist approach, Matali was silenced when it was pointed out to him by `Sakra that a man, by meeting anger with anger, only incurs sin.

The *Gita,* on the other hand, takes just the opposite stand when Arjuna is reminded by Krsna of his svadharma, which when violated brings about sin, besides spoiling worldly fame. The deciding factor, it may be noted, in both Buddhism and the *Gita,* is the moral consideration of sin, but the measuring rod of sin, as indicated above, and is different in the two systems. Similarly, the statements of Buddhism and the *Gita* regarding the future of the warriors killed on the battlefield are in sharp opposition to each other. According to Buddhism such soldiers cannot but go to hell or be born in an animal species whereas the *Gita* promises heaven for them.

Thus it appears that, although the *Gita* absorbs some of the terms, concepts, and ideas of early Buddhism, it is more interested in counteracting the Buddhist tenets of renunciation, atheism, and *Anatta* by putting forward opposite views in keeping with the orthodox tradition. Early Buddhism is quite unambiguous in exalting the life of utter renunciation. According to it, it is hardly possible for a householder to lead a holy life in all its purity and perfection. It is frequently stated:"Full of impediments is the household life, a dusty path (a path of defilements); whereas the life of renunciation is like the open sky (free from hindrances).

It is not easy to lead this holy life in all its perfection and purity like a polished conch-shell by a person living the household life." The life of a householder is, therefore, termed "inferior" (hina) in comparison with the pure life of a recluse. Naturally the idea of practicing the virtuous life while enjoying the life of a householder is not looked upon as an ideal in early

Buddhism. Now the *Gita,* notwithstanding its compromise with the Buddhist ideal of renunciation, reacts against the undermining of the household life and in sharp opposition to Buddhism shows its preference for the life of a householder. It points out that the complete abandonment or renunciation of action is neither possible nor necessary.

The root cause of bondage is not the action, but the desire behind the action, and so what is necessary for salvation is to abandon the desire and not the action as such. "The learned ones (*budhah*) call him the wise whose undertakings are free from desire and selfish motive and whose actions are burnt up in the fire of wisdom. Having abandoned Attachment to the fruit of action, ever content and free from any dependence, he (really) does nothing, even though (apparently) engaged in action".

Such a man "performing mere bodily action incurs no sin" (`sariram kevalem karma kurvan na "pnati kilbisam-*Gita* IV.21) and thus "even when he acts, he is not bound or contaminated" (krtua'pi na nibadhyate-IV.22; kuruann api na lipyate-V. 7). This skilfulness in action, according to the *Gita*, is the true import of Yoga (yoqah karmasu kau`salam-I. 50). This is how the *Gita* shows that the abandonment of action is not necessary for salvation. Then it argues that it is not possible to renounce all actions and remain inactive completely. Taking action in its broad sense (both physical and mental), it points out: "None can remain without doing action even for a moment". So long as life remains, action is unavoidable. All are compelled to engage in action by the force of nature. "Even the maintenance of physical life is not possible without action". Thus, after having shown that the renunciation of action is neither necessary nor possible, the *Gita* further reinforces its argument by pointing out that the performance of action is very desirable even for the maintenance of the world.

It is in this connection that the example of King Janaka Attaining to perfection by disinterested action is adduced, and God himself is cited as an ideal who, without any interest of his own, is engaged in the work of maintaining the world-order. As the origin of the world is traced to God, it becomes the duty of man to live in the world and promote its welfare. One who does not discharge selfle:s service to the world is said to live in vain. Pursuing further the same line of argument, the *Gita* exhorts that work alone is the true worship of God, man's homage to the supreme. "Devoted each to one's own profession... by worshipping him through the performance of his own duty, man attains perfection".

Lastly, the *Gita* tries to score over early Buddhism by pointing out that the path of renunciation of action is difficult and cannot be practiced without cultivating the attitude of disinterestedness. But the path of disinterested action is easy and leads to perfection within a short time. It clearly says: "Renunciation is difficult to attain, O Arjuna, without disinterested action (yoga). But the sage endowed with yoga (following the path of disinterested action) attains to Brahmana in no time". Thus, it is shown that the path of disinterested action (karmayoga) has the advantage of being easier and yet it leads to the same goal which is arrived at by the difficult path of renunciation (V. 2).

The *raison d'^etre* of it, according to the *Gita*, is that the essential factor responsible for salvation, namely, desirelessness or detachment, is wholly contained in disinterested action and in the words of the *Gita*, "He who neither hates nor desires should ever be known as a renouncer (*samnyasi*)". Thus it appears that the *Gita* is making a conscious effort to highlight the path of action (*pravrtti*) in preference to that of renunciation (*nivrtti*) as championed by early Buddhism. In its treatment of God, also, the *Gita* seems to make a similar conscious effort to vindicate its position and take care of the charges levelled by early Buddhism against the existence of God.

The theism with which early Buddhism seems to be acquainted with frequently brings in for criticism is at best the idea of Brahma as creator and controller of the World. The Buddha exposes the absurdity of the eternity of Brahma by pointing out that Brahma is only a first-born being who appears at the beginning of the world-process (vivat tamane lake). Despite his very long span of life, he is as much subject to birth and death as are all of the beings who are born after him. But both Brahma and other beings feel, under delusion, that the former is the supreme one, the creator and controller of the world.

Now it is interesting to note that the *Gita* is clearly averse to such crude theism. It explicitly states that God is superior to Brahma, the creator-god (gariyase Brahmano "py adikartre-XI.37). Brahma and `Siva and hosts of other gods and demigods are all shown to be contained within the Supreme Divinity. Arjuna is clearly told that worlds up to the realm of Brahma are subject to birth and death. One attains freedom from this cycle of birth and death only after reaching the Supreme God. But there is a still more serious objection. Whatever the nature of divinity, if God is the creator and controller of all, "then people commit murder, theft and unchaste deeds due to God's act of creation; they are covetous, full of hate and hold wrong views due to God's act of creation."

The *Gita* seems to offer a reply to this charge when it asserts that God is only the impartial operator of the universal law of karma which is but a manifestation of His own nature (*prakrti* or *suabhava*). It is repeatedly pointed out that God is not tainted by actions (na mam karmani limpanti), for He has no yearning for the fruits of action. Referring to the acts of creation and dissolution, Krsna, the incarnate God, declares: "These actions do not bind me, O Arjuna, for I am seated as if indifferent and unattached in those actions".

The *Gita* points out that people, because of sheer ignorance, hold God responsible for the good and evil of the world. In the words of the *Gita*: "The all-pervading spirit does neither take on the sin nor the merit of anyone. Knowledge is enveloped by ignorance and hence is creatures deluded". It is again pointed out by Buddhism that reliance on the supernatural creator is detrimental to moral incentive and self-effort. "Those who fall back on God's act of creation as the essential factor lack the impulse and effort regarding what should be done and what should not be done." Such people, relying on God's mercy and help, abandon effort and offer vain prayers for the fulfillment of their desires. These prayers, the Buddha points out, are as futile as calling the other shore of the river to come to the opposite side.

The *Gita* tries to escape this difficulty by giving an activistic orientation to its theistic ideas. Work itself is considered the best worship of God. It is said that "man Attain s perfection by worshipping Him through his own action". God Himself is conceived as ceaselessly active, placing his ideal before man. This introduction of action into the tenet of devotion enables the *Gita* to maintain that absolute dedication or surrender to God means ceaseless discharge of one's duties. Krsna says: "With perfect resignation to me, one while doing all actions attain s by My grace the eternal undecaying abode".

Arjuna is, therefore, exhorted to perform his duty to the best of his ability by dedicating all his works to God. Having thus fortified itself with an activistic faith in God, the *Gita* mounts its offensive against atheists and warns them in bitter words. Krsna says: "The evil-doers, stupid and lowly men, possessed of demoniac nature, do not seek refuge in Me, because their minds are carried away by ignorance". "Such fools are born in demoniac species life after life, and, not attaining to Me, go down to the lowest state".

Thus, a closer examination of this polemic style and combative character of the *Gita*, which is significantly different from the vast mass of earlier traditional literature, suggests that the impact of early Buddhism had begun to make itself felt on Indian thought by the time the *Gita* was composed. Even while highlighting its doctrine of soul in contradistinction to the Buddhist doctrine of *Anatta* (soullessness), it is remarkable to note that the *Gita* speaks in a somewhat Buddhist fashion of the impermanence of worldly objects, as also of their being a source of suffering. But, unlike the Buddha, it does not go to the length of deducing therefrom the doctrine of soullessness. By analyzing the entire personality of man, the Buddha frequently shows that each one of its constituents is transitory and, consequently, a source of suffering. He then asks, "Is it proper to look upon that which is impermanent, sorrowful and changeable as 'this is mine, I am this, this is my self?" "And the obvious reply comes: "Certainly not, Lord." The *Gita*, while initiating its doctrine of an immortal soul in the second chapter, observes in a like manner: "Contacts with objects, O Arjuna, give rise to cold and heat, pleasure and pain. They come and go and are impermanent (*anittyah*).

And subsequently it adds: "Whatever pleasures are born of contacts are only sources of suffering (dukkhayonayah). They have a beginning and an end, O Arjuna. No wise man delights in them". Thus it appears that the *Gita*, like Buddhism, arrives at the fact of worldly suffering from the impermanence of worldly objects and imparts the teaching of detachment from them. But it does not go all the way with Buddhism and Parts Company with it when the latter comes in open conflict with its avowed doctrine of the soul. On the basis of these evidences, it appears fairly reasonable to conclude that the *Gita*, in the light of the new approach to life heralded by early Buddhism, makes necessary changes and adjustments in the traditional orthodoxy and absorbs some of those ideas and expressions of the new movement which could be conveniently fitted into its scheme, while trying at the same time to counteract vigorously the growing Buddhist influence of renunciation, atheism, and *Anatta*.

These trends on the part of the *Gita* are ample indications of the fact that Buddhism from its very early stages had begun to make its influence felt on traditional Indian thought. Was early Buddhism a revolt against Brahmana ritualism and the Upanisadic philosophy? Or was its opposition confined to the former, while it accepted its main ideas from the latter? For unspecified reason(s), since the beginning of Pali researches, it has been taken for granted that as far as the relationship between early Buddhism and the Upanishads was concerned, these were the only possible alternatives. What obliges us thus to limit ourselves has never been adequately discussed.

A moment's reflection, however, will convince us that secondary or derivative evidence, its usefulness notwithstanding, is not enough without corroboration from the primary sources. The main question, therefore, should be: Do we have reliable evidence from the Pali Canon and other early texts which lends support to either alternative? This chapter proposes to examine the issue of relating early Buddhism to the Upanishads one way or the other, questioning the fashionable view that early Buddhism was indebted to the Upanishads for its fundamental tenets.

Let us make it clear at the outset that the term "Upanisadic philosophy" is not being used to denote the exact words contained in the extant Upanisadic texts. There is no reason to think that these very texts were available to the Buddha and his followers. Pointing out the absence of references to actual Upanisadic passages will be at best inconclusive negative evidence. By "Upanisadic philosophy" we mean only the peculiarly Upanisadic ideas, values, and modes of thinking. These include: there is a spiritual ultimate reality underlying the phenomenal world, known as Brahmana or *Atman*; the individual soul is essentially one with this reality; we are in bondage due to the ignorance of our true nature; and, finally, we can, and should, try to win liberation by Attaining true insight.

The Upanisads, as the name suggests, are esoteric and mystical in their values and mode of thinking. They subscribe to the doctrine of moral retribution (karma) in the field of ethics. Whether the Pali Canon was in any way influenced by the Upanishads really ought to be determined by evidence concerning its acquaintance with the Upanisadic tenets mentioned above. Another stipulation concerns the anteriority of the Upanishads and their similarity in certain aspects with early Buddhism.

There cannot be much doubt that the oldest and most important Upanishads - the Brhadaranyaka, the Chandogya, and the Aitereya, in particular - were pre-Buddhistic, though not in their finally redacted form. Similarly, it is quite obvious that both the Upanishads and early Buddhism believed in the undesirability of worldly existence and sought emancipation from it, both shared a faith in moral retribution, and neither had much respect for priestly rites and rituals. These considerations have always strengthened the feeling that early Buddhism was influenced by, or indebted to, the Upanishads.

The Buddha's (supposed) indebtedness to the Upanishads is affirmed by some scholars, while other scholars appear keen to establish the "supremacy" of the Upanishads, using this indebtedness as a supporting argument. Monier Monier Williams believes that "the Buddha, like all Indians, was by nature a metaphysician. He had great sympathy with the philosophy of the Upanishads." Nevertheless, the Buddha denied the reality of soul because "it is obvious that to believe in the ultimate merging of man's personal spirit in One Impersonal Spirit is virtually to deny the ultimate existence of any human spirit at all."

Albrecht F. Weber is more specific: "This teaching [Buddhism] contains, in itself, absolutely nothing new; on the contrary, it is entirely identical with the corresponding Brahmanical doctrines; only the fashion in which Buddha proclaimed and disseminated it was something novel and unwonted." A. B. Keith has fixed the "lower limit" of the date of the Upanishads on the basis of his conjecture that "Buddhism accepts from the Upanishads the doctrines of transmigration and pessimism." Coming to the other group, comprising chiefly Indian scholars, we find Ramchandra D. Ranade trying to trace the "sources of Buddhism" in the Upanishads, asking us to remember "that the end of the Upanishadic period and the beginning of the Buddhistic period are contemporaneous, and that the one gradually and imperceptibly merges into the other."

It is his contention that "all the main rudiments of Buddhism are present in embryo the Upanishads." T. M. P. Mahadevan is also of the same opinion: "It is no exaggeration to say that the Upanishads constitute the basic springs of Indian thought and culture. They have inspired not only the orthodox systems of Indian philosophy but also some of the so-called heterodox Schools like those of Buddhism."

Radhakrishnan is certainly the best representative of this point of view and should be quoted in detail. "Early Buddhism is not an absolutely original doctrine," he declares.

"It is no freak in the evolution of Indian thought.... Early Buddhism, we venture to hazard a conjecture, is only a restatement of the thought of the Upanishads from a new standpoint." He is quite explicit that "for a revelation of the struggle of spirit and the experience of soul, Buddha had ready at hand that supreme work of Indian genius, the Upanishads." Moreover, "Buddha himself was not aware of any incongruity between his theory and that of the Upanishads. He felt that he had the support and sympathy of the Upanishads and their followers."

The Upanisadic influence on the Buddha would logically lead to this conclusion: "Those who tell us that for the Buddha there is religious experience but there is no religious object are violating the texts and needlessly convicting him of selfcontradiction. He implies the reality of what the Upanishads call Brahmana, though he takes the liberty of giving it another name, dharma, to indicate its essentially ethical value for us on the empirical plane." In short, it has been uncritically assumed that in ancient India all philosophy and religious ideas flowed from the Upanishads, and attempts then were made to fit early Buddhism into this picture. Naturally, there was no alternative but to establish somehow that early Buddhism was indebted to the Upanishads. We now turn to examine evidence from the Pali Canon and elsewhere to see how far this conclusion can be sustained.

The problem can be attacked from many angles. First, there are reasons to think that the early Buddhists, or at least the Buddha, not only were ignorant of the Upanisadic ideas, but also that they did not have any acquaintance with the Upanisadic idiom. Hermann von Oldenberg very correctly observes that "of all the texts in which the Brahmanical speculations as to the delivering power of knowledge are contained, perhaps not even one was known except by hearsay to the founder of the Buddhist community of believers." This is supported by many pertinent considerations.

Many passages from the Pali Canon feature debates between the Buddha and the inquisitive Brahmans. To cite an example, in the Tevijja-sutta of the *Digha Nikaya*, some young Brahmans are discussing with the Buddha the problem of reaching the god Brahma. The Buddha stops after declaring that these Brahmans or even their ancestors were not qualified to speak on this subject, being without any personal knowledge about the Brahma-gods. The point to note is the absence of "Brahmana" in the neuter in a context where it reasonably should have been expected. Reaching "Brahma" (which was, in the Pali Canon, only a class of gods) was never considered to be a problem either by the priests or by the seers of the Upanishads.

What could make the editors of the Canon attach importance to this except ignorance? The Upanishads always use "Brahmana" in the neuter, while the Pali Canon seems to know only of "Brahma" in the masculine. "This neuter Brahma is never mentioned by the Buddhists," says Edward T. Thomas, "nor do they ever discuss the Upanisadic doctrine of Attaining to this Brahma or becoming identified with it." He is quite correct in holding that had this doctrine been known to the early Buddhists, it would have been the subject of severest refutation, being, in his opinion, "utterly opposed to Buddhist teaching."

It should be noted that "Brahma-" as a qualifying prefix is certainly not unknown to the Pali Canon. We frequently come across expressions like "Brahma-jala," "Brahma-cariya," and "Brahma-bhuuta." In all these cases it has been translated as "perfect" or "excellent," which appears to be warranted by the context. Nevertheless, the champions of the indebtedness theory prefer to break up the conjunction and read metaphysical implications into the prefix. "The Buddha calls himself Brahma-bhuta, he who has become Brahmana," says Radhakrishnan.

Quite apart from the fact that this rendering is supported neither by the context nor by Pali grammar and usage, the question arises, Is it imaginable that a true follower of the

Upanishads - and that is what Radhakrishnan believes the Buddha must have been - would content himself merely with a prefix to denote the highest reality? Do we really deduce metaphysical doctrines from conjunctive usages? The nearest that the Pali Canon comes to the Upanisadic position is perhaps in its treatment of one type of "heresy of individuality" (*sakkayaditthi*) wherein the self is identified not with one of the five factors of existence (*khandhas*) but with the whole universe.

The belief is described as so loko, so *Atta*: "the world around me is the Self which I shall hereafter become, eternal and permanent, everlasting and unchangeable, standing fast like heaven and earth." In other words, a person, out of ignorance (*avijja*), can delude himself with the thought that he is essentially one with the whole world. However, this can at best be a naive misrepresentation of the true Upanisadic position - in fact, it is indistinguishable from materialism - and of course it is not quoted with approval. This type of thinking is supposed to be as ill-founded as any other heresy. All we can say on the basis of this passage is that probably the Buddha heard some such idea and felt, without understanding it properly, that it militated against his ideas.

Second, coupled with this ignorance of the Upanisadic way of thinking is another significant fact. Brahmans figure in the Pali Canon time and again, but always as priests and never as philosophers or even as propagators of rival creeds. "On the one hand," to quote E. J. Thomas again, "there was the view of the Brahmain priests that by due performance of the sacrifices and other duties of life rebirth in heaven might be won, and on the other the secret doctrine of Brahmain recluses that freedom from rebirth might be won by Attaining a certain knowledge. It is only the first that we find discussed by the Buddhists."

The few Brahmans who are shown as being interested in speculative tenets - for instance, Potthapada and Jaliya, both of whom figure in the *Digha Nikaya* - never talk in the Upanisadic vein and in fact do not appear to be acquainted with any higher type of thinking. The Pali Canon is certainly not very accurate in reporting rival views, but it never ignores them. We do see Jain and Ajivika tenets mentioned time and again and then, why not the views of Brahmana recluses? A study of the names of religious teachers that figure in the Pali Canon also leads to some interesting results.

The Tevijja-sutta, referred to earlier, mentions the names of well-known seers like Vessamitta and Vasisattha (Vi'svamitra and Vasistha). But not once do we come across the names of the seers and sage-philosophers of the Upanishads. Not that the Pali Canon is averse to mentioning names of other religious teachers, with both approval and disapproval. The Buddha himself is shown referring to Uddaka Ramaputta and Alara Kalama with great reverence. He repeatedly acknowledges his debt to them. Six "heretical" teachers - including the Jain Tirthamkara, the Ajivika leaders, and a materialist - are mentioned many times, with vehement disapproval. What could prevent the editors of the Pali Canon from mentioning the Upanisadic sages in one way or another?

Third, it has been customary to regard the Upanishads as the orthodox or preponderant philosophy of that day, from which other sects borrowed ideas. This presupposition also seems to have acted as a prop for the indebtedness theory and thus deserves to be examined. Now, have we any evidence, in the Upanishads themselves or in the Buddhist and Jain scriptures, which lends credence to this view? In fact, a close study of the Pali Canon leads one to believe that Brahmans, that is, the priestly class, were merely one group among many that were active in those days and with whose approach to the religious questions the Buddha did not agree. Their activities and beliefs never seemed to have received any more importance or attention than did those of the other sects.

There is every reason to agree with Oldenberg's observation that "the champions of the Veda, the Brahmins, are really not more than one among many parties, and, indeed, to all appearance, by no means an especially powerful one." When the Brahmans, as a class, did not have the important place in the social setup in which the Buddha moved that they acquired in the succeeding centuries, why should it be presumed that their philosophy had precedence over all other systems? In these circumstances, there is no reason to think that the Buddha was obliged either to agree with and follow the Upanisadic tradition or to oppose it. The lack of acquaintance with the Upanisadic ideas and idiom considerably strengthens this feeling.

In an age quite unaware of copyright laws, the term "borrowing" is not a suitable choice. Every age has its own commonwealth of ideas. These are the ideas which are held by all irrespective of other differences. Such ideas are accepted and inherited in the same manner as linguistic usages are accepted and inherited. Individual freedom is one such idea in Western culture.

No one feels obliged to express indebtedness for it to some earlier thinker, simply because it is a common property now. In a similar way, the doctrine of moral retribution was a common property in the day of the Buddha. In any case, it is not held by anyone that the Upanisadic seers originated it, though it was first mentioned by them. According to the well-known Brhadaranyaka Upanishad passage, this doctrine was not even known to the Brahmans.

Similarly, as Bimala C. Law has pointed out, the Pali texts dearly indicate that "the doctrine was propounded before the advent of the Buddha by an Indian teacher who was a householder." Thus, both the Upanishads and the Pali Canon treat this doctrine as a common property. Where is the question of its being borrowed by one from the other? A closer look will reveal that this doctrine was the outcome of what T. W. Rhys Davids has called "normalism." Since the beginning of philosophizing in India, it has been firmly believed that things happen according to some law (*rta*). How could rebirth be possible without such laws? Thus, it is clear that the Buddha's faith in moral retribution in no way makes him indebted to the Upanishads.

Fourth, we shall discuss a psychological consideration which is relevant to the present issue, though it has yet to be given due importance. Philosophical differences, as has been well said, are temperamental in the last analysis. Broadly speaking, thinking people are either imaginative or matter-of-fact; the terms "tender-minded" and "tough-minded" have been advisedly used for these types. The tender-minded try to solve all the basic problems speculatively, by positing another plane of existence which is free of the evils faced by us. All idealists and religious teachers accepting a personal godhead come under this class.

On the contrary, the tough-minded prefer to deal with the hard facts, to analyze actual experiences. The former hardly take any interest in the mundane world, the ordinary, day-to-day, prosaic life. The iatter regard all speculation as a waste of time.

It would be both difficult and needless to enumerate all the passages from the Upanishads and the Pali Canon to show that while the former represent the cream of tender-minded thinking in ancient India, the latter were at the other extreme. The Upanishads seldom care for actual experiences; their aim is to discover a suprasensuous, supraphenomenal reality, entirely free of change and the laws of the world, which could be the basis as well as the goal of all becoming and with which we could identify ourselves in some way and thus win liberation from this existence.

Psychological analyses may not be absent in the Upanishads, but they hardly form any significant part of them. Early Buddhism, on the contrary, uncompromisingly refuses to transcend the empirical; passages featuring the Buddha making fun of those who talk about things not amenable to experience are legion, and his firm opposition to all speculation is well known. The difference of outlook is too clear to escape the notice of any careful observer. Keeping all this in view, any talk of one school influencing the other or being indebted to the other hardly sounds well founded, however emotionally satisfying it may be to some.

Let us now return to the main question. Undoubtedly, the Upanisads were pre-Buddhistic, and early Buddhism had some similarities with them. But it is equally clear that the Pali Canon hardly gives us any reason to think that the early Buddhists were even properly acquainted with the Upanishads. The Upanishads were admittedly esoteric and mystical while the Buddha took pride in not having the "closed fist of the teacher." The two were obviously the products of very different types of temperaments. The question is: Can mere anteriority and similarity to some extent, by themselves and unaided by internal evidence, serve as sufficient ground to think in terms of indebtedness! The answer is too obvious.

If we disabuse our minds of preconceived notions, another possibility emerges in the light of the preceding discussion. The fact that the Pali Canon appears to be ignorant of the philosophy of the Brahmans but not of their ritualistic practices is very suggestive. Probably both the Upanishads and early Buddhism developed independently of each other as reactions to the same type of situation. Soon after the eclipse of the sacrificial ideas, the need must have been felt for a more philosophical explanation of the value and destiny of human life. The doctrine of moral retribution, the need for liberation from the rounds of rebirths, and such other ideas, were already taking shape, apparently independently of both. They only made use of these ideas in accordance with their different philosophical attitudes, one taking the speculative road and developing a "substance view," while the other dealt with the hard facts on the basis of a "becoming view."

3

Indian Religion at the Time of the Buddha

India has been an important part of three major world religions - Hinduism, Buddhism, and Islam. Buddhism began in India and spread to other places in Asia. Islam came into India from West Asia. The origins of Hinduism are less clear, but are certainly related to the arrival of the Indo-European Aryans from West Asia. We don't know very much about the earliest Indian religion, of the Harappa people, but certainly it was polytheistic. Based on the art of that time, some people think the later Hindu gods were already being worshipped.

With the arrival of the Aryans about 1500 BC, the Indo-European gods entered India as well. This was the beginning of modern Hinduism. Hinduism was (and is) polytheistic - Hindus believe in many gods. Stories about these gods were written down in the Rig Veda and other epic poems. In this kind of Hinduism, people believed in reincarnation - that people could be reborn into other bodies after they died. But in the 600's BC, Indian people were interested in some other way to get a good rebirth than through sacrifice and the priests. This search is seen in the Upanishads, written about this time. And it is seen in the teachings of the Buddha in the 500's BC.

According to Gautama Buddha, people can get free of the cycle of reincarnation by being good people, by learning not to care about the things of the body, and through meditation.

Buddhism became very popular in India and quickly spread throughout East Asia. But even Buddhists still paid attention to the Hindu gods. About the same time, another religious leader, Mahavira, also encouraged people to try to get out of the cycle of reincarnation. His followers were called Jains. Jains thought that the best way to escape reincarnation was to be good - to be kind to people and animals, and to tell the truth, and not to be greedy.

By the 600's AD, even though Buddhism remained popular in East Asia, many people in India had begun to go back to Hinduism. They still remembered the Buddha, but he became just one of many Hindu gods to them. Jainism continued, but among a small group of people in India. In the 1100's AD, Indian people began to convert to Islam under a series of conquests by Muslim people from the north. Islam demanded that people give up worshipping any god but Allah, and so many people did give up their old Hindu gods at this time. But many people, especially in southern India, also stayed Hindus.

In the 500's BC, during the later part of the Aryan period in India, the idea of reincarnation became very strong among Hindus. Most people believed that after you died, you would be reborn in another form, and then reborn again, and again, forever. But then people started to not like this idea. They didn't want reincarnation to just go on and on forever. Wasn't there any way to stop this; to get off the wheel of reincarnation and just be? A young Indian prince named Siddhartha Gautama Buddha had an idea. He thought that you could get off the wheel of reincarnation if you were good and pure enough. He refused to be a prince anymore, and tried to spend his life being good and pure so he could get off the wheel. Gautama Buddha had many followers during his lifetime, and after he died he had even more.

Most of Buddha's followers tried to be good while still living their normal lives - working in the fields or as soldiers, getting married, taking care of their parents and their children. But some of his followers adopted a Jain idea of getting away from the world so they could work full-time on being good and pure. These people were called monks or nuns. In the 300's BC, one of the great Mauryan kings, Asoka, became a Buddhist, which helped Buddhism to succeed. Asoka convinced many other Indian people to become Buddhists. At first, most Buddhists were in India. But by 500 AD Buddhism spread to China and other parts of East Asia. By the 600's AD most of the Buddhists in India had gone back to being Hindus again. They still remembered Buddha, but as one of many Hindu gods.

In China, on the other hand, Buddhism got stronger and stronger. Soon most of the Buddhists were in China and not India. In China, as in India, most Buddhist people continued to lead more or less ordinary lives, but some Buddhist men and women left their jobs and their families in order to live in Buddhist monasteries as monks or nuns. Religion and philosophy that developed from the teachings of the Buddha (Sanskrit: "awakened one"), a teacher who lived in northern India between the mid-6th and the mid-4th centuries bce (before the Common Era or Christian era). Spreading from India to Central and Southeast Asia, China, Korea, and Japan, Buddhism has played a central role in the spiritual, cultural, and social life of Asia, and during the 20th century it spread to the West.

Ancient Buddhist scripture and doctrine developed in several closely related literary languages of ancient India, especially in Pali and Sanskrit. In this chapter Pali and Sanskrit words that have gained currency in English are treated as English words and are rendered in the form in which they appear in English-language dictionaries. Exceptions occur in special circumstances- as, for example, in the case of the Sanskrit term *dharma* (Pali: *dhamma*), which has meanings that are not usually associated with the English "dharma."

Pali forms are given in the sections on the core teachings of early Buddhism that are reconstructed primarily from Pali texts and in sections that deal with Buddhist traditions in which the primary sacred language is Pali. Sanskrit forms are given in the sections that deal with Buddhist traditions whose primary sacred language is Sanskrit and in other sections that deal with traditions whose primary sacred texts were translated from Sanskrit into a Central or East Asian language such as Tibetan or Chinese.

THE CULTURAL CONTEXT

Buddhism arose in northeastern India sometime between the late 6th century and the early 4th century BCE, a period of great social change and intense religious activity. There is disagreement among scholars about the dates of the Buddha's birth and death. Many modern scholars believe that the historical Buddha lived from about 563 to about 483 BCE. Many others believe that he lived about 100 years later (from about 448 to 368 BCE). At this time in India, there was much discontent with Brahmanic (Hindu high-caste) sacrifice and ritual.

In northwestern India there were ascetics who tried to create a more personal and spiritual religious experience than that found in the Vedas (Hindu sacred scriptures). In the literature that grew out of this movement, the Upanishads, a new emphasis on renunciation and transcendental knowledge can be found. Northeastern India, which was less influenced by the Aryans who had developed the main tenets and practices of the Vedic Hindu faith, became the breeding ground of many new sects. Society in this area was troubled by the breakdown of tribal unity and the expansion of several petty kingdoms. Religiously, this was a time of doubt, turmoil, and experimentation.

A proto-Samkhya group (i.e., one based on the Samkhya school of Hinduism founded by Kapila) was already well established in the area. New sects abounded, including various skeptics (e.g., Sanjaya Belatthiputta), atomists (e.g., Pakudha Kaccayana), materialists (e.g., Ajita Kesakambali), and antinomians (i.e., those against rules or laws- e.g., Purana Kassapa). The most important sects to arise at the time of the Buddha, however, were the Ajivikas (Ajivakas), who emphasized the rule of fate (*niyati*), and the Jains, who stressed the need to free the soul from matter. Although the Jains, like the Buddhists, have often been regarded as atheists, their beliefs are actually more complicated.

Unlike early Buddhists, both the Ajivikas and the Jains believed in the permanence of the elements that constitute the universe, as well as in the existence of the soul. Despite the bewildering variety of religious communities, many shared the same vocabulary-*Nirvana* (transcendent freedom), *Atman* ("self" or "soul"), *yoga* ("union"), *karma* ("causality"), *Tathagata* ("one who has come" or "one who has thus gone"), *Buddha* ("enlightened one"), *Samsara* ("eternal recurrence" or "becoming"), and *dhamma* ("rule" or "law")-and most involved the practice of yoga. According to tradition, the Buddha himself was a yogi- that is, a miracle-working ascetic.

Buddhism, like many of the sects that developed in northeastern India at the time, was constituted by the presence of a charismatic teacher, by the teachings this leader promulgated, and by a community of adherents that was often made up of renunciant members and lay supporters. In the case of Buddhism, this pattern is reflected in the Triratna- i.e., the "Three Jewels" of Buddha (the teacher), *dharma* (the teaching), and *Sangha* (the community). In the centuries following the founder's death, Buddhism developed in two directions represented by two different groups. One was called the Hinayana (Sanskrit: "Lesser Vehicle"), a term given to it by its Buddhist opponents.

This more conservative group, which included what is now called the Theravada (Pali: "Way of the Elders") community, compiled versions of the Buddha's teachings that had been preserved in collections called the *Sutta Pitaka* and the *Vinaya Pitaka* and retained them as normative. The other major group, which calls itself the Mahayana (Sanskrit: "Greater Vehicle"), recognized the authority of other teachings that, from the group's point of view, made salvation available to a greater number of people. These supposedly more advanced teachings were expressed in sutras that the Buddha purportedly made available only to his more advanced disciples.

As Buddhism spread, it encountered new currents of thought and religion. In some Mahayana communities, for example, the strict law of karma (the belief that virtuous actions create pleasure in the future and nonvirtuous actions create pain) was modified to accommodate new emphases on the efficacy of ritual actions and devotional practices. During the second half of the 1st millennium CE, a third major Buddhist movement, Vajrayana (Sanskrit: "Diamond Vehicle"), or Esoteric Buddhism, developed in India. This movement was influenced by gnostic and magical currents pervasive at that time, and its aim was to obtain spiritual liberation and purity more speedily.

Despite these vicissitudes, Buddhism did not abandon its basic principles. Instead, they were reinterpreted, rethought, and reformulated in a process that led to the creation of a great body of literature. This literature includes the Pali *Tipitaka* ("Three Baskets")-the *Sutta Pitaka* ("Basket of Discourse"), which contains the Buddha's sermons; the *Vinaya Pitaka* ("Basket of Discipline"), which contains the rule governing the monastic order; and the *Abhidhamma Pitaka* ("Basket of Special [Further] Doctrine"), which contains doctrinal systematizations and summaries. These Pali texts have served as the basis for a long and very rich tradition of commentaries that were written and preserved by adherents of the Theravada community.

The Mahayana and Vajrayana/Esoteric traditions have accepted as *Buddhavacana* (the word of the Buddha) many other sutras and tantras, along with extensive treatises and commentaries based on these texts. Consequently, from the first sermon of the Buddha at Sarnath to the most recent derivations, there is an indisputable continuity-a development or metamorphosis around a central nucleus-by virtue of which Buddhism is differentiated from other religions.

EXPANSION OF BUDDHISM

The Buddha was a charismatic leader who founded a distinctive religious community based on his unique teachings. Some of the members of that community were, like the Buddha himself, wandering ascetics. Others were laypersons who venerated the Buddha, followed certain aspects of his teachings, and provided the wandering ascetics with the material support that they required. In the centuries following the Buddha's death, the story of his life was remembered and embellished, his teachings were preserved and developed, and the community that he had established became a significant religious force. Many of the wandering ascetics who followed the Buddha settled in permanent monastic establishments and developed monastic rules.

At the same time, the Buddhist laity came to include important members of the economic and political elite. During its first century of existence, Buddhism spread from its place of origin in Magadha and Kosala throughout much of northern India, including the areas of Mathura and Ujjayani in the west. According to Buddhist tradition, invitations to the Council of Vesali (Sanskrit: Vaishali), held just over a century after the Buddha's death, were sent to monks living throughout northern and central India. By the middle of the 3rd century BCE, Buddhism had gained the favour of a Mauryan king, Asoka, who had established an empire that extended from the Himalayas in the north to almost as far as Sri Lanka in the south.

To the rulers of the republics and kingdoms arising in northeastern India, the patronage of newly emerging sects such as Buddhism was one way of counterbalancing the political power exercised by Brahmans (high-caste Hindus). The first Mauryan emperor, Chandragupta (*c.* 321–*c.* 297 BCE), patronized Jainism and, according to some traditions, finally became a Jain monk. His grandson, Asoka, who ruled over the greater part of the subcontinent from about 268 to 232 BCE, traditionally played an important role in Buddhist history because of his support of Buddhism during his lifetime. He exerted even more influence posthumously, through stories that depicted him as a *chakravartin* ("a great wheel-rolling monarch").

He is portrayed as a paragon of Buddhist kingship who accomplished many fabulous feats of piety and devotion. It is therefore very difficult to distinguish the Asoka of history from the Asoka of Buddhist legend and myth. The first actual Buddhist "texts" that are still extant are inscriptions (including a number of well-known Asokan pillars) that Asoka had written and displayed in various places throughout his vast kingdom. According to these inscriptions, Asoka attempted to establish in his realm a "true *dhamma*" based on the virtues of self-control, impartiality, cheerfulness, truthfulness, and goodness. Although he promoted Buddhism, he did not found a state church, and he was known for his respect for other religious traditions.

He sought to maintain unity in the Buddhist monastic community, however, and he promoted an ethic that focused on the layman's obligations in this world. His aim, as articulated in his edicts, was to create a religious and social milieu that would enable all "children of the king" to live happily in this life and to attain heaven in the next. Thus, he set up medical assistance for human beings and beasts, maintained reservoirs and canals, and promoted trade. He established a system of *dhamma* officers (*dhamma-mahamattas*) in order to help govern the empire. And he sent diplomatic emissaries to areas beyond his direct political control.

Asoka's empire began to crumble soon after his death, and the Mauryan dynasty was finally overthrown in the early decades of the 2nd century BCE. There is some evidence to suggest that Buddhism in India suffered persecution during the Shunga-Kanva period (185–28 BCE). Despite occasional setbacks, however, Buddhists persevered; and before the emergence of the Gupta dynasty, which created the next great pan-Indian empire in the 4th century CE, Buddhism had become a leading if not dominant religious tradition in India. During the approximately five centuries between the fall of the Mauryan dynasty and the rise of the Gupta dynasty, major developments occurred in all aspects of Buddhist belief and practice.

Well before the beginning of the Common Era, stories about the Buddha's many previous lives, accounts of important events in his life as Gautama, stories of his "extended life" in his relics, and other aspects of his sacred biography were elaborated on. In the centuries that followed, groups of these stories were collected and compiled in various styles and combinations. Beginning in the 3rd century BCE, and possibly earlier, magnificent Buddhist monuments such as the great stupas at Bharhut and Sanchi were built. During the early centuries of the 1st millennium CE, similar monuments were established virtually throughout the subcontinent. Numerous monasteries emerged too, some in close association with the great monuments and pilgrimage sites. Considerable evidence including inscriptional evidence points to extensive support from local rulers, including the women of the various royal courts.

During this period Buddhist monastic centres proliferated, and there developed diverse schools of interpretation concerning matters of doctrine and monastic discipline. Within the Hinayana tradition there emerged many different schools, most of which preserved a variant of the *Tipitaka* (which had taken the form of written scriptures by the early centuries of the Common Era), held distinctive doctrinal positions, and practiced unique forms of monastic discipline. The traditional number of schools is 18, but the situation was very complicated, and exact identifications are hard to make.

About the beginning of the Common Era, distinctively Mahayana tendencies began to take shape. It should be emphasized, however, that many Hinayana and Mahayana adherents continued to live together in the same monastic institutions. In the 2nd or 3rd century, the Madhyamika School, which has remained one of the major schools of Mahayana philosophy, was established, and many other expressions of Mahayana belief, practice, and communal life appeared. By the beginning of the Gupta era, the Mahayana had become the most dynamic and creative Buddhist tradition in India.

At this time Buddhism also expanded beyond the Indian subcontinent. It is most likely that Asoka sent a diplomatic mission to Sri Lanka and that Buddhism was established there during his reign. By the beginning of the Common Era, Buddhism, which had become very strong in northwestern India, had followed the great trade routes into Central Asia and China. According to later tradition, this expansion was greatly facilitated by Kanishka, a great Kushana king of the 1st or 2nd century CE, who ruled over an area that included portions of northern India and Central Asia.

BUDDHISM UNDER THE GUPTAS AND PALAS

By the time of the Gupta dynasty (*c.* 320–*c.* 600 CE), Buddhism in India was being influenced by the revival of Brahmanic religion and the rising tide of bhakti (a devotional movement that emphasized the intense love of a devotee for a personal god). During this period, for example, some Hindus practiced devotion to the Buddha, whom they regarded as an avatar (incarnation) of the Hindu deity Vishnu, and some Buddhists venerated Hindu deities who were an integral part of the wider religious context in which they lived. Throughout the Gupta and Pala periods, Hinayana Buddhists remained a major segment of the Indian Buddhist community.

Their continued cultivation of various aspects of Buddhist teaching led to the emergence of the Yogacara School, the second great tradition of Mahayana philosophy. A third major Buddhist tradition, the Vajrayana or Esoteric tradition developed out of the Mahayana school and became a powerful and dynamic religious force. The new form of text associated with this tradition, the tantras, appeared during the Gupta period, and there are indications that distinctively Tantric rituals began to be employed at this time as well. It was during the Pala period (8th–12th centuries), however, that the Vajrayana/Esoteric tradition emerged as the most dynamic component of Indian Buddhist life.

Also during the Gupta period, there emerged a new Buddhist institution, the Mahavihara ("Great Monastery"), which often functioned as a university. This institution enjoyed great success during the reign of the Pala kings. The most famous of these Mahaviharas, located at Nalanda, became a major centre for the study of Buddhist texts and the refinement of Buddhist thought, particularly Mahayana and Vajrayana thought. The monks at Nalanda also developed a curriculum that went far beyond traditional Buddhism and included much Indian scientific and cultural knowledge. In subsequent years other important Mahaviharas were established, each with its own distinctive emphases and characteristics.

These great Buddhist monastic research and educational institutions exerted a profound religious and cultural influence not only in India but throughout many other parts of Asia as well. Although Buddhist institutions seemed to be faring well under the Guptas, Chinese pilgrims visiting India between 400 and 700 CE discerned a decline in the Buddhist community and the beginning of the absorption of Indian Buddhism by Hinduism. Among these pilgrims was Faxian, who left China in 399, crossed the Gobi Desert, visited various holy places in India, and returned to China with numerous Buddhist scriptures and statues.

The most famous of the Chinese travelers, however, was the 7th-century monk Xuanzang. When he arrived in northwestern India, he found "millions of monasteries" reduced to ruins by the Huns, a nomadic Central Asian people. In the northeast Xuanzang visited various holy places and studied Yogacara philosophy at Nalanda. After visiting Assam and southern India, he returned to China, carrying with him copies of more than 600 sutras. After the destruction of numerous Buddhist monasteries in the 6th century CE by the Huns, Buddhism revived, especially in the northeast, where it flourished for many more centuries under the kings of the Pala dynasty.

The kings protected the Mahaviharas, built new centres at Odantapuri, near Nalanda, and established a system of supervision for all such institutions. Under the Palas the Vajrayana/Esoteric form of Buddhism became a major intellectual and religious force. Its adherents introduced important innovations into Buddhist doctrine and symbolism. They also advocated the practice of new Tantric forms of ritual practice that were designed both to generate magical power and to facilitate more rapid progress along the path to enlightenment. During the reigns of the later Pala kings, contacts with China decreased as Indian Buddhists turned their attention toward Tibet and Southeast Asia.

THE DEMISE OF BUDDHISM IN INDIA

With the collapse of the Pala dynasty in the 12th century, Indian Buddhism suffered yet another setback, from which it did not recover. Although small pockets of influence remained, the Buddhist presence in India became negligible. Scholars do not know all the factors that contributed to Buddhism's demise in its homeland. Some have maintained that it was so tolerant of other faiths that it was simply reabsorbed by a revitalized Hindu tradition. This did occur, though Indian Mahayanists were occasionally hostile toward bhakti and toward Hinduism in general.

Another factor, however, was probably much more important. Indian Buddhism, having become primarily a monastic movement, seems to have lost touch with its lay supporters. Many monasteries had become very wealthy, so much so that they were able to employ indentured slaves and paid labourers to care for the monks and to tend the lands they owned. Thus, after the Muslim invaders sacked the Indian monasteries in the 12th and 13th centuries, the Buddhist laity showed little interest in resurgence.

CONTEMPORARY REVIVAL

In the 19th century Buddhism was virtually extinct in India. In far eastern Bengal and Assam, a few Buddhists preserved a tradition that dated back to pre-Muslim times, and some of them experienced a Theravada-oriented reform that was initiated by a Burmese monk who visited the area in the mid-19th century. By the end of that century, a very small number of Indian intellectuals had become interested in Buddhism through Western scholarship or through the activities of the Theosophical Society, one of whose leaders was the American Henry Olcott. The Sinhalese reformer Anagarika Dharmapala also exerted some influence, particularly through his work as one of the founders of the Mahabodhi Society, which focused its initial efforts on restoring Buddhist control of the pilgrimage site at Bodh Gaya, the presumed site of the Buddha's enlightenment.

Beginning in the early 20th century, a few Indian intellectuals became increasingly interested in Buddhism as a more rational and egalitarian alternative to Hinduism. Although this interest remained limited to a very tiny segment of the intellectual elite, a small Buddhist movement with a broader constituency developed in South India. Even as late as 1950, however, an official government census identified fewer than 200,000 Buddhists in the country, most of them residing in east Bengal and Assam. Since 1950 the number of Buddhists in India has increased dramatically. One very small factor in this increase was the flood of Buddhist refugees from Tibet following the Chinese invasion of that country in 1959.

The centre of the Tibetan refugee community, both in India and around the world, was established in Dharmsala, but many Tibetan refugees settled in other areas of the subcontinent as well. Another very small factor was the incorporation of Sikkim- a region with a predominantly Buddhist population now in the northeastern part of India- into the Republic of India in 1975. The most important cause of the contemporary revival of Buddhism in India was the mass conversion, in 1956, of hundreds of thousands of Hindus living primarily in Maharashtra state who had previously been members of the so-called scheduled castes (formerly called untouchables).

This conversion was initiated by Bhimrao Ramji Ambedkar, a leader of the scheduled castes who was also a major figure in the Indian independence movement, a critic of the caste policies of Mahatma Gandhi, a framer of India's constitution, and a member of India's first independent government. As early as 1935 Ambedkar decided to lead his people away from Hinduism in favour of a religion that did not recognize caste distinctions. After a delay of more than 20 years, he determined that Buddhism was the appropriate choice. He also decided that 1956- the year in which Theravada

Buddhists were celebrating the 2,500th year of the death of the Buddha- was the appropriate time.

A dramatic conversion ceremony, held in Nagpur, was attended by hundreds of thousands of people. Since 1956 more than three million persons (a very conservative estimate) have joined the new Buddhist community. The Buddhism of Ambedkar's community is based on the teachings found in the ancient Pali texts and has much in common with the Theravada Buddhist communities of Sri Lanka and Southeast Asia. There are important differences that distinguish the new group, however.

They include the community's reliance on Ambedkar's own interpretations, which are presented in his book *The Buddha and His Dhamma*; the community's emphasis on a mythology concerning the Buddhist and aristocratic character of the Mahar (the largest of the scheduled castes); and its recognition of Ambedkar himself as a saviour figure who is often considered to be a bodhisattva (future buddha). Another distinguishing characteristic of the Mahar Buddhists is the absence of a strong monastic community, which has allowed laypersons to assume the primary leadership roles. During the last several decades, the group has produced its own corpus of Buddhist songs and many vernacular books and pamphlets that deal with various aspects of Buddhist doctrine, practice, and community life.

The Buddha's relation with Hinduism is so close that it's easy to confuse Buddhism with Hinduism. The two religions have close connections, and yet they are distinct. This was because of Buddha's reform movements and his refining of Hindu beliefs. It would not be wrong to state, then, that Buddha founded a noble religion by distilling Hinduism, and offering a commonsense approach to self-betterment to which the people can relate easily. Swami Kriyananda (J Donald Walters) in his book The Hindu Way of Awakening perspicaciously notes how Westerners confuse between these two closely connected religions, and why people mistakenly consider Buddhism and not Hinduism as the religion of India:

"Hinduism is often omitted from rosters of the world's great religions. Everyone knows, of course, that Hinduism exists. Even so, it is confused in many people's minds with what they think of as Buddhism. For Buddhism fits into their concepts of what a religion ought to be...

"Even if the Westerner holds good intention towards India... he may see Hinduism as containing some of the worst examples of Paganism. Small wonder, then, that many people look upon Buddhism as the noblest representative of India's religion, and turn to it when wanting an Indian religion to place among the great religions of the world.

"While Buddhism is relatively simple, Hinduism is complex...Buddhism seems, to Westerners especially, to offer a benign and palatable form of the Indian religious experience. Most students of religion know that Buddha tried to reform some of the ancient practices; they think of him as having brought order and sophistication to primitive chaos. When they prepare lists of the great world religions they think of themselves as demonstrating respect for the religion of India by calling it Buddhism. Most of them are not conscious of their mistake."

Buddha, as we know, began his meditation as a Hindu. He was awakened with a new enlightenment only to denounce Hinduism and emerge as the founder of a new religion. Therefore, to understand Buddhism fully, one should not separate it from Hinduism; while at the same time view it separately from Hinduism. Buddha's way of life was "the golden mean" and a relief from the pagan stigmas and caste system prevalent in Hinduism. The Hindu caste system defined a person's position in society as determined by their birth. Buddha condemned the Hindu caste system and said that it is karma or the good and bad actions of a person and not birth that should determine a person's caste. He introduced the idea of placing morality and equality on a higher place than genealogy of a person.

Jesus had the same relationship to Judaism as Buddha to Hinduism. Both Hinduism and Judaism are ethnic and non-missionary traditions, and are characterised by an element of segregation between the castes and races, unlike Buddhism and Christianity. Swami Kriyananda compares Buddha's position relative to Hinduism with Martin Luther's to the Roman Catholic Church: "Both men were reformers, and the structure reformed by each was not supplanted by his teachings. The Catholic Church survives to this day, and has in many ways been strengthened by Luther's reforms. Hinduism similarly was purified and strengthened by the teachings of Buddha, and was in no way replaced by them. Most Hindus today look upon Buddha as one of their own Avatars or Divine Incarnations."

Hindus believe that the purpose of the avatar of Buddha, like all divine avatars, was to re-establish dharma where "adharma" (irreligiousness) had become prevalent. Buddha is regarded by some sects of Hindus as an incarnation of Vishnu, or even as a Hindu. This is because Buddha's theistic beliefs are not contrary to Hinduism, but only a step ahead. This is also because the nature of Hinduism itself is such that all beliefs are recognized as being facets of the Ultimate Truth. It is interesting to note that the word "Nirvana"- used by Lord Buddha to describe the state of permanent bliss- is indeed a Vedic term. The great unification of Buddhism and Hinduism is still prevalent in Nepal, the birthplace of Buddha. Ironically, Nepal is the world's only Hindu nation, where people don't consider the two religions distinct from each other.

HARAPPA-MOHENJADARO

The Harappa-Mohenjodaro civilization flourished in the Indus River valley during the third and second millennia B.C.E. It had commercial contact with the pre-Babylonian Sumerians of the Mesopotamian area in modern-day Iraq, but little cul-tural influence from them. The people were most likely proto-Dravi-di-ans, with a religion having a supreme god who, representing fertility, creation, ascetic yogis with supernatural powers, and the lord of cattle, was somewhat like a prototype of the later Hindu god Shiva. The religious beliefs also included a mother goddess, ritual ablu-tion, phallic worship, and reverence of the sacred peepul (Skt. pipala) tree and of holy animals such as the cow. The peepal is a type of banyan fig tree, known in Buddhism as the bodhi tree.

Starting in the second half of the second millennium B.C.E., Indo-Iranian tribes invaded and conquered the Indus River valley. Subsequently, they settled there and beyond, to the east, in northern India. These tribes most likely originated in the area of Afghanis-tan, eastern Iran, and southern West Turkistan, and were known as the "Aryans," the "noble ones." The word Iran-, in fact, derives from the same source as the word Aryan. Early Iranian and Indian cul-tures share certain linguistic and religious features in com-mon through these tribes. With the Aryan invasion, many of the darker-skinned Harappa-Mohenjodaro native people became silaves, while others moved to South India. The class division of the Aryans into nobility and tribesmen was expanded to become the caste system of In-dia. The Sanskrit word for caste, varna, also means colour.

THE VEDAS

In the thirteenth century B.C.E., the Aryans established the Paurava Empire in northern India. By the ninth century B.C.E., their religion was codified in the Vedas. The Vedic gods are less humanized than their an-cient Greek counterparts. They are the maintainers of cosmic order and the upholders of moral good. During its earliest periods, practice of the Vedic religion entailed mostly singing hymns of praise and request to its gods. With the codification of the Vedas, however, society entrusted a caste of priests to make sacrificial offerings into a sacred fire to the gods.

The priests were known a "Brahmins." The offerings were required in order to compel the gods to maintain order; otherwise, the gods would not do so. The ceremonial offer-ings fed into the sacred fire consisted of milk, clarified butter (ghee), grains, and especially "soma," -the intoxicating juice of a possibly psycho-ac-tive plant. The ritual act of making of-ferings was ven-erated even more than the gods them-selves and, conse-quently, the Brahmain priests played an essential role in society. In other words, society believed that its welfare derived not so much from the favor of the gods, but rather from the Brahmins' correct performance of the offering ritual.

Because of this, early Hinduism is usually referred to as "Brahmanism." Further, society viewed the making of offerings as a debt owed to the gods. This belief gave rise to the Brahmanic concept of positive acts being the per-formance of one's duty. "Mantras" were originally the metric hymns of the Vedas, specifically the Rg Veda, to be sung at the ritual offerings to the gods. Their sound was viewed as having special power, and they were venerated as being unchanging and eternal.

Further, according to the Brahmanic teachings, the universe was created through the sacrifice of Brahma, who was somewhat like a primal giant. In other words, Brahma was the original being out of whom the universe evolved and who then sustains the universe and all life. The parts of his body became different as-pects of the universe and the castes of society. Thus, society viewed the universe as an organic whole, mirrored in the human body. After death, human spirits travel through the pathway of the cremation fire to the highest heaven of eternal light. Those who are negative sink into underground darkness.

A large literature evolved from the Vedas. The Brahmanas, in prose, explained the Vedic rituals and aided in their perfor-mance. The Puranas gave accounts of history. One epic history in particular, the Mahabharata, became seminal for the development of later, popular Hinduism. It was composed in the ninth century B.C.E. Also during this period, early ideas developed about another great god, Vishnu.

THE UPANISHADS

The Paurava Empire began to decline in the eighth century B.C.E., after a great flood caused the relocation of its capital. Slowly, the Empire broke into many smaller states. Some were kingdoms; others were republics. These major changes in

Indian society marked the beginning of a period of philosophical and religious speculation. The final portion of the Brahmanas was the Upanishads, a body of literature that developed, more fully, the philosophical basis for Brahmanism. Writ-ten over several hundred years, beginning around the end of the seventh century B.C.E., twelve of the Upanishads predated Buddha. Although each of the twelve presented slightly different teachings, they shared many general themes.

From the Brahmanic idea of the parallel between human beings and the primal giant, the Upanishads developed the assertion of the identity of *Atman* - the individual self or "soul"- with Brahma. Further, they explained that, as the primary cause of the universe, Brahma periodically created the world out of him and retracted it back into himself. Depending on the specific Upanishad, this process occurs in one of two ways. Either Brahma evolves into the universe or all the living beings in it; or the universe and all its living beings are merely the ap-pearances of Brahma. In either case, the true reality is the unity of everything and everyone as Brahma. The world of appearances of separate objects and individual beings is illusion (Skt. *maya*). Individual *Atmans*, or souls, are all, in fact, identical with Brahma.

The Upanishads also introduced the assertions of karma and rebirth. These assertions accord with their explanation that the universe undergoes repeated cycles of creation and destruction over huge spans of time. Similarly, indivi-dual souls experience repeated birth and death over countless lifetimes. This cycle of repeated rebirth (Skt. *Samsara*) occurs be-cause of their unawareness of the identity of themselves and Brahma. Moreover, it is driven by the force of their "karma" - their actions based on their unawareness that all is illusion. When one realizes what has always been the case, namely the basic unity between oneself and Brahma, with the separa-tion between the two being a total illu-sion, one attains liberation (Skt. *moksha*).

The path to liberation involves developing detachment and cultiva-ting a correct understanding of reality through hearing, think-ing, and meditating about the unity of the universe. The usual course of human spiritual development, however, passes through four life stages:

- Leading the celibate life of a student (Skt. *brahmacharya*),
- Becoming a married householder (Skt. *grhastha*) and raising a family,
- Retiring to the forests (Skt. *vanaprastha*) and living as a hermit,
- Renouncing everything (Skt. *sannyasa*) and, while still living alone in the forests, following intensive spiritual practice for gaining liberation.

Thus, the Upanishads emphasized that the universe is understandable and that to gain liberation from the sufferings of repeated rebirth due to unawareness and karma, one must see the true nature of reality and experience it for oneself. Buddhism and many of the other later Indian philosophical and religious systems accept these premises.

THE TIME OF SHAKYAMUNI BUDDHA

The division of northern India into republics and kingdoms continued into the time of Shakyamuni Buddha (566 - 485 B.C.E.). The two major ones were the Vrji Republic, with public assemblies and democratic institutions, and the autocratic kingdom of Magadha. Both types of state, however, functioned within the ritual structure of Brahmanism. This is because Brahmanism described the duties of a ruler, rather than his powers and form of government. Buddha was born in the tiny Shaka Republic, located to the north of Magadha, and taught in both these larger states.

Buddha's time saw the rise of the merchant class and the accumulation of great fortunes, measured now in money, rather than in cattle. The merchants became wealthier than the kings, and so the kings fought back by taking more autocratic measures to control commerce and society in general. Thus, within the kingdoms, the main preoccupations were gaining economic and political power. Consequently, with their emphasis on money and the use of violent force, the kingdoms became much stronger than the republics - economically, politically, and militarily. As a result, people experienced their freedom becoming increasingly more restricted and their suffering becoming increasingly greater. Many philosophers of the time, including Buddha, sought liberation through spiritual means.

There were two main spiritual groups offering paths to liberation in response to this difficult situation.

- The Brahmanas were the orthodoxy, who stayed with the old Brahmanic rituals. They followed the Upanishads as their philosophical basis, but within the context of first leading a life of duty within society and only becoming celibate renunciates after retiring. They were exclusively from the Brahmain caste and pursued their path to liberation as solitary ascetics living in the forests.
- The shramanas were wandering mendicant spiritual seekers. They came from castes other than the Brahmins and sought liberation by leaving society from the start. They lived together in the forests, with no caste differences, as a spiritual community (Skt. Sangha), rather than as solitary ascetics. They organized their autonomous communities on the model of the republics, with decisions made by assemblies. Moreover, all of them rejected a supreme god, such as Brahma, or any other form of a creator. Although the shramana communities had no caste differences within them, the laypeople that followed their teachings to a lesser extent and supported them still lived with the structure of the caste system.

THE FIVE MAIN SHRAMANA SCHOOLS

When Shakyamuni Buddha renounced his princely life, he joined the shramanas. Accordingly, after his enlightenment, he organized the spiritual seekers who followed him into autonomous communities along the same lines as other shramana groups. Thus, Buddhism became the fifth of the five shramana schools of the time.

The five shramana schools and their basic views were as follows:

- The Ajivika School, founded by Gosala, was deterministic and thus rejected the causal process of karma. They asserted that the constituent elements of the universe - earth, water, fire, wind, happiness, unhappiness, and living souls (Skt. *jiva*) - are uncreated, partless atoms or monads that do not interact with each other. Because everything is predetermined, although actions do occur through the atoms of these constituents; nevertheless, neither the actions themselves nor the atoms actually cause anything to happen. Living souls pass through an enormous number of rebirths and, after experiencing every possible life, they automatically enter a state of peace and are thus free of rebirth. Liberation, therefore, does not depend on what anyone actually does.
- The Lokayata or Charvaka School, taught by Ajita, also rejected karma. Not only that, it also rejected rebirth and any such thing as a living soul. It advocated hedonism, teaching that all actions should be spontaneous and should come from one's own nature (Skt. *svabhava*) - in other words, they should be natural. The aim of life was to experience as much sensual pleasure as possible. This school rejected all forms of logic and reasoning as valid ways of knowing anything.
- The Jain or Nirgrantha School, founded by Mahavira, broke away from the Lokayata School as a strong reaction against it. It therefore asserted living souls undergoing rebirth through the force of karma. Jainism, still existent as today as one of the major Indian religious systems, teaches extremely strict ethical behavior and, in fact, extreme asceticism as the means for gaining liberation.
- The Ajnana School of Agnostics, led by Sanjayin, asserted that it was impossible to gain conclusive knowledge about anything through philosophical speculation or debates based on logic. It advocated living in celibate communities that placed their emphasis merely on friendship.

- Buddhism developed as a shramana school that accepted rebirth under the force of karma, while rejecting the existence of the type of soul that other schools asserted. In addition, Buddha accepted as parts of the path to liberation the use of logic and reasoning, as well as ethical behavior, but not to the degree of Jain asceticism. In this way, Buddhism avoided the extremes of the previous four shramana schools.

THE BUDDHA'S PLACE IN INDIAN THOUGHT

The Buddha is the greatest personality that India has produced in the many millennia of her history For the people of Asia's wide expanses, to day as centuries ago, the Buddha is the great exponent of the spirit of India, His name is known to the uncivilized nomad in the icy steppes of Siberia as well as to the cultured son of China.

To him turn in homage the gentle Sinhalese of tropical Ceylon and the war - like Japanese of Nippon's Moderate climes When early last century scholars of the West began to study the spiritual life of Asia, the Sage of the Sakyans, as no other genius of the East, became the prime focus of interest; no other has been so often mentioned, praised and blamed; no other has exercised, even 2500 years after his death, such a significant influence on the philosophy of Western thinkers among them I mention only Schopenhauer as an example.

When searching for the cause of this extraordinary phenomenon, we ask ourselves why just the Buddha could make such a strong and long - lasting impact, while many other Indian thinkers and prophets who at their times were equally popular, did not penetrate beyond India's borders and were even forgotten in their own home country. In looking for the reasons we find that in the personality of the Buddha several features are united which only in their totality were able to produce that universal effect which the founders of other Indian religions could not achieve.

The first among these features is the fact that in the course of his preaching the Buddha summarized the results of prior philosophical thought and did so in a or that was precise and yet intelligible to the unlearned; sSecondly, the fact that the Buddha himself practiced and embodied up to the highest point the ethical principles which he taught; and thirdly, he made his way of salvation quite independent from the limitations of Indian tradition and its caste system and therefore offered it to the whole of humanity. Like all great teachers of mankind, the Buddha was also a child of his time. From his predecesscrs he took over the teachings of Karma, rebirth, the sorrow yielding transiency of all craving, asceticism, liberation through knowledge and Nirvana. But by giving these teachings a distinctive philosophical character that took them out of their connection with Brahmainical tradition, the Buddha created a teaching of deliverance that was meant for all men. Unlike them he did not speak of sacrifices or of Brahma, but he may be called a phenomenologist who, restricting himself to the actualities of the inner and outer world as perceived by man, explained the nature of suffering, its cause, its cessation, and the noble eightfold path leading to Nirvana Similarly as his contemporary, Heraklitus of Ephesus, he taught the Panta Rhei, the eternal flux of all phenomena.

The Brahmins taught as Parmenides did a state of Being, abiding and eternal, in which every individual self has its roots. The Buddha proclaimed the very antithesis of it: there is no abiding Being, no immutable self there is only a becoming, flux, only by understanding the nature not only of the external world but also of the ego, is it possible to attain to the highest selflessness that brings about Nirvana, the dissolution of the imaginary personality - complex.

The Buddha's teaching could not have had such an enormous success in India and beyond its borders if not for his so very attractive personality. The Buddha was not a theoretician who offered good counsel to others, but he was one who by his own example put the final, authentic seal on the ethical teachings he proclaimed.

Aged 29, he left the luxurious court of his royal father at Kapilavatthu (in the Himalayas) and donned a mendicant's robe for seeking after salvation. In vain he searched for ultimate wisdom among other teachers: in vain he undertook the severest ascetical self - mortification for many years, Finally, after seven years of spiritual struggle, the Eye of understanding opened within him, under the holy fig tree (the Bodhi Tree) which can still be seen at Bodh Gaya.

Thus he became a Holy One, an Awakened One, and a Buddha. For over forty years he then walked through the northern parts of India, in ascetic's garb, living on collected alms food, and preaching his doctrine. Up to his death at eighty he did not shirk the hardships of the fatiguing peregrinations on foot, for the sake of spreading his message. The texts describe him as a majestic personality, a man of self - abnegation and of a rare kindness of heart, the embodiment of passion -free serenity. Pious faith may have later glorified the Buddha, surrounding him with a divine aura and with a dense overgrowth of legends and miracles. But below that sacral over painting of the original picture there remains the image of a man of rare equipoise and serenity: the figure of a Saint who has transcended the world and whose features radiate the perfect stillness of his mind.

The Buddha was no revolutionary in the Western sense. Though he was opposed to the Brahmins arrogance, his aim was not a revolution against the social order as represented by the caste system in India A graded structural organization of society appeared to him, the aristocrat, a necessity by natural law, as natural as the gradation of beinigs in general, starting with the lowest animals and rising, through men and spirits, to the gods: because, according to the Buddha, even gods are subject to Karma as are men, and therefore enjoy their present position only for a limited time.

What he challenged was the claim of Brahmins to be superior to the other castes, by virtue of being the guardians of the sacred Vedic tradition. For the Buddha, no class or caste privileges existed as far as salvation was concerned. Hence his emphatic statement: "Not by birth is one a Brahmain, but only by knowledge and moral conduct'.

It is only the moral qualities that determine an individual's rank in the stages of his gradual progress towards deliverance. Hence also members of the lower castes were admitted to his monastic order. So we find among his disciples, side by side with Brahmins and warriors, those who had been scavengers or had other despised occupations, even a converted robber chief For the Buddha neither noble birth nor wealth were decisive, but solely a man's understanding and his moral conduct. The monks and nuns who, withdrawn from worldliness, lived either singly or in communities a life of renunciation and of active lovingkindness for all that lives, had always been only a minority among the Buddha's followers, as they represented only the upper ranks of his disciples. Below them were numerous lay devotees who, at various stages of dedication and inner development, observed only a part of the rules binding on monks; and finally there were the still larger numbers of those who were in Sympathy with the teaching and participated in its rites, but who, without exclusive allegiance and with the Indian's typical tolerance, were devoted also to other religious cults.

Hence, from the Buddhist point of view, the teaching of deliverance can be understood and practised by different people to a very different extent, according to their inclinations and capacities. The "road to enlightenment" starts even as far down as on the level of animals; we hear, for instance, of pious elephants and hares, or of a frog who as reward of homage paid to the Buddha, was reborn in a devout huiman family and, progressing steadily, finally gained deliverance.

If one wishes to have a correct idea of the Buddhist "Weltanschauung" and outlook on life, one has to familiarize oneself with the Buddhist conception that an incalculably large number of living beings, through thousands of years, in thousands of lives, proceed on their way to the light, slowly though not without relapses. The Western concept that salvation depends on the moral quality of one single life must not be used as a basis for judgingBuddhist ethics.

Hence the widely spread opinion that because the Buddha taught renunciation to his monks, he wanted all men to be monks, is quite erroneous and so also the idea derived from it, that Buddhism is averse to culture. Because only a few among the countless beings will reach Nirvana after slow progress, therefore Buddhism, from its very start, has provided less stringent ethical precepts for those who only gradually can achieve that maturity required for final liberation.

Hence, in Buddhist countries, art and sciences have always been cultivated, and it is not by chance that Buddhists have been among the founders of Indian medicine, as it was one of their foremost endeavours to help suffering humanity. For the great majority of Buddhists and this I found also in present - day Burma, Siam, China and Japan Nirvana is only the ultimate, distant goal to which practically only the monk is devoted.

Buddhism when it flourished, was certainly not a pessimistic and life denying religion. This can be seen from the fact that some of the greatest rulers of ancient India, Ashoka (250 B.C.), Kanishka (100 A.C.) and Harsha (650 A. C.) were Buddhists. Buddhism did not establish in India an organized Church in the Western sense, and it had no central ecclesiastical authority laying down what was the true faith and what was not.

Hence there arose many schools and sects who differed from each other in several doctrinal issues, though all of them revered the Buddha as their master. As enforced concersion is alien to Buddhism and as it did not demand exclusive allegiance or a formal repudiation of other religions, the total number of Buddhists underwent strong fluctuations. Buddhism was never the dominant religion of India, and it was always only a section of the population that professed it.

Even at periods of its widest dissemination on the Indian subcontinent, Brahmanism always remained a strong force. When, since about the 8th century A.C., Brahmanism came to the fore again and vigorous religious movements arose in its midst to which an ageing Buddhism was no match, Gautama Buddha's teaching almost vanished in India. Similarly as

Christianity which in present day Palestine counts only very few followers but instead had conquered a large part of the world, so also Buddhism found in the Far East and in South – East Asia rich compensation for the loss in India.

In Burma, Thailand, Cambodia and Laos, in Tibet, Sikkim and Bhutan almost the whole population is Buddhist: in Ceylon It is a large majority, and in China, Korea and Vietnam Buddhism have a large number of followers, while in Japan it is the predominant religion. Within the long history of Indian religion, the one and a half millennia of Buddhist history on Indian soil are only an episode but it is an episode of a significance that can hardly be rated highly enough.

Buddhism has amalgamated the currents of Indian thought in a system of ingenious synthesis which decisively influenced minds at a time of India's political and cultural greatness. It was through Buddhism that Indian ideas became known in most parts of Asia, and this was an achievement of cultural propaganda of a vast extent but also in contemporary India. The impact of the Buddha, his teaching and his community of monks is still very much in evidence.

The formulations given by the Buddha and his disciples for fundamental concepts of the Indian world view have partly been adapted by the opponents and made parts of their systems. This applies, for instance, to formulations connected with the law of moral causality (Karma), the teachings on a gradual path to enlightenment, liberation by knowledge, and Nirvana. Also the towering personality of the Buddha could not be overlooked or by passed: hence they gave to him, the great heterodox, rank or an incarnation (*avatar*) of God Vishnu.

4

Early Buddhist Doctrine

When we use the term Buddhists, we do not mean to imply by it either the exoteric Buddhism instituted by the followers of Gautama Buddha, or the modern Buddhistic religion, but the secret philosophy of Sakyamuni, which in its essence is certainly identical with the ancient Wisdom-Religion of the sanctuary, the pre-Vedic Brahmanism. Buddha, Pythagoras, Orpheus, Socrates, or even Jesus, left behind them any writings. The esoteric teachings of Buddha were the Gupta Vidya (secret knowledge) of the ancient Brahmins, the key to which their modern successors have, with few exceptions, completely lost. And this Vidya has passed into what is now known as the inner teachings of the Mahayana school of Northern Buddhism.

In fact, Buddhism in the present age cannot be justly judged by one or the other of its exoteric popular forms. Real Buddhism can be appreciated only by blending the philosophy of the Southern Church and the metaphysics of the Northern Schools. If one seems too iconoclastic and stern, and the other too metaphysical and transcendental, even to being overgrown with the weeds of Indian exotericism - many of the gods of its Pantheon having been transplanted under new names to Tibetan soil - it is entirely due to the popular expression of Buddhism in both Churches.

The Hindu Reformer limited his public teachings to the purely moral and physiological aspect of the Wisdom-Religion, to Ethics and Man alone. Things "unseen and incorporeal," the mystery of being outside our terrestrial sphere, the great Teacher left entirely untouched in his public lectures, reserving the hidden Truths for a select circle of his Arhats. Time and imagination made short work of the purity and philosophy of these teachings, once that they were transplanted from the secret and sacred circle of the Arhats, during the course of their work of proselytism, into a soil less prepared for metaphysical conceptions than India; i.e., once they were transferred into China, Japan, Siam, and Burma.

How the pristine purity of these grand revelations was dealt with may be seen in studying some of the so-called "esoteric" Buddhist schools of antiquity in their modern garb, not only in China and other Buddhist countries in general, but even in not a few schools in Tibet, left to the care of uninitiated Lamas and Mongolian innovators. One great distinction between Theosophy and exoteric Buddhism is that the latter, represented by the Southern Church [Theravada], entirely denies (a) the existence of any Deity, and (b) any conscious post-mortem life, or even any self-conscious surviving individuality in man. Such at least is the teaching of the Siamese sect, not considered the purest form of exoteric Buddhism.

And it is so, if we refer only to Buddha's public teachings. The schools of the Northern Buddhist Church, established in those countries to which his initiated Arhats retired after the Master's death, teach all that is now called Theosophical doctrines, because they form part of the knowledge of the initiates - thus proving how the truth has been sacrificed to the dead-letter by the too-zealous orthodoxy of Southern Buddhism. But how much grander and more noble, more philosophical and scientific, even in its dead-letter, is this teaching than that of any other Church or religion.

"The one Universal Light, which to Man is Darkness, is ever existent," says the Chaldean "Book of Numbers." From it precedes periodically the energy, which is reflected in the "Deep" or Chaos, the storehouse of future worlds, and, once awakened, stirs up and fructifies the latent Forces, which are the ever present eternal potentialities in it. Then awake anew the Brahmas and Buddhas - the co-eternal Forces - and a new Universe springs into being.... The doctrine of God being the Universal Mind diffused through all things underlies all ancient philosophies.

The Buddhist tenets which can never be better comprehended than when studying Pythagorean philosophy - its faithful reflection - are derived from this source as well as the Brahmanical religion and early Christianity. Archaic Occultism would remain incomprehensible to all, if it were rendered otherwise than through the more familiar channels of Buddhism and Hinduism. For the former is the emanation of the latter; and both are the children of one mother - ancient Lemuro-Atlantean Wisdom. It is by the spirit of the teachings of both Buddha and Pythagoras that we can so easily recognize the identity of their doctrines.

The all-pervading universal soul, the Anima Mundi, is Nirvana; and Buddha, as a generic name, is the anthropomorphized monad of Pythagoras. When resting in Nirvana, the final bliss, Buddha is the silent Monad, dwelling in darkness and silence. He is also the formless Brahma, the sublime but unknowable Deity, which pervades invisibly the whole Universe. Whenever it is manifested, desiring to impress itself upon humanity in a shape intelligent to our intellect, whether we call it an avatar, or a King Messiah, or a permutation of Divine Spirit, Logos, Christos, it is all one and the same thing. In each case it is the "Father," who is in the Son, and the Son in "the Father."

The immortal spirit overshadows the mortal man. It enters into him, and pervading his whole being, makes of him a god, who descends into his earthly tabernacle. Every man may become a Buddha, says the doctrine. In the esoteric and even exoteric Buddhism of the North, Adi Buddha, the One unknown, without beginning or end, identical with Parabrahma and Ain-Soph, emits a bright ray from its darkness. This is the Logos (the first), or Vajradhara, the

Supreme Buddha. As the Lord of all Mysteries he cannot manifest, but sends into the world of manifestation his heart - the "diamond heart," Vajrasattva. This is the second logos of creation, from whom emanate the seven Dhyani Buddhas, called the Anupadaka, "the parentless."

These Buddhas are the primeval monads from the world of incorporeal being, the *Arupa* world, wherein the Intelligences (on that plane only) have neither shape nor name, in the exoteric system, but have their distinct seven names in esoteric philosophy. These Dhyani Buddhas emanate, or create from themselves, by virtue of *Dhyana*, celestial Selves - the superhuman *Bodhisattvas*. These incarnations at the beginning of every human cycle on earth as mortal men, become occasionally, owing to their personal merit, Bodhisattvas among the Sons of Humanity, after which they may re-appear as Manushi (human) Buddhas.

The Anupadaka (or Dhyani Buddhas) are thus identical with the Brahmanical Manasaputra, "mind-born sons" - whether of Brahma or either of the other two Trimurtian Hypostases, hence identical also with the *Rishis* and *Prajapatis*. As the reader is supposed not to be acquainted with the Dhyani-Buddhas, it is as well to say at once that, according to the Orientalists, there are five Dhyanis who are the "celestial" Buddhas, of whom the human Buddhas are the manifestations in the world of form and matter.

Esoterically, however, the Dhyani-Buddhas are seven, of whom five only have hitherto manifested, and two are to come in the sixth and seventh Root-races. They are, so to speak, the eternal prototypes of the Buddhas who appear on this earth, each of whom has his particular divine prototype. So, for instance, Amitabha is the Dhyani-Buddha of Gautama Sakyamuni, manifesting through him whenever this great Soul incarnates on earth as He did in Tzon-kha-pa [who was] the first and greatest Reformer who founded the "Yellow-Caps," Gyalugpas. He was born in the year 1355 A.D. in Amdo, and was the Avatar of Amitabha, the celestial name of Gautama Buddha.

The term Anupadaka, "parentless," or without progenitors, is a mystical designation having several meanings in the philosophy. By these name celestial beings, the Dhyan-Chohans or Dhyani-Buddhas are generally meant. But as these correspond mystically to the human Buddhas and Bodhisattvas, known as the "Manushi (or human) Buddhas," the latter are also designated "Anupadaka," once that their whole personality is merged in their compound sixth and seventh principles - or Atma-Buddhi, and that they have become "diamond-souled" (*Vajrasattvas*), the full Mahatmas.

The mystery in the hierarchy of the Anupadaka is great; its apex being the universal Spirit-Soul, and the lower rung the Manushi-Buddha; and even every Soul-endowed man is an Anupadaka in a latent state. As the synthesis of the seven Dhyani-Buddhas, Avalokiteswara was the first Buddha (the Logos), so Amitabha is the inner "God" of Gautama, who, in China, is called Amita (Buddha). They are, as Mr. Rhys Davids correctly states, "the glorious counterparts in the mystic world, free from the debasing conditions of this material life" of every earthly mortal Buddha - the liberated Manushi-Buddhas appointed to govern the Earth in this Round.

They are the "Buddhas of Contemplation," and are all Anupadaka (parentless), i.e., self-born of divine essence. The exoteric teaching which says that every Dhyani-Buddha has the faculty of creating from himself, an equally celestial son - a Dhyani-Bodhisattva - who, after the decease of the Manushi Buddha, has to carry out the work of the latter, rests on the fact that owing to the highest initiation performed by one overshadowed by the "Spirit of Buddha" a candidate becomes virtually a Bodhisattva, created such by the High Initiator. As to Gautama's being one of the true and undeniable Saviours of the World, suffice it to say that the most rabid orthodox missionary, unless he is hopelessly insane, or has not the least regard for historical truth, cannot find one smallest accusation against the life and personal character of the "Buddha."

Without any claim to divinity, allowing his followers to fall into atheism rather than into the degrading superstition of deva or idol-worship, his walk in life is from beginning to the end, holy and divine. During the forty-five years of his mission, it is as blameless and pure as that of a god - or as the latter should be. He is a perfect example of a divine, godly man. He reached Buddhaship - i.e., complete enlightenment - entirely by his own merit and owing to his own individual exertions, no god being supposed to have any personal merit in the exercise of goodness and holiness.

His is the only absolutely bloodless religion among all the existing religions: tolerant and liberal, teaching universal compassion and charity, love and self-sacrifice, poverty and contentment with one's lot, whatever it may be. No persecutions, and enforcement of faith by fire and sword, have ever disgraced it. No thunder-and-lightning-vomiting god has interfered with its chaste commandments; and if the simple, human philosophical code of daily life left to us by the greatest Man-Reformer ever known, should ever come to be adopted by mankind at large, then indeed an era of bliss and peace would dawn on humanity. To become a Buddha one has to reach a complete detachment from all that is evanescent and finite, and live while yet on Earth in the immortal and everlasting alone, in a supreme state of holiness.

To become a Buddha one has to break through the bondage of sense and personality; to acquire a complete perception of the real self and learn not to separate it from all other selves; to learn by experience the utter unreality of all phenomena of the visible Kosmos foremost of all. The spiritual entity breaks loose for ever from particle of matter, then only it enters upon the eternal and unchanging Nirvana. He exists in spirit, in nothing; as a form, a shape, a semblance, he is completely annihilated, and thus will die no more, and for spirit alone is no Maya, but the only reality in an illusionary universe of ever-passing forms.

Esoteric teachings claim that Buddha renounced Nirvana and gave up the Dharmakaya vesture to remain a "Buddha of Compassion" within the reach of the miseries of this world. And the religious philosophy he left to it has produced for over 2,000 year's generations of good and unselfish men. Every Orientalist and Pundit knows by heart the story of Gautama, the Buddha, the most perfect of mortal men that the world has ever seen, but none of them seem to suspect the esoteric meaning underlying his prenatal biography, i.e., the significance of the popular story.

The Lalitavistara tells the tale, but abstains from hinting at the truth. The 5,000 Jatakas or the events of former births (re-incarnations) are taken literally instead of esoterically. Gautama, the Buddha, would not have been a mortal man, had he not passed through hundreds and thousands of births previous to his last. Yet the detailed account of these, and the statement that during them he worked his way up through every stage of transmigration from the lowest animate and inanimate atom and insect, up to the highest - or man, - contains simply the well-known occult aphorism, "a stone becomes a plant, a plant an animal, and an animal a man."

Every human being who has ever existed has passed through the same evolution. But the hidden symbolism in the sequence of these rebirths (*jatakas*) contains a perfect history of the evolution on this earth, pre and post human, and is a scientific exposition of natural facts. One truth not veiled but bare and open is found in their nomenclature, viz., that as soon as Gautama had reached the human form he began exhibiting in every personality the utmost unselfishness, self-sacrifice and charity. The name "Gautama" means - "on earth (*gau*) the most victorious (*tama*)."

The ethics of Theosophy are identical with those taught by Buddha, being the soul of the Wisdom-Religion, and once the common property of the initiates of all nations. But Buddha was the first to embody these lofty ethics in his public teachings, and to make them the foundation and the very essence of his public system. It is herein that lays the immense difference between the exoteric Buddhism and every other religion. For while in other religions ritualism and dogma hold the first and most important place, in Buddhism it is the ethics which have always been the most insisted upon.

Christianity becomes every day more a religion of pure emotionalism; the root philosophy of both Adwaita and Buddhist scholars is identical, and both have the same respect for animal life, for both believe that every creature on earth, however small and humble, "is an immortal portion of the immortal matter" - for matter with them has quite another significance than it has with either Christian or materialist - and that every creature is subject to Karma. The anatmavada doctrine was one of the most important ideas of the primitive Buddhism which distinctly distinguished it from orthodox Brahmanism as well as from Jainism, or other religious and philosophical doctrines of the Indian origin.

In its classical form preserved in the Pali Theravada tradition it proclaims the absence of substantial eternal self, or *Atman* as empirical phenomenon replacing it by five skanhas, or groups of elements (dharma) which may be understood as elementary and ever-changing psycho-physical states as well as units of description of these states. Nevertheless, early Buddhist texts said nothing about *Atman* in its Upanishadic sense, i.e. about Universal Self beyond empirical states of consciousness. The Madhyamika branch of the Mahayana Buddhist thought developed this notion of the anatmavada doctrine in the direction of the dharma nairatmya teaching (the theory of essenceless nature of dharmas, or their devoidness of intrinsic self-being, svabhava).

Another school of the Mahayana Buddhism, Yogacara (Vijnanavada) was very interested in the problem of the sources of the empirical forms of consciousness (the sarvastivadins and sautrantikas were engaged only in the analysis of the psychical experience as such though the roots of the Yogacara approach may be found in the ideas of early mahisasakas).

They developed the doctrine of the seventh (*manas*) and the eighth (*alaya-vijnana*) kinds of consciousness. Certainly, *alaya-vijnana* of Asanga and Vasubandhu is not *Atman* at all but the attention to the problem of substratum of consciousness was a key to the development of some kind of the Buddhist ontology / metaphysics restoring the idea of *Atman* in the purely Buddhist context.

The Yogacara School did not represent the homogenous and coherent unity. It seems to be possible to divide this school into three relative but different branches:

1. The phenomenology or phenomenological psychology of Vasubandhu and Asanga;
2. Logical and epistemological branch of Dignaga and Dharmakirti
3. Metaphysical / ontological branch of Maitrey-Asanga: a kind of the Yogacara and Tathagatagarbha synthesis represented by Asanga's Mahayanasutralamkara and purely the Tathagatagarbhist treatise of Maitreya (according to Chinese tradition its author was Saramati)
4. Ratnagotravibhaga / Uttaratantra.

The theory of the Tathagatagarbha was the logical and natural result of the evolution of the Buddhist Mahayana thought. It proclaimed the positive character of the Buddhist Absolute (*dharmakaya, ekacitta*) as non-empty (*asunya*) by itself. It has four good qualities which can not be separated from it (compare with the abhidharmist dharma-theory, where the holder-dharma is the same as the quality held by it, unlike the substance of the Brahmanists, which is absolutely different from its qualities): *nitya* (eternity), *sukha* (bliss), *Atman* (self; essence) and *subha* (purity).

The Yogacara-Tathagatagarbha synthesis marked the climax of the development of metaphysical trend of the Buddhist thought (*Lankavatara sutra, Mahayanasutralamkara* and probably Chinese compendium of this synthesis known as Mahayana sraddhotpada sastra). Certainly, it is absolutism but specifically Buddhist one, the absolutism preserving the main Buddhist approaches and features. Does it contradict to the classical anatmavada doctrine? I suppose, definitely no. The classical anatmavada proclaimed the skandhas instead of *Atman* as empirical reality.

The Tathagatagarbha doctrine proclaimed the *Atman* behind skandhas as super empirical absolute reality Attain able only in the state of enlightenment / awakening (making in the same time the nature of every kind of consciousness as semsnyid in rdzogs-chen, or fo xin in Chan). The historical fate of the Tathagatagarbhist absolutism was different in India and other regions of the Mahayana Buddhism. The most remarkable event in the history of this doctrine is its exclusive prevalence in the Chinese and Far Eastern Buddhist schools where the Tathagatagarbha doctrine became the core of such schools as Tiantai, Huayan and Chan.

Peace is the essential teaching of Buddhism. As the means of practice, peace cultivated in a person's mind is a source of an act of peace and a moral deed. Only a peaceful mind can originate a peaceful act. Many passages of the Buddhist teachings encourage a person to keep his/her mind in peace and demand peace from others. A passage here may illustrate the point:

All men tremble at punishment,

All men fear death;

Remembering that thou art like unto them,

Do not strike or sila.

He who, seeking his own happiness,

Does not injure or kill beings

Who also long for happiness,

will find happiness after death.

All phenomena (originating from a sentient being)

Dhamma- are preceded by (the activity of) the mind,

have as their chief agent the mind;

And are made up of the mind.

If one were to speak or act

with a pure mind,

Happiness follows one as a consequence,

Even as the shadow that never leaves one. - The *Dhammapada*

Like Mahatma Gandhi's ahimsa, the Buddhist loving-kindness (metta) and altruistic practices should be cultivated internally. It is not proved to exist by means of a helpful act, white or yellow clothing, a smiling face, and so on. It is essentially the sincerity and purity of a person's heart. It cannot exist without a peaceful mind. A peaceful mind yields wisdom and all virtues. Thus, in Buddhism, meditation is a crucial means to attain a peaceful mind. The principle of meditation is the training of mindfulness. Whenever we pay attention to our own thoughts, words, and deeds, we are conscious of ourselves and are aware of our movements. Being aware of our own selves, we feel ashamed of doing evil and thus do not let ourselves go wrong.

There are many places in Thailand which offer free courses in meditation to Thais and foreigners. For example, the meditation teaching at the Non Pah Pong Monastery and meditation lectures and training at the World Meditation of Buddhists headquarters are well known to a considerable number of meditators. In the view of Ajahn Chah, the former abbot of the Non Pah Pong Monastery, meditation practices are the cultivation of mindfulness and insight. First, we must find a meditation subject which is suitable to our particular tendencies, a way of practice which is right for our character and for example, going over and over the parts of the body: hair of the head, nails, teeth, and skin can be very calming.

The mind can become very peaceful from this practice. If contemplating these five things leads to calm, it is because they are appropriate objects for contemplation according to our tendencies. Whatever we find to be appropriate in this way, we can consider being our practice and using it to subdue defilements. If such practice does not work, we may try again with another meditation subject, e.g. the recollection of death. For those who still have strong greed, aversion, and delusion, it is useful to take this subject of personal death for meditation.

We shall see that everybody must die some day. Developing this practice, we find that an attitude of dispassion arises. The more we practise, the more we find peace. This is because it is a suitable and appropriate practice for us.

According to the Buddhist Scriptures, the tipitaka, the Buddha searched for peace and enlightenment in the forest. Thus, it is a tradition and preference for monks to go to the forest and live in solitude. There they practise meditation and find peace in their ascetic lives. In addition, the Buddhist discipline prescribes that monks should live not too close to and not too far from a village so that they can live a peaceful life, find some food, and preach the doctrine to lay people. Since, in Buddhism, the meditation subject can be anything suitable for each meditator, the meditation practice is beneficial to all, even to non-Buddhists. It is the universal way of peace. Christians may concentrate on Jesus as their meditation subject. Hindus may meditate on Shiva or Vishnu and Muslims on Allah. If all human beings practise meditation everyday, the world will be free from wars.

Apart from being the means of practice, peace is also the goal and the ideal of Buddhist life. The final goal of Buddhist moral practices is the attainment of peace both worldly and other-worldly. The goal of the monastic life is nibbana or the ultimate peace as follows:

The bhikkhu (monk) who lives in loving-kindness,

And is pleased in the Buddha's teaching,

Attains the peaceful state (nibbana),

Which is happiness at the allaying of conditioned things?

The Dhammapada

And the goal of everyone, monks and laity, in this world is nibbana.

Those whose minds are rightly trained in the factors of enlightenment, and who changing to nothing,

And delighting in such dissociation,

They- the resplendent ones- attain nibbana even in this world.

In order to form the habit of peace offering, Buddhists are taught to diffuse loving-kindness to all beings as often as they can everyday. For example, before they go to bed at night, Buddhists recite the verse from the Buddhist Scriptures as follows:

Let creatures all, all things that live,

All beings of whatever kind,

See nothing that will bode them ill!

May naught of evil come to them!

The Culla-Vagga

Having the habit of peace offering, one's mind always rests in peaceful happiness and in peace with others. Buddhists who reject peace and do not try to live in peace with others are wayward followers of the Buddha and can hardly be called Buddhists.

Buddhadasa-bhikkhu (1906-93), an eminent monk of Thailand, once gave a lecture on the subject 'Till the World Is With Peace'1 asserting that peace should be fulfilled through qualified peace-makers as follows:

1. Peace-makers should be well educated and moral people. Education here aims at spiritual growth and moral wisdom. On the contrary, education today emphasizes only academic knowledge, intellectual capacities, and technology. Thus, it rouses desire and selfishness and ignores the religious truth guiding human beings to right thought and right conduct. Ideally and properly, education should cultivate our basic human-ness in order to make humankind righteous and peaceful.
2. Peace-makers should be physically, mentally and spiritually healthy. In order to be healthy physically, one should be free from all excessive enjoyments and indulgence. To be healthy mentally is to be free from all

defilements and fetters. To be healthy spiritually is to be free from false conceptions and blind faith. The unhealthy are those who are slaves to their own selfishness, defilements, worldly enjoyments and other trivialities of worldly life. They disregard and dislike the Buddhist doctrine. They cannot form a good society. Indeed, only healthy social members can establish a peaceful society.

3. Peace-makers should come from righteous and peaceful families. Righteous and peaceful families know their duties and obligations to others. They act according to the Buddhist doctrine. Those who come from righteous and peaceful families are responsible social members. For example, if they are the superiors, they will treat inferiors with compassion; if they are children, they will respect and care for their parents. They can always secure peace in their society.
4. Peace-makers should live according to a dhammic economic plan that is moderate in living, in spending and in possessing, being neither too poor nor too rich. If we live moderately, we shall feel content with ourselves. We shall not struggle for anything more than we need to survive. If we are too poor and our morality is not strong enough, we may be trapped into misconduct and be harmful to ourselves and others in order to survive, e.g. stealing or even killing others for some money. On the other hand, if we are too rich, we may be indulgent and careless about others. In Thailand today, rich people are generally extravagant. The word sresthi in Thai means the rich. In Pali and Sanskrit, it originally and literally means the noblest. At the time of the Buddha, the Buddhist rich people were philanthropic and righteous. They built alms-houses to serve the poor, ascetics and all in need. Peace-makers should adopt the spirit and practices of the rich in the Buddha's time so that all members of society can live happily and peacefully together.
5. Peace-makers should know and practise the dhamma, the life duty of all human beings. Such duty demands all

human beings to work and live for the sake of all beings and in accordance with the law of nature. In order to fulfil one's duty, one needs to get rid of one's selfishness and cultivate concern and responsibility for the sake of the world.

6. Peace-makers should be unselfish and altruistic, realizing that all people are companions in the process of birth, old age, sickness, and death. They should try to cooperate with others in order to establish a peaceful and loving society.
7. Peace-makers should be moral in thoughts, words, and actions. Morality keeps the world in balance and equilibrium. Those who think, speak or act morally always keep themselves to this normative balance leading to peace and happiness of others. On the other hand, those who act against this equilibrium create disturbances. Thus, morality is indispensable for the realization of peace on earth.
8. Peace-makers should have the right view (*samma-ditthi*). The right view is the knowledge of morality in the fundamental sense. One cannot conduct oneself morally unless one understands the real meaning and value of morality. The right view is the only means to free oneself from all suffering and is crucial for overcoming one's selfishness. It gives us the true knowledge of the world and thus asserts the necessity of world peace.
9. Peace-makers should have a 'cooled' life. Whenever all defilements are eliminated from our minds, our lives are 'cooled down' (*nibbana*), which can be experienced in this life, is generally understood as two stages of a peaceful life, ordinary and ultimate. The ordinary or worldly stage is the peaceful lives of ordinary people. The ultimate stage is absolute freedom from all pains and is exclusively experienced by holy people or the enlightened ones. If all people had 'cooled' lives, the world would certainly be in peace.

Apart from meditation and moral cultivation, peace can be attained through all religious arts, e.g. paintings, sculptures, images, and so on. In Thailand, Buddha images are intentionally made to inspire peace in the hearts of all who see them. The smiling face of a Buddha image and his eyes gazing downward seem to invite all sufferers to come and take merciful guidance from him. Entering the consecrated assembly hall of a Thai Buddhist temple, one finds the Buddha image presiding at the end of the hall. Looking around, one can see murals depicting the history of the Buddha's life showing his moral activities and compassion for all beings. Going to a temple for an appreciation of religious arts is thus a way to create peace in one's heart.

Besides, all Buddhist temples are sanctuaries. They are places of peace and protection of all lives. Formerly, those who had a death sentence and could escape to a temple and be ordained as monks were forgiven and freed. Nowadays, all kinds of people love to free animals, such as dogs, cats, birds and small turtles in a temple or a monastery compound. They know that the animals will be safe there since it is a Buddhist tradition not to harm any being in a temple. It is important to call for peace education.

All institutions should teach people to love peace. A proper educational system should be established to promote humaneness and moral wisdom. Since the word manussa (human being) in its original sense means 'one of noble heart', the right educational system should endow students with noble hearts and make them complete human beings. Once people become human beings, peace can be restored to the entire world.

THE CONCEPT OF PEACE

In Vietnam since early times, peace has been largely conceived of as peace in one's mind, peace towards one's fellows, and peace with nature. Those aspects of peace are greatly influenced by Buddhism. Each social stratum has its own approach to the serenity of mind through Buddhism. The intelligentsia practised Zen (*dhyana*) firstly through Zen masters coming from India and later from China to ultimately establish their own Zen sect in the thirteenth century called the Thien Truc Lam (Bamboo Forest Zen Sect). They abided by the teachings of Buddha:

Those who practise meditation steadfastly,

Always strong in determination and perseverance,

The wise ones enjoy nibbana,

Safe from any bondage, the highest - *Dhammapada*, 234

Or

... He does not cleave to sense-desires,

Cool he is, and without germs to a new life,

All clinging are cut down,

Pains in the heart are overcome,

Serene and calm, he leads a life of happiness,

And his mind has Attained peace and calmness - *Samyutta Nikaya*, I, 2635

Learned Buddhist scholars enjoyed great influence on the daily life of the common people. Through them the commoners could have an understanding of the gist of Buddha's teachings on His attitude towards other religions and antagonistic doctrines, His love and compassion for the world, and on fundamental topics of daily life such as dispute and harmony, anger and gentleness, harmfulness and harmlessness, hatred and friendliness, killing and respect for life, etc. Among many teachings they were most impressed by such words as:

One should take oneself as one's own refuge,

Because there is no other refuge,

By a self well tamed and restrained,

One obtains a refuge that is very difficult to obtain - *Dhammapada*, 1606

Or

By oneself, evil deed is done,

By oneself, one is defiled,

By oneself, evil deed is not done,
By oneself, one becomes purified.
Purity and impurity are done by oneself,
No one can purify another

Dhammapada

They were fully aware of the value of self-reliance on the way of deliverance to obtain fundamental peace, that in one's mind. They had an insight into the expression of Buddhism, that to be born as human is the most advantageous status for every living being, as it is only he who may realize the Four Holy Truths and practise the Eightfold Holy Path to deliverance. It is the human, rather than any deity or other supra-human force, who determines his own happiness, his own destiny. They understood the statement by Buddha: 'Over is Sky, under is Earth, only the Self is exclusive.' Peace in one's mind lays the foundations of peace in the community and the world, as was expounded by Buddha:

Oh Bhikkhu, you should go forth for the welfare of the many, for the happiness of the many, out of compassion for the world, for the advantage, for the welfare, for the happiness of the deities and human beings.... Oh Bhikkhu, teach the Dhamma, that is good at the beginning, good in the middle, good at the end, with meaning and with form. Reveal the holy life that is completely and entirely pure.

That is the work to be done by the Samgha. As for common people, they try their best to exercise the Four Cardinal Virtues put forth by Buddhism to maintain and expand harmony and peace in their community. These are loving-kindness (*metta*); compassion (*karuna*); happiness (*piti*); sacrifice (*upekkha*) under the disinterested and altruistic spirit. People understand *metta* as bringing happiness and tranquillity to others; *karuna* as relieving suffering and danger to others; *piti* as being happy with the achievements- material and mental- of others; *upekkha* as being ready to give up personal belongings, including body, wealth and happiness for the benefit of others; disinterested as acting fairly, not being influenced by personal advantage; and altruistic as being forgiving towards those who sincerely show repentance after having been led astray.

These virtues have had a strong impact on the minds of the Vietnamese people and together with Confucianism have shaped their behaviour. If Buddhism provided the Vietnamese people with a good-natured heart, Confucianism provided them with wisdom translated into the sense of order, discipline and responsibility. Two major contributions of Confucianism to traditional Vietnamese society are the materialization and institutionalization of benevolence as advocated by Buddhism into regulations and laws; and defining the responsibility and duty of each individual towards himself and the community in which he is living, including family, village, and the country, out of the concept of the Five Constant Virtues (Ngu Thuong). They are humanity (Nhan), righteousness (Nghia), rites (Le), wisdom (Tri), and trust (Tin); the first three have been set great store by.

Humanity is conceived of as benevolence and charity. Righteousness means that speaking and acting should be in accordance with the conscience, in line with the right way. He who can respond to these two criteria is worthy of being human. It was written in the Book of Changes: 'Yin and Yang are the principle of Sky, Rigid (Hard) and Flexible (Soft) are the principles of Earth, Humanity and Righteousness are the principles of Humanity.' Rites are regulations, discipline, order in society and respect towards these institutions. Rites were set up to ensure the maintenance of Humanity and Righteousness. Obviously, these five Confucian virtues complement the four Buddhist virtues for the peaceful behaviour of the Vietnamese people, especially the sense of tolerance and benevolence towards their fellows. Buddhism and Confucianism constituted the basis of Vietnamese people's individual and social behaviour in every circumstance, especially in peace-making and peace-keeping.

BUDDHIST EXPERIENCE

The Buddhist contribution to peace in Vietnam could be seen through various aspects prevailing in four major instances:

In times when people suffered the atrocities of foreign domination, aggression and wars- At those junctures, Buddhism was closely connected with national independence, which was considered indispensable to a socio-political environment for peace. Without national independence there is neither freedom nor happiness, which is seen as two major factors of the peaceful life. Buddhism then came up as a mental support to the striving for peace of the Vietnamese people. It served as a means for rallying people against the tyranny of oppressors by its basic tenets of democracy, self-reliance and self-deliverance as happened in the sixth century when an insurrection against Chinese domination burst forth under the leadership of a leader who named himself Ly Phat Tu (Ly the son of Buddha) versus Thien Tu (son of Heaven), the appellation of the Emperor of China.

In and after resistance wars against aggressors- The typical Buddhist sense of humanism and forgiveness has been extended to war prisoners. They were treated with humanity, as was shown during the wars against the French colonialists and the American imperialists in the second half of this century. They were provided with food and means of transport to return home, as were Chinese war prisoners in the fifteenth century. The Vietnamese people considered them victims and dupes of their ruling circles; and such an act was just aiming at maintaining peace between nations.

In times when people could live in peace to rebuild their country after disastrous wars- Buddhism served as a means for relieving people's sufferings caused by wars and natural calamities out of its spirit of mutual help, its sense of tolerance and benevolence. This tolerance policy prevailed in eleventh to early thirteenth centuries under the Ly dynasty, and was expressed through edicts of exemption from reducing taxes, declaring amnesty and reduction of sentences. A very compassionate word of Emperor Ly Thanh Tong (eleventh century) has been recorded in the Annals: 'My affection for my daughter [princess] is the same as for the common people to whom I assume the role of parents. They are guilty due to their lack of knowledge. I am full of pity for them. From now on, howsoever serious or light guilt may be, the sentence should be reduced.'

It was by practising the benevolence policy that the Tran Dynasty (thirteenth to fifteenth century) could raise the living standards of the people and ensure stability by defeating the Mongolian invaders. Especially in the era of the Democratic Republic, such great events as the Dien Bien Phu victory (1954) or National Reunification (1975) could have not happened if the people could not exercise their freedom, democracy, equality in specific conditions of war under a national spirit imbued with the Buddhist sense of self-reliance and benevolence.

Nowadays Vietnam is practising renovation and developing the market economy in the situation of peace and stability inside the country and the boom of the information revolution over the world. Stability is the basic condition for healthy and sustainable development. Social stability requires, first, the stability in each person, or in other words the peace in one's mind. The Vietnamese people always keep cheerfully in mind the philosophy: keeping still coping with changes. Still does not mean motionless, immobile or frozen but rather a state of equilibrium and harmony. Equilibrium implies inner motion of each element sharing the structure. And the harmony of something is the way in which the parts of it are combined into a suitable and desirable arrangement. Equilibrium and harmony bring about force, just as the practising of Buddha's teachings gives us peace in our minds.

By the practice of this philosophy the Vietnamese people could overcome many historical vicissitudes. Now, in the market economy, there are many negative aspects, especially the 'superstition' of money and supra-consumerism, and the endangering of Vietnamese ethical values. The question is how to combat them successfully. Administrative measures to tackle this problem are necessary but not radical. That requires rather the enhancement of the spiritual life, or in other words equilibrium between material and spiritual life. At this juncture Buddhism, combined with Confucianism, is playing a significant role in Vietnam. Buddhism in fact does not deny the material life, rather it preaches the ethical and spiritual life by encouraging good deeds and shunning evil actions which are deeply rooted in the selfish cravings of human beings. It is indeed somewhat unrealistic to destroy thoroughly the selfish craving in human behaviour. It would be better to tame and restrain it, first in oneself, and further to behave as such towards others as is taught by Buddha:

You should do to yourself

What you have instructed others to do.

Well tamed yourself, you should tame others.

Truly difficult indeed, is self tamed - *Dhammapada*, 15911

Or

Thinking of his own benefits, he does harm to others.

When other do harm to him in return,

Being harmed, he harms others.

Such is what the fool thinks,

When his wicked actions do not mature- *Samyutta Nikaya*, 10312

Vietnam is a latecomer on the way of industrialization and modernization. However, this could be advantageous as the country could draw experience from the success as well as failure of other more advanced countries in the reducing of negative aspects of the market economy. The most appropriate approach should be relying on traditional culture, in which ethical values of religion are salient features. In the case of Vietnam, these are Buddhistic combined with Confucian ones. Actually, there is a Government Committee for Religious Affairs to regulate the activities of various religions for the benefit of the many; an Institute for Buddhist Study, in the framework of the Vietnam Buddhist Congregation with its various periodicals to deepen Buddhist knowledge and popularize Buddha's teachings, especially on ethical values and peace.

Noteworthy are a good many humanitarian societies operating in the Buddhist spirit of benevolence and under the motto 'untorn leaves protect and help torn leaves', aiming at relieving the pain and suffering of the disadvantaged. Many central and local funds initiated by Buddhist monks and named 'funds for eradicating starvation and reducing poverty' were raised and responded to warmly by people from various social strata. Now Buddhist monks and laymen are among the most fervent humanitarian activists in foreign relations. In the course of history Vietnam has had two aspects of foreign relations: peaceful and conflicting. In these two, Buddhism had made contributions to positive solutions. No great matter is to be commented on the first issue, as Buddhism is a champion of peace- peace in one's mind and peace among humankind. As far as conflict is concerned, some remarks need to be made in this context as it is related to peace.

Among the commandments of Buddhism, the first deals with non-killing. That is to ensure peace and harmony between humans. Non-killing is the antagonist of killing. As the act of killing, like every act of a human, is generated from the mind, the question is how to generate a good thought rather than an evil one in one's mind. That could be achieved through Right Meditation, one stage in the Eightfold Path. So, an act could be asserted as good or evil only when it is considered from its motivation. There is no room here for the concept of 'the end justifies the means'.

An act is good if it is done for the benefit of others or to help others. On the other hand, Buddhism preaches that the origin of evil acts lies in one's selfish craving. That is the concept of peace and war of the Vietnamese people. They had to face repeated invasions by enemy forces. They had to safeguard their Fatherland by every means available, including killing aggressors, for the sake of peace for their country and their fellows.

While practising Buddhism, the Vietnamese leaders and people had to undertake resistance wars to fight against aggressors, wars waged by those people excited by so much selfish craving. And, as always, after such wars, wherein they always came out victorious, the Vietnamese leaders resumed their policy of good relations with those states who were once invaders. Even some of them, such as Emperor Ly Thai Tong (eleventh century), Emperors Tran Thai Tong and Tran Nhan Tong (thirteenth century), had cast off their monastic dress to put on armour and lead the whole people to defeat the Chinese and Mongolian invaders.

Especially Emperor Tran Nhan Tong, after his sound victory over the Mongolian troops, re-took his monastic dress and went into the forest to found the national Buddhist Sect of Zen, the Truc Lam (Bamboo Forest) Zen Sect. Deeply imbued with the sense of Buddhist benevolence and tolerance, the vast majority of Vietnamese always support the state policy of good relations with foreign countries. Nobody other than the Viet people, who suffered great hardships caused by wars, eagerly wish for peace and stability of society and peace and good relations with other countries in order to improve their living standards, their quality of life.

Buddhism in Vietnam is becoming a factor in traditional and national culture. It is so combined with Confucianism that it is hard to define it explicitly. Buddhism is so closely connected with national consciousness that one cannot understand it thoroughly unless it is seen in the context of national history.

It has made significant contributions to the maintaining and preserving of peace and stability for Vietnamese society during periods of peace as well as war. Now, when Vietnam is practising renovation and the market economy and the open-door policy, Buddhism is proving indispensable, especially for the maintenance and improvement of ethical values of restraint and to reduce socially negative aspects. Its sense of benevolence and tolerance is of great support to peaceful coexistence and friendly relations between various countries.

As we are told in our Buddhist books, the development of the human personality should be based on four moral foundations:

(i) *Metta*, loving kindness;

(ii) *Karuna*, compassion for all who suffer;

(iii) *Muditha*, sympathetic joy. (To be happy in others' happiness, in their prosperity and success, thereby counteracting feelings of jealousy and unhealthy rivalry between individuals and groups.); and

(iv) *Upekkha*, equanimity, the maintenance of a balanced mind when faced with the ups and downs inherent in life.

These moral qualities are known as Brahma-viharas, the four sublime states. It is by cultivating these noble qualities and practising them that we will be able to maintain a healthy mind and a healthy body.

All these qualities convey a universal message. They give the most satisfactory way of living in harmony with one's fellow men and women, the path to true happiness, to everlasting world peace. Here I must stress that one has to first practice and experience these moral values and create peace within. Only then can one radiate its effect in all ten directions of space to create the desired effect on others, to build the desired peace around the world.

In my own life this kind of moral cultivation started at home, in my childhood, guided by my parents and elders. I can remember we were trained to practise five precepts. These are to refrain from killing, stealing, lying, sexual misconduct and the use of intoxicants, and it is these precepts that formed the foundation stones for the development of true loving-kindness later in my life. There is no particular time in life at which one must practise these moral qualities.

They must be continually practised at all stages of life as students, as family members and fellow members of the community at large. By regular meditation on loving-kindness one can successfully realize inner peace. This is an energy which can be radiated to the whole world.

Today most people are blind to the norms and value systems of their forefathers. In the Buddhist world, the value systems of our forefathers guided us to live a simple, happy and contended life, following the middle path in our day-to-day activities. Extremes are avoided. The ability to live in harmony with ourselves, with nature around us, and with all living beings amidst us is the very objective of that value system.

To conclude one can quote the words of a great son of India, Shri Jawaharlal Nehru.

If we follow the principles enunciated by the Buddha We will ultimately win peace and tranquillity for the world.

5

The Establishment of the Early Buddhist Canon

How the Buddha presented himself to the people of his time and how his disciples perceived him are important to ascertain the veracity of the statement that the "Buddha stood as a human being before human beings to teach a goal of spiritual attainment within the reach of humanity." Did he only preach a way out of life, emphasizing in the process renunciation and total commitment to meditation in isolation, aloof from society and life of the people? Did he also preach to the laity and enable them to reach ethical and spiritual development within family and society? What was his attitude to lay life and secular matters? How concerned was he of such human issues as equality, caste and class privileges, socioeconomic exploitation, gender prejudices, economic viability, government, tolerance and co-existence, violence, security and peace?

The chapter will then examine how many of the Buddha's precepts and examples persist in the current teachings and practices of the Southern School of Buddhism as followed by well nigh 200 million Buddhists in Sri Lanka, Myanamar, Thailand, Cambodia, Laos and parts of India, Bangladesh, Nepal and Vietnam. A brief digression into the history of Buddhism becomes necessary to clarify the meaning and usage of the term Theravada: its general use in current literature is based on a basic misunderstanding that what obtains in these countries is identical with Early Buddhism in every respect.

But the main emphasis is on how Buddhism is actually viewed and practiced in South and Southeast Asia today. Of special interest are the role of the Sangha, the place of the temple in the community, and the part played by the laity and lay organizations. An explanation is to be sought for the leading role which Buddhism plays in the region with regard to literacy and education, sociocultural development, environment and biodiversity, conflict resolution and peace.

HUMANISM AND EARLY BUDDHISM

An analysis of humanistic elements in Early Buddhism and the Theravada tradition has to begin with the definition of the terms: Humanism, Early Buddhism and Theravada Tradition.

HUMANISM

The relevant definitions of humanism in dictionaries are the following:

1. The quality of being human; human nature; any system or way of thought or action concerned with the interests and ideals of people
2. The character or quality of being human; a system or attitude in thought, religion etc., in which human ideals and the perfection of human personality are made central, so that cultural and practical interests rather than theology and metaphysics are at the focus of attention;
3. Position philosophique qui place l'homme et les valeurs humains au-dessus des autres valeurs.
4. The character or quality of being human; devotion to human interests; Any system of thought or action which is concerned with merely human interests (as distinguished from divine), or with those of the human race in general (as distinguished from individual); the 'Religion of Humanity;' A pragmatic system of thought

introduced by F. C. S. Schiller and William James which emphasizes that man can only comprehend and investigate what is within the resources of the human mind, and discounts abstract theorizing; so, more generally, implying that technological advance must be guided by awareness of widely understood human needs.

Humanism in the case of Buddhism stems from the centrality of the human being as its founder, subject and primary concern. Human interests, ideals and values and the perfection of human personality are fundamental to the Buddha's dual approach of ensuring happiness and well-being for the human being both here in this world and hereafter. The Buddha's teachings provide practical guidelines to refashion one's life on one's own initiative and at one's own pace. He has categorically discouraged metaphysical and philosophical speculation and argumentation and advocated pragmatism. Thus all elements highlighted in the above definitions of humanism, including the system of thought expounded by Schiller and William James, ale prima facie applicable to the examination of the subject.

EARLY BUDDHISM

By Early Buddhism is meant the teachings of the Buddha and his immediate disciples as can be traced from the available literature. From circa 528 to 483 BCE (according to the widely accepted chronology), the Buddha as a wandering teacher carried on an extensive mission in and around Magadha (more or less the State of Bihar in modern India). He entered into dialogue and debate with many people on a wide variety of subjects and, on occasion, delivered on his own initiative well structured discourses on various aspects of his Path of Deliverance. The establishment of the Sangha as a self-regulating and self-renewing monastic organization created an effective mechanism for the compilation and transmission of his teachings.

The underlying credo of Buddhism as it evolved into a religion centered round the trinity comprising the Buddha the founder, Dhamma his teachings and the Sangha his disciples.

Elevated to the rank of Three Refuges, this Trinity came to be called Triple Gem or Three Treasures. Inherent in this development was the commitment of the Sangha to preserve the integrity and the authenticity of the Dhamma, which after the Buddha's death represented the Buddha himself as a permanent teacher. It is in the earliest compilations of the Dhamma, as in the Vinaya and Sutta Pi.takas of the Pali Canon and corresponding works of the Agama Suutras of the Buddhist Canon in Chinese as well as fragments of the now lost Sanskrit Canon that we look for traces of Early Buddhism.

A rule-of-thumb criterion in assessing the authenticity and the antiquity of these sources is threefold:

1. The Buddha is presented as a human being with only a minimum of faith-evoking embellishments such as miraculous, supernatural or divine trappings;
2. His interlocutors are themselves human and express human concerns and interests while they meet the Buddha in situations which are normal and plausible; and
3. The moral perfection and ultimate liberation of the human being is the fundamental purpose of the teachings and yet matters of a secular nature like interpersonal relations, gender issues, economic and social considerations are extensively dealt with.

As the title of this chapter seeks to suggest, Theravada tradition is distinguished from Early Buddhism and this calls for an explanation.

THERAVADA TRADITION

EARLY USAGE OF THE TERM THERAVADA

The earliest occurrence of the term Theravada in the Pali Canon is in the Ariyapariyesanasutta of Majjhimanikaya with reference to the doctrines which the ascetic Siddhartha studied under Alara-Kalama and Uddaka-Ramaputta. A cliche, purporting to be a comment of the Buddha-to-be on his erstwhile teachers, is translated by I. B. Horner as "I, as far as mere lip service, mere repetition were concerned, spoke the doctrine of knowledge (Nanavada) and the doctrine of the elders (Theravada), and claimed - I as well as others - that 'I know, I see.'" On the basis of the Commentary, Horner interprets the expression to be "a profession of strength."

What is more likely, however, is that, in the contemporary systems of spiritual training, two distinct aspects were noted: namely, the doctrines as known (i.e. the teachings per se of the founder or exponent) and their compilation or interpretation by elders or long-standing members. And Ascetic Siddhartha had mastered both aspects. The first point to be noted is that the term itself was pre-Buddhistic and was not invented by the Buddha or his disciples. It is in the latter sense of compilation and/or interpretation by elders of the system that we meet the word theriya in the Pali Chronicles of Sri Lanka in relation to the Buddha's teachings, (e.g. *Dipavamsa* - circa fourth century CE - IV, 6, 13 and *Mahavamsa* - circa sixth century CE - II, 40; V, 1).

The first recital of the Doctrine and Discipline done at Rajagaha within three months of the Buddha's death is called Theriya because it was done by the theras or elders (therehe'va katatatta ca theriya'yam parampara - because it was done by the theras themselves, it is the tradition of the theras). The record of the First Council in the Pali Canon, however, adopts a more neutral epithet for this recital: namely, "That of the Five Hundred" because there were five hundred participants in the Council.

The term Theravada when it occurs in *Mahavamsa* V, 6 and 10 is already the generic name of twelve sects, schools or traditions which was contrasted with Acariyavada - doctrines or traditions of teachers. Assumed in the distinction is that Theravada was the orthodoxy while the Acariyavadas were not so. The historicity of the schism in the Buddhist Sangha after the Second Council is undisputed. Both Pali and Sanskrit sources agree, even though they differ in details, that the originally united Sangha split into two main sects or schools as Theras (in Pali) or Sthaviras (in Sanskrit) and Mahasanghikas and that they continued to evolve into as many as eighteen sects.

DIVERSITY OF SRI LANKAN BUDDHISM

It was one of the sects or schools of Theravada/ Sthaviravada, known as Vibhajjavada or Analytical Tradition that Mahinda and Sanghamitta, son and daughter of Emperor Asoka, estabiished in Sri Lanka in circa 247 BCE. It held sway for over two centuries with the Mahavihara, the Great Monastery, as its bastion. The establishment of the Abhayagiri monastery in the first century BCE and the Jetavanarama in the fourth century CE paved the way for the sectarian developments of the mainland to have their impact in Sri Lanka. While the Mahavihara remained conservative and held on to the Pali Canon, the Abhayagiri and Jetavanarama monasteries adopted Sanskrit and the new doctrines of Mahayana schools.

In due course, they were respectively identified with the Dharmarucika and Sagaliya schools. Fa-Xian in circa 412 CE found five thousand monks in Abhayagiri while Theravadins in the Mahavihara were three thousand. That the Mahayana tradition had at least a millennium of widespread presence in Sri Lanka is amply borne out by impressive monuments, inscriptions in Sanskrit with indisputably Mahayana content, images of Buddhas, Bodhisattvas and Taras, and literature. Among the most widely admired works of Buddhist art from Sri Lanka are the gilt bronze Bodhisatva Avalokitesvara of Galewela and colossal monolithic Bodhisattva image of Dambegoda. The text of Prajnaparamitasuutra in Sanskrit inscribed in the Sinhala script on seven gold sheets was discovered when the site of Jetavanarama was excavated.

Verses in Sanskrit in praise of the three bodies or Kayas of the Buddha occur in a rock inscription at Mihintale, the cradle of Buddhism of the Island. At Tiriyay on the north-eastern coast is another Sanskrit incription with eleven verses. (Ibid. 314) A form of Bodhisattva cult was associated with kingship. King Siri Sanghabodhi (300 - 302 CE) is often called a Bodhisattva and an inscription of King Mahinda IV (956-972 CE) states that "none but a Bodhisattva would become a king of Lanka." Literary sources record that Dharmaruci, Sagalika and Vaitulyavadi sects flourished alongside the Theravada tradition of the Mahavihara right up to the middle of the twelfth century.

UNIFICATION OF SCHOOLS OR SECTS OF BUDDHISM IN THE TWELFTH CENTURY

Parakramabahu I (1153 - 1186) launched the reunification of the three fraternities of Mahavihara, Abhayagiri and Jetavanarama. The royal authority prevailed and the reunification of the Sangha into one organization resulted in reform measures with far-reaching results. The most important among them is the precedence given to the Pali Canon and its traditional commentaries and sub-commentaries. Sanskrit was replaced by Pali as the language of worship throughout the country.

Consequently, the Mahayanasuutras, which were upheld by the other two monasteries up to this time, went into disuse and virtually disappeared leaving no traces of their influence especially in the religious works in Sinhala written by a number of lay scholars in the thirteenth century. The loss of the Mahayana scriptures was more than compensated by the adoption and popularization of rites and ritual, including mantra or dharani and mandala or yantra from the Mahayana. The concept of the Buddha too underwent a change. Supernatural or even divine attributes came to be associated with him. While writers of the earlier period had no problem in referring to the Buddha simply as Budun in Sinhala, later writers would humbly address only the "shadow of the footwear of King Buddha".

Devotional worship gained in popularity. Repeating the formula Namo Buddhaya or the nine or ten qualities of the Buddha in the litany "Iti'pi so bhagava arahan sammasambuddho etc." was prescribed as an antidote for fear and insecurity. The Bodhisatva Avalokitesvara figured as God Natha to be worshipped and prayed to in Buddhist temples. Possibly, Samantabhadra similarly became the Buddhist deity Saman. Maitreya, the Bodhisatva who is believed to become the next Buddha, assumed a special position in that the popularly expressed wish after a good deed is to go through the cycle of life and death with all happiness and luxury in both human and heavenly existences and to be reborn at the time of Buddha Maitreya to be instructed and liberated by him.

The most fervent way of expressing gratitude is to wish that the doer of the good act be born a Buddha. As regards one's ultimate liberation, the availability of several paths was recognized and the oft-repeated wish was to enter Nibba.na through any one of the three modes of enlightenment (Tuntara bodhiyen ektara bodhiyakin - from one form of enlightenment out of the three forms - namely, as Buddha, *Paccekabuddha* or *Arahant)*. Hence what developed thus since the twelfth century Sri Lanka was an amalgam of Buddhist traditions which seemed to satisfy diverse spiritual and religious needs of the people. Not only did it take root in Sri Lanka but was eagerly adopted by Myanamar and Thailand and consequently Cambodia and Laos: monks from these countries came to receive higher ordination and education in Sri Lanka: and Sri Lankan missionary monks took the new form of Buddhism to the royal courts of these countries.

The Theravada Pali Canon along with the exceedingly meticulous exegetical commentaries and sub-commentaries and the other literary works in Pali provided an intellectual base for the popular elements which came from the Mahayana. It was, nevertheless, a far cry from the Theravada of the pre-Christian era in both India and Sri Lanka and also from what the Mahavihara maintained as its orthodoxy right up to the time of Parakramabahu I. As the fountain of inspiration and seat of authority for reformed Buddhism, Sri Lanka became the religious metropolis of South and Southeast Asia.

PROTESTANT BUDDHISM OF THE TWENTIETH CENTURY

There is a further element which has to be taken into consideration in defining the "Theravada" Tradition of modern times. Buddhism in Sri Lanka degenerated rapidly in the sixteenth and seventeenth centuries as a result of the occupation of its maritime region by the Portuguese and the Dutch and their frequent incursions into the central hills. As in all instances of such degeneration, the first to be undermined was the intellectual base of Buddhism and consequently animistic and ritualistic elements entered the belief system of the people, as exemplified by astrology, devil dancing, and magic. A revival in which a team of monks from Thailand played a key role revamped the Buddhist Sangha in 1753. A remarkable cultural and literary renaissance ensued. The increasing interest on the part of Western scholars in literary and archaeological research gave a further fillip to the popularization of Buddhism.

The collaboration of the Sangha with these foreign scholars, on the one hand, and the attraction of activists of the caliber of Colonel Henry Steel Olcott of USA, on the other, brought about an unprecedented renaissance of Buddhism. Lay involvement in the study and propagation of Buddhism went hand in hand with the establishment of Buddhist schools and institutions for social services. The net result of the growth and incessant activity in Buddhist circles of Sri Lanka of this period was the emergence of a form of practical and people-oriented Buddhism which scholars like Richard Gombrich and Gananath Obeyesekere called "Protestant Buddhism." Modernizing impact of Western science and technology as well as of Christian institutions and practices resulted in highlighting those aspects of the wide-ranging teachings of the Buddha, which appealed to modern times.

In this process of re-interpreting Buddhism as a religion in conformity with new sociopolitical and scientific tendencies, stress was laid on the humanistic elements of Early Buddhism as are contained in the Pali Canon and its commentaries. The principal players were scholar-monks like Hikkaduwe Sri Sumangala, Waskaduwe Sri Subhuti and Weligama Sri Sumangala and lay activists like Olcott and his Sri Lankan proteges, Anagarika Dharmapala and Sir Don Baron Jayatilaka. As a result Sri Lanka resumed its historic role as a center for the propagation of another new form of Buddhism from the last decade of the nineteenth century.

None of these scholars or activists, however, used the term Theravada to describe the form of Buddhism which they had begun to propagate. When students of comparative religion needed to distinguish this form of Buddhism from what prevailed mainly in China, Korea and Japan, the term Theravada was found to be the most convenient.

But is that an accurate description? Do its users recognize that the form of Buddhism for which it was applied in the pre-Christian era had long ceased to exist other than in books? What prevails in Sri Lanka, Myanamar, Thailand, Cambodia, Laos and parts of India, Bangladesh, Nepal and Vietnam is better and more precisely described by the neutral geographical expression "Southern School of Buddhism." But the early scholars who either ignored or were ignorant of the historical development of Buddhism in Sri Lanka and Southeast Asia equated the Southern School of Buddhism to Theravada. They even speak in terms of "compassion-based, altruistic Mahayana - the Big Raft" and "wisdom-oriented, self-centered or selfish Theravada - the Small Raft," and sought to perpetuate the pejorative term used in Mahayana literature by treating the term Hinayana to be synonymous with Theravada.

HALLMARKS OF THERAVADA TRADITION

Perhaps there is no particular objection to calling the Southern School of Buddhism Theravada as long one realizes that it has to be historically dissociated from the schools of that description on account of the developments in the twelfth, the nineteenth and the twentieth century Sri Lanka. But it does not appear to be the case. In three of the current Buddhist dictionaries, Theravada is defined as follows:

Theravada is the only one of the old schools of Buddhism that has survived among those which Mahayanists have called 'Hinayana.' It is sometimes called Southern Buddhism or Pali Buddhism. It is found today in Ceylon, Burma, Thailand, Cambodia, Laos and Chittagong (East Bengal) - Nyanatiloka: Buddhist Dictionary 1952.

Until recently this school was known in the West by its generic name of Hinayana, which means small or lesser vehicle (of salvation), but this term of reproach coined by the Mahayanists, has now been dropped in favor of the more accurate and less discourteous name of Theravada, the Way of the Elders. As the Theravada school covers Ceylon, Burma, Siam and Cambodia it is called Southern School, to distinguish it from the Northern or Mahayana School which covers Tibet, Mongolia, China, Korea and Japan. - Christmas Humphreys: A Popular Dictionary of Buddhism 1962

Theravada fut introduit a Ceylan (actuelle Sri Lanka) par le fils du roi Asoka, Mahendra (pali Mahinda) ou il fut connu sous le nom de bouddhisme du Sud ou il subsiste - *Dictioinnaire du Bouddhisme: Termes et Concepts* (Editions du Rocher) 1983

Richard Gombrich is far more accurate when he justifies the current popular usage of the term Theravada on the following ground:

"Hallmarks of Theravada Buddhism are the use of Pali as its main sacred language and dependence on the Pali version of the Buddhist Canon as its sacred scripture."

This description of Theravada recalls I-Tsing's (Yijing's) statement in the eighth century CE.

"If one worships Bodhisattvas and reads Mahayana scriptures, he will be called a Mahayanist, otherwise [one is] called a Hinayanist" (quoted by Bangwei Wang in Guruge 1992, 69)

This is why a distinction is maintained in this chapter between Early Buddhism and the "Theravada Tradition" of our times.

THE BUDDHA THE MAN

AUTOBIOGRAPHICAL SNIPPETS

The Pali Canon contains a few but significant autobiographical references attributed to the Buddha. He has spoken of the luxury in which he was brought up in his father's home.

"I was delicate, most delicate, and supremely delicate. Lily ponds were made for me at my father's house solely for my benefit.... I used no sandalwood that was not from Benares. My turban, tunic, lower garments and cloak were all made of Benares cloth. A white parasol was held over me day and night so that no cold or heat or dust or grit or dew might inconvenience me."

He has mentioned that three palaces were constructed for him - one for each season. He has referred to his life style by referring to the way the servants were treated:

"Though meals of broken rice with lentil soup are given to servants and retainers in other people's houses, in my father's house white rice and meat were given to them."

He proceeded further,

"While I had such power and good fortune... the vanity of youth... the vanity of health... the vanity of life entirely left me.: (Anguttara Nikaya, 38)

Elsewhere he referred to his youth again and said, "Being subject to birth, aging, ailment, death, sorrow and defilement, I sought after what was also subject to these things".

"Later, while still young, in the first phase of life, I shaved off my hair and beard - though my mother and father wished otherwise and grieved with tearful faces, and I put on yellow cloth and went forth from house life to homelessness.

In these same texts the Buddha has given his experience with the two teachers, A.lara Kalama and Uddaka Ramaputta:

"I soon learned the teaching. I claimed that as far as lip reciting and rehearsal of [their] teaching went I could speak with knowledge (Nanavada) and assurance (Theravada), and that I knew and saw - and there were others who did likewise."

The brief account of his life in the forest as an ascetic underlines the fear and dread he felt as any ordinary person:

"On such especially holy nights... I dwelt in some

awesome abodes as orchard shrines, woodland shrines and tree shrines which make the hair stand up. And while I dwelt there, a deer would approach me or a peacock would knock off a branch or wind would rustle the leaves. Then I thought: Surely this is the fear and dread coming."

He also has described how strenuous practices affected him physically:

"I stopped in-breaths and out-breaths in my mouth. When I did so, there was a loud sound of winds coming from my ear-holes.... I stopped the in-breaths and out-breaths in my mouth, nose and ears. When I did so, violent winds racked my head... there were violent pains in my head... violent winds carved up my belly, and... there was violent burning in my belly."

The same texts attribute to him an account of how the stringent fasting affected his body:

"My body reached a state of extreme emaciation; my limbs became like joint segments of vine or bamboo stems, because of eating so little. My back became like a camel's hoof; the projections of my spine stood forth like corded beads; my ribs jutted out as gaunt as crazy rafters of an old roofless barn; the gleam of my eyes sunk far down in their sockets looked like the gleam of water sunk far down in a deep well; my scalp shriveled and withered as a green gourd shrivels and withers in the wind and sun. If I touched my belly skin, I encountered my backbone; if I touched my backbone, I encountered my belly skin, for my belly skin cleaved to my backbone. If I made water or evacuated my bowels, I fell over on my face there. If I tried to ease my body by rubbing my limbs with my hands, the hair, rotted at the roots, fell away from my body as I rubbed, because of eating so little.

The all too natural inclination to abandon his goal figures in a beautiful poem where the Buddha's sentiments are attributed to Mara the Tempter:

O you are thin and pale,

And you are in the death's presence too.

A thousand parts are pledged to death,
But life still holds one part of you.
Live, sir! Life is the better way;
You can gain merit if you live;
Come live the holy life and pour
Libations on the holy fires,
And thus a world of merit gain.
What can you do by struggling now?
The path of struggling too is rough
And difficult and hard to bear."

What came to his mind at this stage is stated as follows:

"But by this grueling penance, I have attained no distinction higher than the human state.... Might there be another way to enlightenment?" Here is recalled an incident from his childhood:

"I thought of a time when my Sakyan father was working and I was sitting in the cool shade of a rose-apple tree... and entered upon and abode in the First Meditation... Then following that memory there came the recognition that it was the way to enlightenment." The Attainment of enlightenment is further described in his own words. It ends with the explanation:

"As long as I did not know by direct knowledge, as it actually is, so long did I make no claim to have discovered the enlightenment. But as soon as I knew by direct knowledge, as it actually is..... then I claimed to have discovered the enlightenment that is supreme in the world with its deities, its Maras and its divinities, in this generation with its monks and Brahmans, with its princes and men."

It is only here that a reference is made to Maras, divinities and such other supernatural beings. But they are mentioned along with monks and Brahmans and princes and men to describe the world or rather the universe in which enlightenment was supreme.

Two more autobiographical statements occur in the Mahaparinibbanasutta. One is on his renunciation and mission:

But twenty-nine I was when I renounced
The world, Subhadda, seeking after Good.
For fifty years and one year more, Subhadda,
Since I went out, a pilgrim have I been
Through the wide realm of System and of Dhamma –
Outside of that no victory can be won.

The other in a touching tone is on his imminent death:

"I, too, O Ananda, am now grown old and full of years, my journey is drawing to its close, I have readied my sum of days, I am turning eighty years of age; as just as a worn-out cart, Ananda, can be kept going only with thongs, so, methinks, the body of the Buddha can only be kept going by bandaging it."

Another equally moving was the statement in agreement with Ananda:

"So it is, Ananda, so it is. Youth has to age, health has to sicken, and life has to die. All my limbs are flaccid and wrinkled, my body is bent forward, and there seems a change in the sense faculties of my eyes, ears, nose, tongue and bodily sensations.

Shame on you, sordid Age,
Maker of Ugliness.
Age has now trampled down
The form that once had grace.
To live a hundred years
Is not to cheat Decay,
That gives quarter to none
And tramples down all things." (*Samyutta Nikaya* XLVII, 41)

Ananda once observed, "He was injured when a splintered rock hit his foot." When Vakkali in an exceedingly poor state of health excused himself for not visiting the Buddha, the Buddha's reply was "Enough, Vakkali, why do you want to see my filthy body (puutikaya)?" When his struggle with stringent penance and fasting failed, he had no "distinction higher than the human state." Wha. is significant in all these autobiographical statements is that the Buddha appears, speaks and acts as a human being - a mortal with emotions of fear and anxiety, and subject to human conditions. He was subject to illness and old age. He expected to be so weak in his old age that he would have to be carried about in a gurney.

MAN (PURISA) TO SUPERMAN (MAHAPURISA) TO SUPRA-MUNDANE (LOKOTTARA) BEING

In the earliest texts of the Pali Canon, this was how the Buddha was viewed by his disciples. He was a person of human dimensions: only four finger-breadths taller than his half-brother, Nanda. Both Nanda and Mahakassapa are believed to have resembled the Buddha and sometimes confused disciples who mistook them for the Buddha. In the same Vinaya text, the dimensions of the Buddha's robe are given as nine spans by six spans (approximately 9 feet by 6 feet, according to Welivitiye Sorata: Sri Sumangala Sinhala Dictionary). And the Buddha and Mahakassapa are said to have exchanged their robes.

The thirty-two characteristics and eighty secondary characteristics of a great man, which the Buddha is said to have possessed, were believed to be common to both a Buddha and a *Cakkavatti* (Wheel-wielding or universal monarch) and that was according to the Brahmanical lore. How the thirty-two marks of a great man (Superman in translations of T. W. Rhys Davids) entered the Buddhist lore is to be seen in the Lakkhanasutta of the *Digha Nikaya.* The manner in which these marks would affect the life of a universal monarch and that of a Buddha is compared and contrasted, highlighting, of course, the moral and spiritual attributes of a Buddha.

A long list of personality characters occurs in the Brahmayusutta and is said to be the result of a seven-month meticulous scrutiny of the Buddha by Brahmayu's disciple, Uttara. It deals mainly with behavioral aspects as moving about, receiving and partaking of food, washing hands and begging bowl, speaking, preaching etc. The conclusion drawn is that the Buddha was a great man as believed by Brahmans according to their own scriptures.

Apart from a few dubious characteristics (i.e. soles with illustrations, webbed hands, arms reaching the knees, genitals hidden in a sheath and a tongue large enough to cover the forehead), all that had been observed relate to a handsome and well-proportioned man who does everything mindfully in a coordinated manner. Others made similar observations. Saccaka, the Jaina, chided the Buddha for having taken a nap just one hot afternoon after his meals. When asked by members of other sects, Anuradha described the Buddha as "the highest of men and supremest of men, attained to supreme attain- ment."

The charisma of the Buddha induced people to ask who he really was. *Anguttara Nikaya* records a conversation with Brahmana Dona:

Sir, will you be a god (*deva*)?

No, Brahmana.

Will you be a heavenly angel (*gandhabba*)?

No, Brahmana.

Will you be a spirit (*yakkha*)?

No, Brahmana.

Will you be a human being (*manussa*)?

No, Brahmana.

Then, Sir, What indeed will you is? Brahmana, the taints by which I might be a deva, gandhabba, yakkha or manussa have been all abandoned in me, cut off at the root, made like a palm stump, done away with, and are no more subject to arising in the future. Just as a blue or red or white lotus is born in water, grows in water and stands up above the water untouched by it, so too I, who was born in this world and grew in the world, have transcended the world, and I live untouched by the world. Remember me as one who is enlightened. The reason advanced for not being any one other than a Buddha is purely ethical. This as well as numerous other references in the Pali Canon would show that, during the lifetime of the Buddha itself, Buddhahood had become a distinct state, above and different from that of a human being. Thus was set in motion the progressive addition of supernatural, supernormal or supramundane attributes to the Buddha.

In Early Buddhism, itself, the Buddha is seen emerging from the purely human state reflected in the autobiographical snippets, and assuming that of a great man or Superman with miracles associated with his life and miraculous powers "higher than the human state" (uttari-manussa-dhamma). The final product of this development in Early Buddhism is to be found in Acchariyabbhutadhammasutta of *Majjhima Nikaya* and in two of the injunctions in Mahaparinibbanasutta of *Digha Nikaya.*

Acchariyabbhutadhammasutta most interestingly is attributed to Ananda, who punctuates almost every paragraph with the statement, "Face to face have I heard this from the Buddha and face to face have I received" (sammukha me tam, bhante, Bhagavato sutam sammukha patiggahitam). What needed such repeated reassurance from the narrator was an account of the birth of the Buddha-to-be, which was replete with "wondrous and marvelous phenomena" (acchariya abbhutadhamma). The narrative begins with the Buddha's immediately previous life in the Tusita heaven and his decision to descend to earth to become the Buddha. Earthquakes and sudden illumination through out the universe mark this event.

From the time of the conception, the mother observes the five precepts. She is able to see the unborn baby within her womb "with all his limbs and complete sense organs." She carries him exactly for ten months and delivers him standing. When the baby exits from the mother's womb (matukucchisma nikkhamati - naturally and not from the right side as later narrators added and artists illustrated), he was clean as a gem with no blood or mucus and was received in their hands by four gods.

Two sprays of hot and cold water from above, however, wash the mother and the baby. The moment he is born, he stands on his feet, surveys the directions, takes seven steps to the north (not on lotus flowers) and in a lordly voice says, "I am the chief of the world. I am the best in the world. I am the first in the world. This is my last birth.

There is now no existence again." The paradigm for this account is to be found in Mahapadanasutta of the *Digha Nikaya,* where the birth of the previous Buddha Vipassi is described and in a concluding section a resume of the Buddha Gotama is added as a direct quote from gods in a heaven. With these discourses begins the composition of legendary accounts of the Buddha's life to which faith-evoking elements came to be added progressively.

These proliferated as one of the schools of Buddhism concentrated on the representation of the Buddha in Lokottara or supra-mundane form and details. More and more miraculous elements were introduced until the result was a vita sanctorum. It was a Buddha of such a character that St. Clement of Alexandria, Egypt, knew in the third century CE. He spoke of "Indians that obey the precepts of Boutta, who, through exaggeration of his dignity, honor as God." The two injunctions in *Digha Nikaya* 16 reflect the sanctity attached to the Buddha while he was still alive:

1. The Buddha's body was to be cremated and the remains treated as holy relics to be enshrined in cetiyas (mounds or pagodas) and worshipped; and
2. The places connected with his birth, enlightenment, first sermon and death were to be shrines visited by pilgrims.

Unrecorded as an injunction but equally indicative of the sanctity attached to the Buddha was the Early Buddhists' self-imposed prohibition of representing the Buddha in art in human form over almost the first five hundred years of Buddhism. By the time historical evidence on the spread and development of Buddhism becomes available around the time of Asoka the Mauryan Emperor (circa 299-228 BCE), the prevalence of relic-worship and pilgrimage is amply substantiated. Asoka himself has recorded in his edicts his pilgrimage to Lumbini and Buddha Gaya.

The Buddhist sculpture of the next two centuries at Bharhut, Sanchi and Amaravati abounds in aniconic representation of the Buddha. Wherever his presence was indispensable to the event depicted in a panel were used such symbols as foot-print, seat, bodhi-tree, wheel, parasol and column of fire. The adoption of Mahayana Buddhism by the foreign dynasty of Kushans led to the representation of the Buddha in human form, with Greco-Roman gods serving as the model. Within Mahayana, the proliferation of Buddhas, on the one hand and the assumption of supremacy of Primeval (adi) and Meditational (dhyani) Buddhas over Sakyamuni, on the other, changed the perception of the Buddha as a human teacher.

This was visibly reflected in art where the Buddha was progressively made bigger than life - a case of spiritual and moral greatness being represented by physical dimensions. Among the murals of Ajantha is an example of this development: it is an enormous Buddha who meets his erstwhile wife, who with her son is portrayed as midgets in comparison. The impetus to build or construct gigantic Buddha statues came from Mahayana Buddhism.

It is in the traditionally Mahayana countries that the largest number of colossal Buddhas are found. In Sri Lanka, where Mahayana and Early Buddhism of the Theravada type coexisted, the monumental statues appear to be invariably connected with Mahayana institutions: e.g. Buduruvagala (51 feet), Maligawila (34 feet), Polonnaruwa Galvihara (50 and 23 feet) and possibly also Aukana and Sasseruwa (39 feet) and Dowe (13 feet). We shall review the changing perception of the personality of the Buddha when we return to the consideration of how the Buddha is perceived today in "Theravada" Tradition.

HUMAN CONCERNS IN THE TEACHINGS OF THE BUDDHA

PERFECTION OF HUMAN PERSONALITY

What the Buddha taught was a Path of Deliverance from suffering, specifically called in the first sermon itself "the Noble Eightfold Path leading to the Cessation of Suffering" (dukkhanirodha-gamini-patipada ariya atthangika-magga). The major part of the Pali Canon, therefore, consists of detailed examination and exploration of the process of ethical purification through virtuous conduct (*sila*), development and concentration of the mind (*samadhi*) and realization of wisdom.

The Buddha's discourses on this subject are addressed to human beings, who, alone are believed to possess the relevant background and capacity to seek deliverance. It has been specifically stated that the Buddhahood was attainable only by a human being. Though other spirits are mentioned as acquiring various stages in the Path as Stream-enterers, Once-Returners and Non-Returners and only humans figure in the Pali Canon as reaching the ultimate state of an Arhant. All of them were not monks or nuns.

For example, the Buddha's own father is said to have become an Arhant as a lay person. So the teachings of the Buddha qualify as a form of humanism as they are concerned with perfection of human personality. But there is, of course, a major difference. The Buddha points out a way to happiness not only in this life in the world but in both here and hereafter in one or more lives to come. "One rejoices here and having passed away one rejoices. The doer of good rejoices in both" (Idha nandati pecca nandati - punnakari ubhayattha nandati) is the reward that one gets for being good.

MONASTICS AND LAITY

It is true that the soteriological approach of the Buddha places a high premium on the monastic ideal of renunciation and homelessness. In an autobiographical statement on why he renounced lay life, the Buddha says,

Full of obstacles is life in a house

It is an abode of stain (or dust)

Free as space is Going Forth

Seeing this I went forth - *Samyutta Nikaya* II, 1

A significant number of discourses culminate in describing how a person listens to a sermon, discovers the obstacles in lay life to practice the holy path, renounces all that is worldly and takes to the life of few needs of a monk or a nun, which progressively enables him or her to attain deliverance. A substantial discourse preached to King Ajatasattu deals with the benefits of monasticism, commencing with this-worldly advantages and culminating in the realization of Nibbana. In a verse in Itivuttaka, the Buddha lays emphasis on the mutually dependent roles of the monastics and the laity for the development of the Faith:

> The lay and the homeless alike
>
> Each supporting the other
>
> Accomplish the true doctrine
>
> The peerless refuge from Bondage.

An explanation given by Ananda and Sariputta to Anathapindaka, the most generous lay supporter of the Buddha, gives the impression that the Buddha and his disciples differentiated the subject-matter when they preached to monastics and lay persons: "Such talks on the *Dhamma* are not given to the white-clothed laity: they are given to those gone forth from the house life".

TEACHINGS FOR THE LAITY

The humanistic concerns of the Buddha predominate in the numerous discourses addressed to the lay folk on matters of socioeconomic and ethical significance to their life. Equality of humanity was a matter of primary concern to him. He was disturbed by the division of society into caste and impatient with Brahmans who claimed social supremacy on grounds of birth. "Not by birth but by action does one become a revered Brahmana or a degraded outcaste" is the crux of his teachings on caste distinctions which the contemporary society upheld. Among the virtues which qualified a person to be called a Brahmana irrespective of his birth caste are such human values as

> Being without possessions and not seizing any
>
> Having power of patience to endure insults.

Ill-treatment and bondage

Observing religious duties and moral principles

Avoiding violence

Not injuring or destroying living beings, movable or unmovable

Not being hostile among the hostile

Being peaceful among the violent

Being free from greed, hatred, and pride

Not depreciating others

Speaking clearly and truthfully so that none is offended by one's speech and not using harsh language.

On the contrary, one was to be called an outcaste whatever be his birth status if one:

Was angry, grumbling, evil and hypocritical

Failed in vision and was deceitful

Harmed living beings

Had no love for the living

Left unpaid debts saying, "I owe you no debt"

Waylaid people on the highway to take their belongings

Lied as a witness for the sake of money

Seduced or ravished other's wives

Killed or harassed with words ones' parents or relatives

Gave wrong counsel with a concealed motive

Did not return hospitality when an opportunity arose

Praised one's self and denigrated others

Degraded others through arrogance.

Not only did he preach but he also counteracted caste prejudices with action. The Sangha was open to all castes, classes, and occupations. Purely chronological seniority from the moment of entry and no other criterion decided precedence within the Sangha. "Just as waters of various rivers lost their identity when they flowed into the ocean, persons of different castes lost their previous social identities in the Sangha," was how the process was explained. Slaves, courtesans, scavengers, barbers and criminals attained distinction within it. The Buddha upheld that birth as a human being was a rare and difficult-to-attain privilege and relied on the capacity of a human being to think critically and independently for one's self. In matters of personal religious belief and practice, he expected every person to exercise freedom of thought. In this context, Kalamasutta of *Anguttara Nikaya* (II, 65) stands out as a remarkable assertion of the human right to think independently without the pressures and constraints of dogma:

Do not accept anything on mere hearsay or tradition, on account of rumors or because it accords with your scriptures, by mere supposition or inference, by merely considering the reasons or because it agrees with your preconceived notions and, therefore, seems acceptable or because the preacher is a respected person.

But when you know for yourselves that these things are moral and blameless: that they are praised by the wise and that when performed or undertaken they are conducive to the well-being and the happiness of the many, and then should you accept them and act accordingly. At the same time, the Buddha anticipated by two millennia and more the principles of pragmatism of Schiller and William James and persuaded people to restrict their speculation and quest for knowledge to what was immediately essential and what was knowable. The ten unexplained questions and the parable of the surgeon and the wounded man illustrate this aspect of humanism of the Buddha's teachings.

The Buddha desisted from making converts, persuading potential disciples to continue supporting their earlier teachers. The ethical system he presented to humanity had no place for commandments or ex cathedra orders. All deeds one commits volitionally are either skillful or competent (*kusala*) or unskillful and incompetent (*akusala*). A person took upon himself or herself voluntarily the kinds of discipline which constituted a skillful, competent, smart or wholesome conduct: "I take upon myself the discipline of abstaining from (veramani sikkhapadam samadiyami) killing, stealing, sexual misconduct, lying and stupefying liquor and drugs" was the formula with which one resolved to observe the virtuous life. Good and evil were also defined pragmatically. Evil is what

1. One does not wish others to do unto one's self;
2. One repents after committing
3. A wise person criticizes in another, and
4. Does not contribute to the good and the happiness of the many.

Good, likewise, is the opposite of these.

The moral "code" of Early Buddhism as can be culled from many texts in the Pali Canon comprises things to be avoided as well as done and the two main lists of things to do appear as the Four Sublime States (*Brahmavihara*) and Ten Meritorious Deeds.

The Sublime States to practice and abide by are:

Loving kindness (*Metta*) - a sentiment similar to a mother's love for her only child;

Compassion (*Karuna*) - what makes one rush to relieve another's misery;

Sympathetic Joy (*Mudita*) - rejoicing in other's joy; and

Equanimity/Equality (*Upekkha*) - treating all alike.

These are to be extended to all sentient beings in a limitless universe. The most frequently preached and chanted discourse of the Pali Canon on loving kindness - elaborates the universality of beings to be so covered with one's sentiments of loving kindness in a way that the born and the still-to-be born, the seen, the unseen as tiny as an atom, and those nearby and far away are all included. Mettanisamsasutta lists eleven benefits accruing to a person who practices loving kindness and the humanistic base of this list is another example of the Buddha's pragmatism:

i. Sleeps happily;
ii. Awakes happily;
iii. Does not have nightmares;
iv. Is liked by humans;
v. Is liked by non-humans;
vi. Gods protect him/her;
vii. Fire, poison or weapons do not hurt him/her;
viii. Mind reaches concentration quickly;
ix. Complexion of the face clears up;
x. Dies in consciousness; and
xi. Gets reborn in a Brahma-heaven if no higher plain had been reached.

Meritorious deeds to be performed are:

i. Charity or generous giving;
ii. Virtuous life;
iii. Development of the mind through meditation
iv. Reverence to those worthy of reverence;
v. Service to the elderly, the needy, the sick and society at large;
vi. Transference of one's merits to others;
vii. Rejoicing in merits acquired by others;
viii. Expounding or teaching the Dhamma;
ix. Listening to the Dhamma; and
x. Straightening or rectifying one's views.

Things to be avoided are listed similarly. As occurring through deed, word and thought are listed ten unskillful, unwholesome or incompetent actions (*Dasa-akusala-vatthu*): killing, stealing and sexual misconduct from deeds; lying, foul language, slandering and vain talk from words; and greed, malice and wrong views from thoughts. The humanistic foundation of the Buddha's thinking is best exemplified by his definition of wrong thoughts: right views are so universally spelled out that there is not even the slightest trace of bigotry. Presented in various contexts are negative qualities to be progressively eliminated. When they are grouped together the following are the human failings - more precisely, the defilements of the mind - whose eradication was the objective of the ethical teachings of the Buddha:

i. Covetousness, excessive greed;
ii. Malice, ill-will;
iii. Delusion, ignorance;
iv. Anger;
v. Hostility, hatred;
vi. Contempt, denigration;
vii. Presumption, domineering;
viii. Envy;
ix. Jealousy, avarice, selfishness;
x. Deceit, hypocrisy;
xi. Fraud;
xii. Obstinacy;
xiii. Impetuosity, quarrelsomeness, rivalry;
xiv. Conceit;
xv. Haughtiness, superiority complex;
xvi. Vanity, pride;
xvii. Negligence, heedlessness.

"When the mind is clean, a good future must be expected," says the Buddha in the Vatthuupamasutta. The pithy aphoristic statements of *Dhammapada, Udana, Itivuttaka,* and *Suttanipata,* and the deftly compiled lists of ones, twos, threes up to elevens in Anguttara Nikaya, and the brief sermons of *Samyutta Nikaya* of the Pali Canon deal mostly with matters applicable to lay life in this world:

> Hatred ceases with love and not with hatred.
>
> Anger subsides when one stops harboring grievances.
>
> The diligent never die; the negligent are like the dead.
>
> A friend indeed is one who points out one's faults.

A well-tamed mind is one's best friend and an ill-tamed mind the worst enemy.

Good health is the greatest profit; contentment the greatest wealth; and trustworthy persons the best relatives.

They blame those who speak a lot; they blame those who speak a little; and they even blame the silent; there is none who is not blamed in this world. This is only a meager sample from *Dhammapada* alone. In *Udana* occurs the parable of the elephant and the blind men which illustrates the importance of a holistic view of things. Again as illustrative of the Buddha's humanistic approach is the Mangalasutta where the objective is to lead a person to a point where he or she is "victorious everywhere" (sabbattham aparajita) to achieve happiness everywhere with a mind unruffled by life's changing circumstances (putthassa lokadhammehi citta.m yassa na kampati).

Listed in it are thirty-eight blessings and only eight deals with renunciation, asceticism and Path of Deliverance. The other thirty relate to the life of the laity and commence with one's social and material environment. Not associating with the foolish, associating with the wise and honoring the worthy and residing in a genial locality are the first four blessings. The rest in order are the following:

Possessing merits acquired from the past,

To set one's self in the right course,

Erudition and skill,

Besides well-groomed discipline,

And words which are pleasantly spoken.

To tend one's parents,

Caring for wife and children,

Untangled in occupations,

Liberality and righteous conduct,

Cherishing one's relatives,

Engaged in blameless action,
To shun and abstain from evil,
Restraint in the use of intoxicants,
Heedful in the practice of virtue,
Dignity and humility,
Contentment and gratitude,
Listening on time to religious discourses,
Patience and courtesy,
The company of recluses,
And religious discussions at opportune moments.

Literally thousands of similar quotations can be culled from the vast body of discourses attributed to the Buddha and his senior disciples in the Pali Canon.

THE BUDDHA'S POSITION ON SOCIAL ISSUES

GENDER ISSUES

Contrary to the prevailing views on gender issues in India, the Buddha is on record as recognizing the equality of women. To King Pasenadi Kosala who looked unhappy on the birth of a daughter, he had the following advice:

A woman child, O lord of men, may prove
Even a better offspring than a male.
For she may grow up wise and virtuous,
Her husband's mother reverencing, true wife.
The boy she may bear may do great deeds,
And rule great realms, yea, such a son
Of noble wife becomes his country's guide.

In his list of seven factors which contributed to the security and development of a nation, the fourth was that women and girls should be assured protection from harassment. When, after repeated refusal by the Buddha to ordain his step-mother, Ananda asked the specific question, "Are the women folk capable of going forth from home to homelessness in the Dhamma as preached by the Buddha and Attaining the status of a Stream-Enterer, Once-Returner, Non-Returner or Arahant?" the answer of the Buddha was a categorical "Yes." Not only did he say so, but created the Order of Nuns to accommodate women, even though he set additional rules for them.

Of course, the first of the eight rules which makes the most senior nun junior to the just ordained monk has not been convincingly explained. Yet the step-mother as a nun was declared the chief of those with the longest experience. In a non-canonical work, Manorathapuura.ni, the spirit of the Buddhist attitude occurs as "Not on all occasions are men wise. Women, too, are wise and intelligent on various occasions." As many as fourteen short discourses on women occur in the Samyuttanikaya: one of them lists five desirable qualities of a woman as-

- Being beautiful
- Being wealthy
- Being virtuous
- Being skillful and diligent (analaso-not lazy), and
- Producing progeny.

Such a woman is said to be certainly favoured by men. Those without these qualities are shown as disliked by men. Another enumerates the miseries particular to women:

- Has to leave for her husband's home very young and be separated from her own relatives,
- Menstruation,
- Pregnancy,
- Childbirth, and
- Has to be of service to man (purisassa paricariyam upeti)

Though it is not explicitly stated, the purpose of this discourse could have been to sympathize with the natural lot of women and perhaps draw attention to two socially-inflicted miseries (i.e. the first and the fifth). It is significant that the stereotype role of women as a servant of man is considered a traditional (*avenika*) misfortune whereas Hindu law-books of a later age made such service a woman's spiritual duty. The position of woman as wife and mother finds special mention in the Pali Canon. In several texts the mother is called the pubbacariya or first teacher.

Tending father and mother as well as wife and children are viewed as a blessing in the Maṅgalasutta, quoted above. A monk is not only permitted to share the food obtained by begging with one's parents but doing so is commended as an act praised by the wise (pandita idh'eva nam pasamsanti). "The wife is one's best friend" (bhariya ca parama sakha) is a dictum of the Buddha. In an insightful analysis of the role and behaviour of a wife in a marriage, he identifies as many as seven different kinds of wives. Three kinds he condemns as harsh and devoid of virtue and love: namely,

- Torturing wife (*vadhakabhariya*),
- Stealing wife (*coribhariya*) and
- Domineering wife (*ayyabhariya*).

Four others whom he praises are mother-wife (*matubhariya*), who is protective and tends a husband as a mother does a son, sister-wife (*bhaginibhariya*) who is modest and respectful to the husband, friend-wife (*sakhibhariya*), who is noble and chaste, and rejoices at the sight of the husband, and silave-wife (*dasibhariya*), who is free from anger and with a pure heart waits on the husband.

Adultery (paradarasevi: "associating with other's wives") is condemned on grounds of not only ethical impropriety but also this-worldly consequences. In two verses of the *Dhammapada*, he says:

Four misfortunes befall a man who commits adultery: acquisition of demerit, disturbed sleep, humiliation as the third and hell (*niraya*) as the fourth. Acquiring demerit, one has an evil destiny. Frightened man's happiness with a frightened woman is short lived. The king imposes heavy punishment. Hence no man should frequent another's wife. We shall return to the Buddha's knowledge and understanding of a wife's emotional needs when we discuss interpersonal relationships in Sigalovadasutta.

POVERTY AND VIOLENCE

In Kutadantasutta of *Digha Nikaya,* the Buddha makes a direct link between poverty and violence, and argues that law-enforcement and punishment are not an effective solution:

> Perchance his majesty might think, "I will soon put a stop to these scoundrels' game by degradation and punishment, and fines and imprisonment and execution." But the criminal actions of bandits who pillage villages and towns and make roads unsafe cannot be satisfactorily put a stop to. The criminals left unpunished would still go on harassing the realm. Now there is one method to adopt to put a thorough end to this disorder: to those who keep cattle and cultivate farms, let the king give fodder and seed-corn. To those who trade, let the king give capital. To those in government service, let the king give wages and food. Then these people, following each one's own business, will no longer harass the realm. The king's revenue will go up and the realm will be quiet and at peace. The populace, pleased with one another and happy, dancing, their children in their arms, will dwell with open doors.

Government subsidies to the private sector and adequate salaries to service personnel so as to ensure an economically viable society are the proffered answers to the problem of economic instability and resulting violence.

YOUTH PROBLEMS

For a comprehensive survey of the Buddha's opinions on secular matters a primary source is Sigalovadasutta of *Digha Nikaya.* Preached to a teenager, this discourse deals with a wide range of subjects that would be of interest to a lay person:

- What is conducive to a good reputation
- How one's wealth could be safeguarded
- Evils of addiction to intoxicants, frequenting streets at unseemly hours, haunting fairs and clubs, gambling,

association with evil friends and idleness.

- Pseudo-friends to be shunned
- Good friends to be cultivated
- How to handle one's income: consumption, investment and saving.
- Obligations to be fulfilled in interpersonal relationships between parents and children; teacher and pupil; wife and husband; friend and friend; employer and the servant; and religious teachers and the laity.

Studiously avoided are references to matters spiritual or religious and the Buddha's own path of deliverance. A virtuous life in which one avoids killing, stealing, sexual misconduct and lying is the recipe for a good reputation. One risks one's wealth in six ways; namely, by addiction to intoxicants, frequenting streets at unseemly times, haunting fairs and clubs, gambling, keeping company with evil friends and idleness.

As if all items fit a matrix, six evil consequences of each of these aspects are listed. For example, addiction to intoxicants results in actual loss of wealth, proliferation of quarrels, susceptibility to disease, loss of good character, indecent exposure, and impairment of intelligence. Gambling, likewise, results in the addicted gambler being subject to anger as a winner and to grief as a loser, being a loser of actual wealth, being one whose testimony is of no weight in a court of justice, being despised by friends and officials, and being considered unsuitable for marriage on the ground that he is unable to support wife or children. As consequences of idleness are enumerated the neglect of work to be done, and the resulting non-accumulation of new wealth and dwindling of the existing wealth, on account of procrastination with such six excuses as "it is too cold, too hot, too early, too late, too hungry and too full."

The discourse repeats causes of destruction of a person. In one verse the six causes are: Sleeping till after sunrise, adultery (i.e. "going to women who are to others as dear as their lives"), involvement in hate, violence, evil friends and excessive miserliness. In another are listed addiction to dice and women, drinking, and dance and song, sleeping by day, sauntering in streets at the wrong time, evil friends and excessive miserliness. A similar list occurs in Vyagghapajjasutta of *Anguttara Nikaya and* comprises: debauchery (itthidhutta - lit. addicted to women), drunkenness (suradhutta-addicted to liquor), gambling (akkhidhutta-addicted to dice) and companionship with evil persons.

The analysis of four types of pseudo-friends and four types of good friends proceeds with another matrix wherein four comments are made on each pseudo- or good friends. For example, a Buddy-Buddy or word-only friend makes friendly professions as regards the past and the future, treats with useless things, and shows inability when opportunities arise. The Helper-friend, on the contrary, protects one and one's wealth when one is heedless, comes to one's aid in fear, and provides twice as much when a need arises. The importance of good friends is further underscored in Vyagghapajjasutta which, too, is preached to a lay person.

MONEY

The Buddha's advice to Sigala as regards the handling of money is worthy of attention. Not only is he counseled to accumulate wealth for the benefit of the family as a bee collects pollen (i.e. without oppression to the producer of such wealth) but also to see wisely that the wealth grows high like an anthill. Such wealth has to be utilized as follows:

> Divide the income into four,
>
> Binding one's self to friends,
>
> With one part may you enjoy (consume):
>
> Invest two parts in your business.
>
> Save the fourth, so that
>
> It is there in times of distress.

Having money and being wealthy are not decried in the teachings of the Buddha, even though "wanting the least" (*appicchata*) is highly recommended and contentment is commended as the highest wealth. Of course, there are the accounts of Sudinna and Ratthapala whose parents tried to tempt them with wealth to abandon monkhood. Their reply was that the parents should put all their wealth into bags, transport them in carts, and drop them into river Ganga where it was the deepest. Poverty, thus, is appreciated when chosen by monastics. Acquiring wealth in the youth, nevertheless, is declared in the *Dhammapada* as an alternative to life as a monastic:

> Those, who have not led the holy life [or] not acquired wealth in youth, pine away like old herons at a dry pond without fish or lie like worn-out bows, sighing after the past.

Prosperity in this life is regarded as a reward for good Kamma in previous lives as well as the present. In one listing, the possession of wealth is said to generate four kinds of happiness for the laity; namely,

- Happiness of having (*atthisukha*),
- Happiness of consuming (*bhogasukha*),
- Happiness of being free from debt (*ananasukha*), and
- Happiness of blameless conduct (*anavajjasukha*).

In Vyagghapajjasutta, Dighajanu asks the Buddha for advice for people like him who were encumbered with wives and children, used to luxuries like imported perfume, handled silver and gold and decked themselves with garlands, perfumes and unguents. The Buddha's response was to list four achievements each to ensure happiness in this life and hereafter. As regards this life, he enumerated the following:

1. Persistent effort (*utthanasampada*)
2. Security and wariness (*arakkhasampada*)
3. Good friendship (*kalyanamittata*) and
4. Balanced livelihood (*samajivikata*)

The explanation of items 1, 2, and 4 elaborates the Buddha's views on wealth: Persistent effort: "By whatever activity a person earns his livelihood, whether by cultivation, animal husbandry, archery (military service), ministering to kings or any other craft, one is skillful and not lazy, reasons out to ways and means of accomplishing the tasks and is efficient and capable."

Security and wariness: "Whatever wealth a person has justly acquired by dint of effort, strength of arms, the sweat of the brow, or any other right means, one protects it by guarding and watching that kings would not seize it, thieves would not steal it, fire would not burn it, water would not carry it off or ill-disposed heirs would not take it away." Balanced livelihood: "Knowing his income and expenditure, one leads a balanced life without being either too extravagant or too niggardly, thinking, 'My income can be in excess of my expenditure but not my expenditure in excess of income.' Just as a goldsmith or his apprentice knows by holding up a balance that by so much it has dipped down and by so much it has tilled up, one knows his income and expenditure and leads a balanced livelihood."

These principles tally with the definition of Right Livelihood (*samma ajiva*) as one of the elements of the Noble Eightfold Path. The kinds of livelihood which are declared wrong as they bring harm to others include trading in arms, living beings, intoxicants and poison, slaughtering and fishing, soldiering, deceit, treachery, soothsaying, trickery, and usury. As important as these statements in the Pali Canon on the Buddha's position regarding money and wealth are the accounts of very close friendships that he maintained with rich and generous donors like Anathapindika and Visakha. No further proof is needed to dispel the notion that either the Buddha or Buddhism scorned wealth or the wealthy.

GOVERNMENT

The Buddha was equally close to practically all the kings who ruled various kingdoms in the region in which he was active. Though there is no evidence of his having played any direct role in statecraft, be was conscious of separating matters of state from those of religion. For example, no one was permitted to become a monk if he was under obligation to perform any royal duties. When the rising power of Magadha threatened the independence of the tiny Republic of the Vajjis, the Buddha assures that no harm would come to them as long as they adhered to seven principles. With interpretations within parenthesis relevant to modern times, these principles demonstrate another instance of the Buddha's concern with human welfare:

1. Meet frequently in harmony, discuss in harmony and disperse in harmony (That is, participate fully in public life and affairs, observe the democratic principles of consultation, and preserve harmony in spite of differences.)
2. Introduce no revolutionary laws, do not break the established law, and abide by the old-time norm (That is, to make a balance between the tradition and the modern, and make changes slowly and cautiously and not drastically.)
3. Honor, reverence, esteem and worship the elders and deem them worthy of listening to. (That is, recognize the value and relevance of trans-generational wisdom.)
4. Safeguard the women-folk from force, abduction and harassment. (That is, recognize the importance of women and their need for protection.)
5. Honor, revere, esteem and worship both inner and outer shrines (That is, protect the cultural and spiritual heritage.)
6. Perform without neglecting the customary offerings. (That is, safeguard the practice of religion.) and
7. So assure that saints have access to one's territory and having entered dwell there pleasantly (That is, being open to all religions and spiritual influences in a spirit of tolerance).

In later Buddhist literature in Pali occurs frequently a list of ten traditional duties of a ruler (*Dasa-raja-dhamma*). They are:

i. Giving alms,
ii. Virtuous life or morality,
iii. Liberality,
iv. Straightness or honesty,

v. Gentleness,

vi. Self-control (lit. asceticism),

vii. Non-anger or pleasant temperament,

viii. Nonviolence,

ix. Forbearance,

x. Non-opposition.

A list of three things to be avoided by a ruler consists of falsehood, anger and derisive laughter. That the Buddha upheld democratic decision-making is illustrated by rules laid down for the Sangha. To ensure compromise and consensus particularly in conflict-resolution, each question for decision would be put to the assembly thrice by an eloquent speaker and voted upon after discussion.

Arbitration through a committee is enjoined to reach consensus. Only in extremely rare cases would a rule by majority vote be even considered. Early Buddhism, thus, provides some relevant insights in matters pertaining to government and conflict-resolution.

INTERPERSONAL RELATIONS

As noted earlier, the central theme of Sigalovadasutta is the discussion on obligations to be mutually respected in interpersonal relations. Six groups have been identified and each party in a group is shown to owe five obligations to the other. Such a matrix of arithmetical perfection could have led to some degree of artificiality and triteness. But this does not seem to happen. The six groups cover every imaginable form of interpersonal relations - save between siblings. Each set of five obligations has been thought out with an in-depth knowledge and understanding of human material and emotional needs.

The parents, thus, are required to prevent the child from evil, inculcate good qualities, have the child taught an art (i.e. given an education leading to a livelihood), contract a marriage with a suitable partner, and hand over the inheritance in time. The child in return has to nourish them in their old age, perform his or her duties toward them, preserve the family and clan (that is, by procreation), protect the heritage, and make offerings when they are dead and gone.

The teacher's obligations to the student are to lead him or her to perfect discipline, to ensure that he or she holds on to well-established norms or traditions, to instruct him or her in the knowledge of every art, to spread his or her reputation among his friends and companions, and to provide for his or her safety in every direction. The student has to reciprocate by standing up to receive the teacher, by waiting upon him, by obedience, by personal service, and by studying the art or subject diligently.

The husband fulfilled his duties toward the wife by respecting her, by not humiliating her, by being faithful, by handing over authority, and by presenting jewelry. The last of the duties coincides with an analysis elsewhere in the Buddhist literature of "the insatiable desires of a woman" as sexual satisfaction, birth of children, and ornaments and jewelry. The wife in turn performs her duties well, extends hospitality to relatives all around (i. e. to hers as well as her husband's), is faithful to her husband, protects what is earned and acquired, and is proficient and industrious in all duties. Taken together the duties between parents and children and between husband and wife, the picture that emerges as the Buddha's ideal of family values and relations confirms deep concern in the stability of the home as the primary unit of society.

The fourth set of interpersonal rèlations applies to friends. A friend has to treat his or her friend by giving gifts, with pleasant words, by benevolence, by accepting the friend as an equal, and by not disputing. The frind was required to reciprocate by protecting the person and property of the friend whenever he or she was negligent, by being a refuge at times of fear, by not abandoning him or her in adversity, and by showing consideration to his family and relatives. The next set to be identified consists of employer and servant. Though restricted to household servants at the time of the Buddha, the obligations of each party are valid for employer-employee relations in general as will be shown by comments in parenthesis. The employer has to

- Assign work according to strength or capacity (no king-size jobs for man-size employees, as the popular saying goes)
- Provide food and salary (no enforced or unpaid labor)
- Ensure health care (a specific obligation of the employer)
- Share special delicacies (both as a demonstration of human concern and as recognition of good work: e. g. bonuses, perquisites and rewards), and
- Grant leave at times (i. e. periods of rest as earned leave).

The employee in return wakes up earlier and sleeps later than the employer, is content with the wages and rewards given, does his or her work well and diligently, praises the employer and spreads his or her fame (i. e. subscribes to good public relations). The last of the six relationships is between the religious or spiritual teacher and his or her lay devotees. The recluse, priest or minister restrains the lay devotee from evil, establishes him or her in the good, teaches what has not been heard before (new knowledge), elucidates what has been heard (reinforces existing knowledge), and shows the way to heaven. The lay devotee's duties are to extend friendliness to the spiritual teacher in deed, word and thought, keep the door open for him or her for unhindered entrance, and supply his or her material needs and creature comforts.

EXEMPLARS FROM NARRATIVE LITERATURE AND ART

The life of the Buddha is extensively documented. The background for each discourse is described both in the Pali Canon and in the voluminous commentaries on *Dhammapada* and *Jataka*. Together they provide an extensive literary base for the elaboration of the underlying human concerns of the Buddha and his disciples:

The Buddha has time to intervene with children harassing a snake for their delight and to teach an old man a song in praise of his cane so that the public could be aware of the neglect he suffered in the hands of his children. He would not preach to a hungry man but see to it that he is fed before he could join the audience. The Buddha would go miles to save an endangered child or to stop a bandit from killing his own mother.

He would wash and treat the sick with his own hands and tell his disciples, "Those who tend the sick do actually tend me." He would rebuke a die-hard conservative for not accepting new ideas and call him a carrier of jute who foolishly declines to accept gold or silver. He would discourage his disciples from performing any kind of miraculous or magical acts to win over followers and urge that the most effective miracle is that of instruction. To demonstrate the worthlessness of the human body and of the pleasures associated with it, he would auction the body of a dead courtesan until no one was even prepared to accept it free of charge. The Buddha would approach a king to urge that his old state elephant needed better caring. He would similarly go to an outcaste servant woman to prevent her from committing suicide and testify to the innocence of a farmer falsely accused of theft. When disciples quarrel, he takes no side but escapes to the tranquility of the forest. When his own relatives gathered on the battlefield to fight for water to their fields, he would, however, sit amidst the two armies and ask them, "What is more valuable: the life of a human being or water?"

His disciples followed his example:

Ananda gladly begged for water from an untouchable woman to quench his thirst. Punna could not be dissuaded from going to a remote region to preach the Dhamma on the ground that the people there were known to be violent.

The vast narrative literature in Pali consisting of the 547 Jatakas or stories of the Buddha's past lives is replete with tales of human interest where the characters are both human and animal. They provide exemplars of ideal conduct for emulation. Each story illustrates a virtue such as charity, gratitude, compassion, honesty, courage, determination, forbearance, perseverance and devotion.

Early Buddhists who were pioneers in the utilization of visual art for educational purposes had these stories depicted in sculpture at such Stuupa sites as Bharhut, Sanchi, Amaravati and Nagarjunikonda. The technique of compressing several incidents of a story to a single medallion or panel testifies to the wide-spread popularity of the stories. The "artistic shorthand" used in sculpture served a mnemonic purpose for parents or guides or for the pilgrims themselves to recollect the events of a narrative which they already knew well.

THE THERAVADA TRADITION OF MODERN TIMES

EARLY BUDDHISM IN DOCTRINES AND PRACTICES

Sri Lanka, MyaNamar, Thailand, Cambodia, Laos and parts of India, Bangladesh, Nepal and Vietnam have preserved to an incredible degree the tenets, ethics and values of Early Buddhism. The reason for such a faithful transmission is that the Pali Canon along with the voluminous exegetical literature in the form of commentaries (atthakatha), sub-commentaries (tika), explanations (tippani) and glossaries (ganthipada) have remained the basic scriptures ever since they were diffused with the twelfth century reformed Buddhism of Sri Lanka. Along with the scriptures came a rich Pali literature which devoted much attention to the history of Buddhism in India and Sri Lanka.

The historiography of Early Buddhists was intended for the dual purposes of establishing the authenticity of the transmission of the doctrine and the discipline and the commemoration and thereby the promotion of liberal donations to the Sangha. The history also provided role models to be emulated and among them Asoka the Righteous, the third Maurya Emperor of India, and the kings of Sri Lanka such as Devanampiya Tissa and Dutthagamini Abhaya figured prominently. This literature was not only copied and annotated but the literary tradition was further continued in Southeast Asia.

In practice and many of the beliefs held by the adherents, the impact of Mahayana and even Vajrayana remains irrefutable.

Even though the human qualities and personality of Sakyamuni Gotama Buddha has not been overshadowed by the supernormal traits of cosmic and dhyani Buddhas, the popular concept of Buddhahood had undergone much change. It is true that the Buddha is not "prayed" to in traditional worship. Yet, his blessings are invoked as though he is present to grant them. "Budupihitayi" says the Sri Lankan Buddhist, meaning "May you have succor from the Buddha." Offerings of food and beverages are made to the Buddha with the invocation "Adhivasetu no bhante"(Venerable Sir may accept our -).

A formula exists by which the Buddha is actually asked to forgive one's faults: accaya.m khama me bhante (Venerable Sir, forgive my fault). Many stanzas in Pali are used in benediction requesting the Buddha's power (anubhava) to ensure good health, success and blessings. The Buddha is invoked in the course of animistic magical rites as in the liturgy used in such exorcist devil-dance ceremonies of Sri Lanka. An adherent with no modern education, including monastics, would assert the traditional belief that the Buddha was eighteen cubits (27 feet) tall.

This region continues to make Buddha statues of immense dimensions as done in Mahayana countries but would explain the gigantic size as a representation of the spiritual and moral greatness of the human Buddha. The facility with which the concept of a "divine" or supernormal Buddha and that of a teacher who, as a man, preached to human beings are reconciled or allowed to coexist is a special feature in the belief system inherent to Southern Buddhism. The same could be said about the concept of Bodhisatvas and other deities and supernatural beings. Hindu deities are worshipped and prayed to for worldly favors in Buddhist temples. The explanation sometimes is that they are themselves aspirants to Buddhahood or they are friends and protectors of Buddhism. One could see similar parallels in the worship of Nats and Phis in Myanamar and Thailand respectively.

As regards the question of liberation or enlightenment, one looks in vain in Southern Buddhism for the black/white contrast made between the so-called Greater Vehicle and the Lesser Vehicle. Whether such a great divide ever existed in reality or whether it was a figment of imagination of the exponents of Mahayana traditions or whether Mahadeva's four points on Arahants were actually points of controversy between schools or sects are matters for further scrutiny. But as far as the present day Buddhists of South and Southeast Asia are concerned, they are hardly conscious of any restriction for them to aspire for anything but the state of an Arahant. The Bodhisattva-Arahanta dichotomy is totally unknown to them.

As already pointed out, they acknowledge gratitude to a kind and helpful person by wishing him or her to become a Buddha (not an Arahant) and for themselves they wish the eventual entry to Nibbana through any one of the three modes of enlightenment: that is, as a Buddha, a Paccekabuddha or an Arahant. It has also to be conceded that "enlightenment in this very life" is not a priority in the Southern School of Buddhism and the postponement of one's liberation until all sentient beings of all universes had been liberated is an unknown concept.

The emphasis, on the contrary, is on "making merit" so that one is reborn in a better state: in a human existence with long life, good complexion, happiness and power (*ayu, vanna, sukha, bala*) or as a *deva* "shining being" in one of the six sensual-sphere (*kamavacara*) heavens. Few even among monastics would aspire for birth in a *Brahmaloka* with form or in a formless state, attainable through higher mental achievements called *Jhana* (Absorptions or Trances). Other than perhaps the monks in forest hermitages, few are known to concentrate on full-time meditation as a means of immediate or accelerated approach to enlightenment and consequently liberation.

The triple spiritual training of *Dana* (liberality or giving), *Sila* (virtuous or moral life) and *Bhavana* (cultivation of the mind or meditation) is pursued by lay devotees for merit-making and the reward normally expected is happiness and prosperity in this world and the next. Merit making as the main preoccupation of adherents to the Southern School of

Buddhism gives an enormous fillip to the practice of all the humanistic principles and values of Early Buddhism.

Avoiding harm and injury to all sentient beings and working for their well-being comprise all forms of humane and social services. Feeding and clothing the poor and the orphaned, providing shelter to the homeless, educating the ignorant, caring for the sick and the destitute, providing communal amenities and the like are equivalent to religious obligations. "If one has nothing else to give others one could offer others one's personal service," is an oft-quoted principle when people are organized to do community services. By way of motivation is related such stories as of the young man Magha who was said to have become the king of gods by digging ponds, and making canals for the benefit of humans and animals.

Among the community services to which the Southern School of Buddhism assigned importance is education. The temple in even the remotest village is a center of learning and culture. The average monk is a man of learning, even if his knowledge and skills are limited to rudimentary texts on Buddhism and literacy. A basic education leading to sustained literacy has been provided to at least the boys. To monks this is a way of showing their appreciation to the community which nurtures them. Writing and copying books are similarly pursued as meritorious acts and supporting monks in such services is believed to enable the laity to share such merit. Thus are the humanistic elements of Early Buddhism fully incorporated into the doctrines and practices of what is called the "Theravada" Tradition of South and Southeast Asia?

IMPACT OF MODERN INFLUENCES

During the last two hundred years or so a major transformation has taken place in the manner in which doctrines and practices of Early Buddhism are reviewed, conserved and propagated in South and Southeast Asia. Several things, as earlier alluded to, happened all together and all at once. The epicenter of these new developments has been once again Sri Lanka. But their impact extended to the entire region. The discovery of the Pali language and literature by the emerging oriental scholars of the West was the starting point. The earliest known scholarly notices of Pali in the West are "Essai sur le Pali" (1826) and "Observations grammaticales sur quelques passages de l'essai sur le Pali" (1827) by Christian Lassen and Eugene Burnouf.

Within a decade was published George Turnour's editio princeps in Roman script and English translation of the Pali Mahavamsa, the Great Chronicle of Sri Lanka. To it was appended a comprehensive - though introductory - essay on Pali literature. A vast literature restricted hitherto to temple libraries and somewhat sporadically and selectively studied by scholar-monks received the attention of a widening circle of Western scholars as well the English educated inteligentsia of South and Southeast Asia. The initial effort came from an unexpected quarter, namely the Christian missionaries' resident in the British colonies of Ceylon (now Sri Lanka) and Burma (now Myanamar).

The first discourses from the Pali Canon to be translated and published were Sigalovadasutta and Subhasutta by Rev. D. J. Gogerly. He also translated Ratthapalasutta, *Cariyapitaka* and Vinaya texts and Dhammacakkappavattanasutta. His colleague R. Spence Hardy published a list of Pali and Sinhala books and two treatises which for a long time continued to be rated as standard authoritative works: namely, *Eastern Monastcism* (1850) and *A Manual of Buddhism and its Modern Development*. In 1855, Viggo Fausboll of Denamark translated *Dhammapada* from Pali into Latin. Bishop P. Bigandet of Burma utilized the written and oral resources of the country and produced in 1858 "Life or Legend of Gaudama the Buddha of the Burmese."

It was a veritable age of discovery for the missionaries and scholars who were impressed with what the newly found literature unraveled. To the intelligentsia of the traditionally Buddhist countries, it was an age of surprise. They had hitherto no access to this rich literature which presented Buddhism to them in a refreshingly new form. The ethical relevance, the philosophical depth, and the overarching commonsense, evinced by the teachings of the Buddha in his own words, appealed to their secular, scientific mindset. The Eighteen-sixties and -seventies were marked by public debates between Christian missionaries and Buddhist monks of Sri Lanka. Scholars and orators on both sides delved into the scriptures of the opposing party and in some debates a high level of intellectual interest was maintained.

A by-product of the extensive study of Buddhist scriptures was the project initiated as far back as 1865 at Pelmadulla in Sri Lanka to revise and rehearse the Pali Canonical texts. The Great Debate of Panadura in 1873 received the attention of a visiting American journalist, J. M. Peebles, who wrote eight articles on the debate. Later he had them published in book form under the title *The Great Debate: Buddhism and Christianity Face to Face*. While these debates were on, an overall interest in Buddhist studies was shown by young civil servants who were sent from England to administer the colony. One of them, Robert C. Childers, published in 1875 the first Pali-English Dictionary and another, T. W. Rhys Davids, paved the way for Pali and Buddhist Studies to be incorporated in the curriculum of Universities in the United Kingdom and subsequently in USA.

Rhys Davids' pioneering efforts to publish Pali texts along with their transilations in English brought about eventually the establishment of the Pali Text Society in 1881. Teams of European scholars in collaboration with scholar-monks and lay scholars of the region ransacked the temple libraries of Burma, Thailand, Cambodia, Chittagong and Sri Lanka for manuscripts for collation for their critical editions of the Pali Canon. The discovery that Burmese, Thai and Cambodian manuscripts were often superior in accuracy as compared to Sri Lankan manuscripts were hastily copied after the 1753 revival, engendered cooperation among national scholars who were keen to publish texts of the highest quality.

The resulting interest in the Pali Canon and literature as well as national literatures in different languages was unprecedented. Massive publishing ventures flourished specially in Colombo, Yangon, Bangkok, and Chittagong. The most spectacular achievement of the time was the publication of the Pali Canon in full in Thai script under the patronage of the King of Thailand and its distribution to many centers of learning in the world. Hand in hand went the restoration of the traditional system of Buddhist education. Pioneering institutions were established in Sri Lanka in the form of Vidyodaya (1873) and Vidyalankara (1875) Pirive.nas, popualry called Oriental Colleges. The model was followed in other countries of the region and a network of institutions of higher learning came into operation. Questions of monastic education and discipline, with special reference to Vinaya jurisprudence, were discussed by the leading luminaries in the Sangha in the region and Pali was the language of communication among them.

Thousands of letters in the temples of Sri Lanka, Thailand, Myanamar and Chittagong which await scholarly scrutiny and eventual publication speak of a period when Southern Buddhism evolved into a unified regional tradition. Increasing access to literary sources and the renaissance in monastic and lay Buddhist education generated a significant Buddhist revival. At the same time, the academia of the world was taking a keen interest in Buddhism and its culture as a human heritage. For example, the translations of Pali texts by Henry Clarke Warren as "Buddhism in Translations" found a place in the Harvard University's five-foot library of World Classics.

Archeological excavation and research established the antiquity and the wide dispersal of Buddhist monuments revealing magnificent achievements in art and architecture. The discovery of the inscriptions of Asoka and their decipherment and transilation enhanced the credibility of Buddhist historical data. Asoka himself stood out as an exemplar Buddhist ruler and his "edicts" stood as testimony to the efficacy in practice of the values and principles of Early Buddhism. In the meanwhile, the plight of the Buddhists *vis-a-vis* politically supported Christian missionaries attracted the attention of the founders of the Theosophical Society in USA, namely, Colonel Henry Steel Olcott and Helena Petrovna Blavatsky. Peeble's book had reached Olcott and he started communicating with the senior scholar-monks of Sri Lanka.

These links culminated in the visit of Olcott and Blavatsky to Sri Lanka in 1880 and their public acceptance of Buddhism as their personal religion. Olcott devoted the rest of his life to the Buddhist cause and his achievements were numerous. His "Buddhist Catechism", published in Sri Lanka in 1881, was a simple, well-organized and readable introduction to Buddhism and in several translations and many editions reached the general readership of the world within a few years. He championed the cause of lay Buddhist education to counteract the influence of missionaries and he established several schools.

His criss-crossed Asia speaking to diverse audiences on the importance of reviving their Buddhist traditions and in 1891 brought leaders of several Buddhist schools and sects to accept a fourteen-point common platform on which all Buddhists could agree. But his most far-reaching contribution was the involvement of the Buddhist laity in the study and propagation of Buddhism and the establishment of institutions for the purpose. Two of his proteges, namely Anagarika Dharmapala and Don Baron Jayatilaka (later Sir), not only continued his program but became leaders of the growing Buddhist movement on their own right. With the Mahabodhi Society established in India in 1891, Anagarika Dharmapala internationalized the Buddhist movement by setting up branches in many countries in Asia, Europe and America and mobilizing a growing body of enthusiastic friends and admirers of Buddhism.

His campaign in India bad two objectives: first, to reclaim for the Buddhists the holy shrines connected with Buddhism (which either lay in ruins or were in the hands of Hindu priests who had no idea of the sanctity which the Buddhists Attached to these monuments); and, second, to take Buddhism back to its land of origin through well-organized missionary services. With his Mahabodhi Journal, which became a forum for international Buddhists, and his prolific writings in both Sinhala and English, he came to be recognized as the foremost exponent and propagator of Buddhism. Anagarika Dharmapala had also the distinction of being the spokesman for the Buddhists at the Parliament of World's Religions in Chicago in 1893. His principal address was on "World's Debt to Buddha."

Conceived as a veritable manifesto of the new form of Buddhism which has evolved in South and Southeast Asia as a result of the manifold activities outlined above, he delved into the humanistic elements of Early Buddhism which study and research had brought to light. The subheadings demonstrate what he saw as the features of Buddhism which the world had to take note of:

The Dawn of a New Era; His First Message; Human Brotherhood; Religion Characteristic of Humanity; The Theism of Buddhism; Evolution as Taught by Buddha; Moral Teachings of Buddha; The Higher Morality; The Low and Lying Arts; Universal Pity; The Realization of the Unseen; Psychic Experiments; Common Appanage of All Good Men; Prohibited Employments; Universalism of Buddha's Teachings; The Pupil and the Teacher; The Honorable Man; The Master and the Servant; Religious Teachers and Laymen; The Mission of Buddha; The Attributes of Buddha; Buddha's disciples; The Compassionateness shown by Buddhist Missionaries; The Ultimate Goal of Man; The Attainment of Salvation; The Spread of the Religion of Humanity; What the Buddhist Literature has Wrought for Mankind; Religion and the Family; Buddhist Brotherhood; Buddha's Exalted Tolerance; Buddhism and Modern Science; Can the Knowledge of the Religion be Scientific? Religion in Relation to Morals; Different Schemes for the Restoration of the Fallen Man; Religion and Social Problems; Religion and Temperance; Benefits Conferred on Women by Buddhism; Love of country and Observance of Law.

Highlighted in bold font are themes which have been further elaborated by modern exponents of the humanistic elements in Southern Buddhism? These also represent the issues which have dominated study and discussion, research and publication, and formal and informal Buddhist education. The list, of course, has grown. Answers are being sought from Buddhism for pressing issues of modern times such as environmental preservation and biodiversity, violence and insecurity, poverty and imbalances in development, and war, peace, and conflict resolution.

The twentieth century has seen many scholars, teachers, writers and speakers, both monastic and lay, who have given Southern Buddhism a new face and a new meaning. Much has been borrowed from other religious institutions. To Christianity it owes such external trappings as Vesak carols and cards. Young Men's and Women's Buddhist Associations, Sunday Schools, organized lay involvement, some forms of congregational worship and the like. Buddhists, both monastics and lay, work actively for the alleviation of human suffering and have evolved diverse institutions and programs for the purpose. They concern themselves with issues of human survival and development and promote nonviolence, peace and conflict-resolution. They strike a balance between such social services and their own spiritual growth through study and meditation. A significant result is that Vipassana meditation in the context of an active life has emerged as a popular modality.

The burgeoning demand by women for a more active role in spiritual life has manifested itself as humanistic aspects of modern Buddhism are stressed. Even within the narrow window of opportunity provided for them as observers of ten precepts or "silamatas" (lit. mothers of precepts), the number renouncing lay life has increased steadily and institutions for them are being established throughout the region. Their campaign to receive full and higher ordination as *bhikkhunis,* too, has achieved significant though limited success.

The sociocultural influence of the Buddhist temple has increased rapidly. In the region as a whole, it is the temple which served to take modern education to rural areas. A galaxy of learned monks and lay persons has achieved international reputation as promoters of Buddhism in the world. The rational, the scientific and the humanistic nature of the Buddha's teachings are the hallmark of their interpretation. If one calls these developments "Theravada Tradition", its historical evolution up to the point that Gombrich and Obeysekera named it "Protestant Buddhism" should not be overlooked.

This brief survey of humanistic elements in Early Buddhism and the Theravada Tradition of South and Southeast Asia has led us to several conclusions:

- Theravada as a label for Southern Buddhism as prevalent in the region is by and large a misnomer because neither the general belief system nor the teachings upheld and emphasized are identical with those of the Theravada school or sect which existed in the first few centuries after the death of the Buddha.
- The alleged distinction based on the Bodhisatva-Arahant dichotomy no longer applies, even if it ever did, and Southern Buddhism has an open mind as regards how one may reach enlightenment.
- The only thing that has remained unchanged is the reliance on the Buddhist Canon and the ancillary literature in Pali. The Buddhist Canon in Pali which represents the Buddha as a teacher of men and women contains a substantial body of humanistic teachings. Early Buddhism qualifies to be considered Humanistic Buddhism.
- The unification of the Sangha in the twelfth century in Sri Lanka and the modernizing influences of the last two centuries have transformed Southern Buddhism into something entirely new for which an apt designation is not readily available.
- Merit-making predominates as a motivating factor in spiritual practice and the aspirations commonly expressed by devotees relate to success and happiness in this life, rebirth in a happier state after death, and eventual end of suffering through enlightenment as a Buddha, a Pacceka Buddha or an Arahant.

- The broad definition of merit-making enables every form of service to humanity - social, educational, philanthropic, ecological etc, - to be pursued as an integral part of practicing Buddhism.
- Due to the reliance on the Pali Canon and literature, Southern Buddhism preserves the teachings of Early Buddhism, which are effectively diffused to the public through sermons, publications, formal and informal education and electronic media.
- In recent years, scholars, writers and preachers show a tendency to choose for elaboration and propagation those teachings of the Buddha that emphasize his human nature, and concern with the secular well-being of human beings.
- Monastics and the laity, alike, are deeply involved in on-hand activities in community development, poverty alleviation, protection of the environment and promotion of nonviolence, peace, conflict resolution, and overall socioeconomic and cultural development.
- Modern exponents of Southern Buddhism, both monastic and lay, seek to underscore the rational, critical, logical, scientific, tolerant, and open-minded nature of the teachings of the Buddha and, for this purpose, retrieve and reinterpret much data from the rich literature in Pali and equally comprehensive historical evidence and documentation.
- Training in Vipassana Meditation, whether by means of temporary ordination or though periodic retreats, reflects the prevailing need for the pursuit of spiritual goals while being actively engaged in daily life.
- The increasing involvement of women in the new form of Buddhism is characterized by the large numbers who chose to renounce lay life and the steady efforts made to restore in the region the full ordination of women as *bhikkhunis*.

6

The Buddhism of King Asoka

As the legend goes, one day after the war was over, Ashoka ventured out to roam the city and all he could see were burnt houses and scattered corpses. This sight made him sick and he cried the famous monologue, "What have I done? Is this a victory, what's a defeat then! This is a victory or a defeat! This is justice or injustice! It's gallantry or a rout? Is it a valor to kill innocent children and women? I do it for enwide the empire or for prosperity or to destroy the other's kingdom or splendor? Someone has lost her husband, someone father, someone child, someone an unborn infant... what's this debris of the corpses? Are these marks of victory or defeat? Are these vultures, crows, eagles the messengers of death or evil? What have I done!

What have I done" The brutality of the conquest led him to adopt Buddhism and he used his position to propagate the relatively new religion to new heights, as far as ancient Rome and Egypt. He made Vibhajyavada Buddhism his state religion around 260 BC. He propagated the Vibhajyavada school of Buddhism and preached it within his domain and worldwide from about 250 BC. Emperor Ashoka undoubtedly has to be credited with the first serious attempt to develop a Buddhist polity. Prominent in this cause were his son Venerable Mahindra and daughter Sanghamitra (whose name means "friend of the Sangha"), who established Buddhism in Ceylon (now Sri Lanka). He built thousands of Stupas and Viharas for Buddhist followers.

The Stupas of Sanchi are world famous and the stupa named Sanchi Stupa was built by Emperor Ashoka. During the remaining portion of Ashoka's reign, he pursued an official policy of nonviolence (*ahimsa*). Even the unnecessary slaughter or mutilation of animals was immediately abolished. Wildlife became protected by the king's law against sport hunting and branding. Limited hunting was permitted for consumption reasons but Ashoka also promoted the concept of vegetarianism. Ashoka also showed mercy to those imprisoned, allowing them leave for the outside a day of the year. He attempted to raise the professional ambition of the common man by building universities for study and water transit and irrigation systems for trade and agriculture. He treated his subjects as equals regardless of their religion, politics and caste. The kingdoms surrounding his, so easily overthrown, were instead made to be well-respected allies.

He is acclaimed for constructing hospitals for animals and renovating major roads throughout India. After this transformation, Ashoka came to be known as Dhammashoka (Sanskrit), meaning Ashoka, the follower of Dharma. Ashoka defined the main principles of dharma (*dhamma*) as nonviolence, tolerance of all sects and opinions, obedience to parents, respect for the Brahmans and other religious teachers and priests, liberality towards friends, humane treatment of servants, and generosity towards all. These principles suggest a general ethic of behaviour to which no religious or social group could object. Some critics say that Ashoka was afraid of more wars but among his neighbors, including the Seleucid Empire and the Greco-Bactrian kingdom established by Diodotus I, none could match his strength.

He was a contemporary of both Antiochus I Soter and his successor Antiochus I Theos of the Seleucid dynasty as well as Diodotus I and his son Diodotus I of the Greco-Bactrian kingdom. If his inscriptions and edicts are well studied one finds that he was familiar with the Hellenic world but never in awe of it. His edicts, which talk of friendly relations, give the names of both Antiochus of the Seleucid Empire and

Ptolemy II of Egypt. The fame of the Mauryan Empire was widespread from the time that Ashoka's grandfather Chandragupta Maurya defeated Seleucus Nicator, the founder of the Seleucid Dynasty.

The source of much of our knowledge of Ashoka is the many inscriptions he had carved on pillars and rocks throughout the empire. Emperor Ashoka is known as Piyadasi (in Pali) or Priyadarshi (in Sanskrit) meaning "good looking" or "favored by the gods with good blessing." All his inscriptions have the imperial touch and show compassionate loving. He addressed his people as his "children". These inscriptions promoted Buddhist morality and encouraged nonviolence and adherence to Dharma (duty or proper behavior), and they talk of his fame and conquered lands as well as the neighboring kingdoms holding up his might.

One also gets some primary information about the Kalinga War and Ashoka's allies plus some useful knowledge on the civil administration. The Ashoka Pillar at Sarnath is the most popular of the relics left by Ashoka. Made of sandstone, this pillar records the visit of the emperor to Sarnath, in the 3rd century BC. It has a four-lion capital (four lions standing back to back) which was adopted as the emblem of the modern Indian republic. The lion symbolizes both Ashoka's imperial rule and the kingship of the Buddha. In translating these monuments, historians learn the bulk of what is assumed to have been true fact of the Mauryan Empire. It is difficult to determine whether or not some actual events ever happened, but the stone etchings clearly depict how Ashoka wanted to be thought of and remembered.

Ashoka's own words as known from his Edicts are: "All men are my children. I am like a father to them. As every father desires the good and the happiness of his children, I wish that all men should be happy always." Edward D'Cruz interprets the Ashokan dharma as a "religion to be used as a symbol of a new imperial unity and a cementing force to weld the diverse and heterogeneous elements of the empire".

At the time of Emperor Ashoka (270-232 BC) and according to his Edicts in the Edicts of Ashoka, Ashoka mentions the Hellenistic kings of the period as a convert to Buddhist, although no Hellenic historical record of this event remain:

The conquest by Dharma has been won here, on the borders, and even six hundred yojanas (5,400-9,600 km) away, where the Greek king Antiochos rules, beyond there where the four kings named Ptolemy, Antigonos, Magas and Alexander rule, likewise in the south among the Cholas, the Pandyas, and as far as Tamraparni (Sri Lanka). - *Ashoka the Great, Edicts of Ashoka, Rock Edict 13 (S. Dhammika)*

Ashoka also claims that he encouraged the development of herbal medicine, for human and nonhuman animals, in their territories:

Everywhere within Beloved-of-the-Gods, King Piyadasi's [Ashoka's] domain, and among the people beyond the borders, the Cholas, the Pandyas, the Satiyaputras, the Keralaputras, as far as Tamraparni and where the Greek king Antiochos rules, and among the kings who are neighbors of Antiochos, everywhere has Beloved-of-the-Gods, King Piyadasi, made provision for two types of medical treatment: medical treatment for humans and medical treatment for animals. Wherever medical herbs suitable for humans or animals are not available, I have had them imported and grown. Wherever medical roots or fruits are not available I have had them imported and grown. Along roads I have had wells dug and trees planted for the benefit of humans and animals. - *Ashoka the Great, Edicts of Ashoka, Rock Edict 2*

The Greeks in India even seem to have played an active role in the propagation of Buddhism, as some of the emissaries of Ashoka, such as Dharmaraksita, are described in Pali sources as leading Greek (Yona) Buddhist monks, active in spreading Buddhism (the Mahavamsa, XI).

DEATH AND LEGACY

Ashoka ruled for an estimated forty years. After his death, the Mauryan dynasty lasted just fifty more years. Ashoka had many wives and children, but many of their names are lost to time. Mahindra and Sanghamitra were twins born by his first wife, Devi, in the city of Ujjain. He had entrusted to them the job of making his state religion, Buddhism, more popular across the known and the unknown world. Mahindra and Sanghamitra went into Sri Lanka and converted the King, the Queen and their people to Buddhism. They were naturally not handling state affairs after him.

In his old age, he seems to have come under the spell of his youngest wife Tishyaraksha. It is said that she had got his son Kunala, the regent in Takshashila, blinded by a wily stratagem. The official executioners spared Kunala and he became a wandering singer accompanied by his favourite wife Kanchanamala. In Pataliputra, Ashoka hears Kunala's song, and realizes that Kunala's misfortune may have been a punishment for some past sin of the emperor himself and condemns Tishyaraksha to death, restoring Kunala to the court. Kunala was succeeded by his son, Samprati, but his rule did not last long after Ashoka's death. The reign of Ashoka Maurya could easily have disappeared into history as the ages passed by, and would have had he not left behind a record of his trials.

The testimony of this wise king was discovered in the form of magnificently sculpted pillars and boulders with a variety of actions and teachings he wished to be published etched into the stone. What Ashoka left behind was the first written language in India since the ancient city of Harappa. Rather than Sanskrit, the language used for inscription was the current spoken form called Prakrit. In the year 185 BC, about fifty years after Ashoka's death, the last Maurya ruler, Brhadrata, was brutally murdered by the commander-in-chief of the Mauryan armed forces, Pusyamitra Sunga, while he was taking the Guard of Honor of his forces. Pusyamitra Sunga founded the Sunga dynasty (185 BC-78 BC) and ruled just a fragmented part of the Mauryan Empire.

Many of the northwestern territories of the Mauryan Empire (modern-day Iran, Afghanistan and Pakistan) became the Indo-Greek Kingdom. When India gained independence from the British Empire it adopted Ashoka's emblem for its own, placing the Dharmachakra (The Wheel of Righteous Duty) that crowned his many columns on the flag of the newly independent state. In 1992, Ashoka was ranked #53 on Michael H. Hart's list of the most influential figures in history. In 2001, a semi-fictionalized portrayal of Ashoka's life was produced as a motion picture under the title 'Asoka'.

BUDDHIST KINGSHIP

One of the more enduring legacies of Ashoka Maurya was the model that he provided for the relationship between Buddhism and the state. Throughout Theravada Southeastern Asia, the model of ruler ship embodied by Ashoka replaced the notion of divine kingship that had previously dominated (in the Angkor kingdom, for instance). Under this model of 'Buddhist kingship', the king sought to legitimize his rule not through descent from a divine source, but by supporting and earning the approval of the Buddhist Sangha. Following Ashoka's example, kings established monasteries, funded the construction of stupas, and supported the ordination of monks in their kingdom.

Many rulers also took an active role in resolving disputes over the status and regulation of the Sangha, as Ashoka had in calling a conclave to settle a number of contentious issues during his reign. This development ultimately lead to a close association in many Southeast Asian countries between the monarchy and the religious hierarchy, an association that can still be seen today in the state-supported Buddhism of Thailand and the traditional role of the Thai king as both a religious and secular leader. Ashoka also said that all his courtiers were true to their self and governed the people in a moral manner.

Writing not earlier than five years after the event, Emperor Asoka portrays in this Edict the dramatic change of heart he experienced on account of the havoc of death and deportation, famine and pestilence that was caused by his war of conquest against Kalinga. The text, as found at Erragudi, Girnar, Kalsi, Maneshra, Shahbazgarhi and Kandahar, runs as follows: The country of the Kalingas was conquered by King Priyadarsi, Beloved of the Gods, eight years after his coronation. In this war in Kalinga, men and animals numbering one hundred and fifty thousand were carried away captive from that country; as many as one hundred thousand were killed there in action and many times that number perished.

After that, now that the country of the Kalingas has been conquered, the Beloved of the Gods is devoted to an intense practice of the duties relating to Dharma, to a longing for Dharma and to the inculcation of Dharma among the people. This is due to the repentance of the Beloved of the Gods on having conquered the country of the Kalingas. Verily the silaughter, death and deportation of men which take place in the course of the conquest of an unconquered country are now considered extremely painful and deplorable by the Beloved of the Gods.

But what is considered even more deplorable by the Beloved of the Gods is the fact that injury to or silaughter or deportation of the beloved ones falls to the lot of the Brahmanas, the sramanas, the adherents of other sects and the householders, who live in that country and among whom are established such virtues as obedience to superior personages, obedience to mother and father, obedience to elders and proper courtesy and are full of affection towards the former; even though they are themselves well provided for, the said misfortune as well becomes an injury to their own selves. In war, this fate is shared by all classes of men and is considered deplorable by the Beloved of the Gods.

Now really there is no person who is not sincerely devoted to a particular religious sect. Therefore, the silaughter, death or deportation of even a hundredth or thousandth part of all those people who were silain or who died or were carried away captive at that time in Kalinga is now considered very deplorable by the Beloved of the Gods. Now the Beloved of the Gods thinks that, even if a person should wrong him, the offense would be forgiven if it was possible to forgive it. And the forest-folk who live in the dominions of the Beloved of the Gods, even them he entreats and exhorts in regard to their duty. It is hereby explained to them that, in spite of his repentance, the Beloved of the Gods possesses power enough to punish them for their crimes, so that they should turn away from evil ways and would not be killed for their crimes. Verily, the Beloved of the Gods desires the following in respect of all creatures: non-injury to them, restraint in dealing with them, and impartiality in the case of crimes committed by them. So, what is conquest through *Dhamma* is now considered to be the best conquest by the Beloved of the Gods.

And such a conquest has been achieved by the Beloved of the Gods not only here in his own dominions, but also in the territories bordering on his dominions, as far away as at a distance of six hundred yojanas, where the Yavana king named Antiyoka is ruling and where, beyond the kingdom of the said Antiyoka, four other kings named Turamaya, Antikini, Maka and Alikasundara are also ruling, and, towards the south where the Cho7as and Pandyas are living as far as Tamraparni. Likewise here in the dominions of His Majesty, the Beloved of the Gods-in the countries of Yavanas and Kambojas, of the Nabhakas and Nabhapanktis, of the Bhoja-paitryanikas and of the Andhras and Paulindas- everywhere people are conforming to the instruction in Dharma imparted by the Beloved of the Gods.

Even where the envoys of the Beloved of the Gods have not penetrated, there too men have heard of the practices of Dharma and the ordinances issued and the instruction in Dharma imparted by the Beloved of the Gods, and are conforming to Dharma and will continue to conform to it. So, whatever conquest is achieved in this way, verily that conquest creates an atmosphere of satisfaction everywhere both among the victors and the vanquished. In the conquest through Dharma, the satisfaction is derived by both the parties. But that satisfaction is indeed of little consequence. Only happiness of the people in the next world is what is regarded by the Beloved of the Gods as a great thing resulting from such a conquest.

And this record relating to Dharma has been written on stone for the following purpose, that my sons and great-grandsons should not think of a fresh conquest by arms as worth achieving, that they should adopt the policy of forbearance and light punishment towards the vanquished even if they conquer a people by arms, and that they should regard the conquest through Dharma as the true conquest.

Such a conquest brings happiness to all concerned both in this world and in the next. And let all their intense joys be what is pleasure associated with Dharma. For this brings happiness in this world as in the next. It also appears in a somewhat condensed version in Kandahar and its opening paragraph is as follows: In the eighth year of his reign, Priyadarsi conquered Kalinga.

One hundred and fifty thousand persons were captured there and deported from there; one hundred thousand others were killed, and almost as many perished. Since that time, pity and compassion gripped him, and he was overwhelmed by that. Just as he prescribed to abstain from consuming living beings, he established zeal in the organization of piety. And, behold, what the king was still more afflicted by: all those who inhabited that country, the Brahmanas or sramanas or other followers of piety as well- those who lived there had to be concerned about the interests of the king, to revere and respect their teacher and their father and mother, to love and not to deceive their friends and companions, and to treat their silaves and servants as mildly as possible- if, from among those who were behaving there like that, one was dead or deported, other people are also indirectly affected by this, and the king is extremely afflicted by it.

And, with other peoples, there is no place in the country where men are not indeed sincerely devoted to one sect or another. In spite of its convincing candour and tone of credibility, this Edict, when analyzed vis-a-vis the plethora of legendary and literary information on Emperor Asoka, poses a number of important issues which have baffled six to eight generations of Asokan scholars since the 1830's.

The most significant among them relates to Asoka's connection with Buddhism. The purpose of this chapter is to examine the evidence from all available sources with a view to ascertaining the relative veracity and reliability of the three identifiable sources of information, namely:

i. The Theravada tradition as recorded in Pali in the Chronicles and the commentarial literature of Sri Lanka;

ii. The Mahayana tradition as preserved in Sanskrit and Chinese literary works and records; and

iii. Over two hundred lithic records which the Emperor had caused to be inscribed on rock faces, pillars and caves all over his far-flung empire.

In order to avoid the most distasteful display of unmitigated personal prejudices which had characterized the writings of several Asokan scholars of the past, no one source will be considered prima facie to be more reliable than another. This rigour will be applied with equal care to the lithic records in spite of the obvious temptation to assign them a higher degree of reliability on grounds of either contemporaneity with the protagonist or immutability in transmission. A lesson learnt specially from the epigraphical extravagances of Nissankamalla in Sri Lankan history is that inscriptions per se are no more reliable than other sources of historical information.

On the contrary, they could even be more misleading. The questions for which we shall seek answers will be the following:

1. Was Asoka converted to Buddhism? If so, when and by whom?
2. What role did the Kalinga war play in either his conversion to Buddhism or the change of his imperialist policy?
3. How consistent were his statements in edicts and inscriptions in terms of time and place?
4. Was he actually involved in the propagation of Buddhism

within and outside his empire?

CONVERSION OF ASOKA TO BUDDHISM

According to Joseph M. Kitagawa, the rulers of kingdoms and republics of northeast India extended their patronage to "heteropax sects" (i.e. unorthodox sects when viewed from the Vedic or Brahmanical standpoint) as "one way of avoiding the meddling of Brahmans (high-caste Hindus) in the affairs of the state." While more evidence will be needed before one accepts this view in toto, the fact remains that Asoka's ancestors were associated with Jains and Ajivakas according to both tradition and literary sources.

The founder of the Mauryan dynasty, Candragupta, was in all probability propelled to and sustained in power by the Brahmana political theoretician Kautilya, reputedly the author of the Arthasastra. But the Jain tradition asserts that he abdicated the throne, adopted the life of a Jain ascetic and fasted to death at Sravana Belgola near Mysore.

As regards the religious affiliations of his son, Bindusara, the Sri Lankan Buddhist records portray him as a devotee of Brahmanism - providing alms to 60,000 Brahmans daily at Pataliputra. According to Greek sources, he had appealed to the Seleucid king of Syria, Antiochus I, for a Greek philosopher to instruct him. Bindusara's wife, Dharma- the mother of Asoka- is mentioned in Buddhist sources as a devotee of Ajivakas and her family preceptor is named in Pali sources as Janasana (Jarasana, Jarasona) and in Sanskrit as Pingalavatsa. Asoka, too, dedicated at least two caves to the Ajivakas in the twelfth year from his coronation.

What becomes very clear from these records is that at this particular time in India, and possibly even in Sri Lanka where Pandukabhaya had built them a residence, the Ajivakas constituted a strong and vibrant religious movement. It is stated in Buddhist sources that when Asoka was disenchanted with the Brahmans (whom he supported in continuation of his father's practice) and sought for new religious guidance, the saints and teachers whom the Emperor's men could summon were Ajivakas, Jains and Pandranga Parivrajakas. The Sri Lankan Vinaya Commentary, the Samantapasadika states emphatically that for three years after his coronation, Asoka was a follower of other sects (bahirakapasanda -non-Buddhistic).

Neither tradition nor literary sources associate Buddhism with either Chandragupta or Bindusara, even though an effort had been made to trace the genealogy of the Mauryas to the kinsmen of the Buddha, the Sakyas. Thus the first Maurya emperor to come under the influence of Buddhism or to support Buddhist institutions was Asoka. The fact that Asoka embraced Buddhism and gave Buddhist institutions his special patronage and support is no longer debated. Even if tradition and literary sources are discounted, the following inscriptions leave no more room for doubt.

1. Minor Rock Edict (MRE) I (available in 13 versions): A little more than two years and a half have passed since I have been avowedly a lay follower (*upasaka*) of the Buddha. It is now more than a year since the Sangha has been intimately associated with me (sanghe upayite) and I have been exerting myself in the cause of the Dharma.
2. Same MRE (Ahraura version): This declaration has been made by me while I am on a tour of pilgrimage for 256 nights since the relics of the Buddha ascended the platform (i.e. were caused to be installed by me on the platform for worship).
3. MRE II, a unique text found only in a single version at Bairat (Bhabur) and now at the Indian Museum, Calcutta: King Priyadarsi of Magadha salutes the monks of the Sangha, wishes them good health and comfort in their movement, and addresses them in the following words: It is known to you, Venerable Sirs, how far is my reverence for and faith in the Buddha, the Dharma and the Sangha.

   Whatever, Venerable Sirs, has been said by the Lord Buddha is well said. But, Venerable Sirs, I deem it proper to speak out what appears to me the way as to how the true Dharma may be of long duration. I desire, Venerable Sirs, that the largest number of monks and nuns should constantly listen to and reflect on the following which are texts of the Dharma: Vinayasamutkarsha or the Exaltation of Discipline; Aryavasa or the Noble States of Living; Anagatabhayani or the Fears to Come; Munigatha or the Song of the Hermit; Mauneyasûtram or the Discourse on the State of a Hermit; Upatisyaprasna or the Question of Upatisya; and Rahulavavada or the Exhortation to Rahula, which was delivered by the Lord on the subject of falsehood. In the same way the lay followers of the Buddha, both male and female, should listen to and reflect on the sacred texts. This record, Venerable Sirs, is caused to be written by me for the following purpose, viz., that people may know my intention.

4. RE VII (in seven versions): Now King Priyadarsi, Beloved of the Gods, visited Sambodhi (i.e. the Sacred Bodhi Tree at Buddha Gaya) ten years after his coronation. Thence started these pilgrimages for Dharma.
5. Minor Pillar Edict (MPE) I (Allahabad-Kosambi text): This is the order of the beloved of the Gods. The Mahamatras stationed at Kausambi are to be addressed in the following words: I have made both the Sangha of the monks and Sangha of the nuns united. No heretical monk should be admitted into the Sangha. Whosoever be it a monk, be it a nun, shall break up the unity of the Sangha should be made to wear white robes unworthy of the Order and to reside in what is not fit for the residence of a recluse.
6. MPE I (Sanchi text): You should act in such a way that the Sangha cannot be divided by any heretical monk. Both the Sangha of the monks and the Sangha of the nuns have each been made by me a united whole to last as long as my sons and great-grandsons shall reign and the moon and the sun shall shine. The monk or nun who shall break up the Sangha should be made to put on white robes and to reside in what is not fit for the residence of a recluse.

For my desire is that the Sangha may remain united and flourish for a long time.

7. MPE I and MPE I (Sarnath text): You should act in such a way that the Sangha cannot be divided by anyone. But verily that monk or nun, who shall break up the Sangha, should be compelled to put on white robes and to reside in what is unfit for the residence of a recluse. Thus should this order be communicated to the Sangha of the monks as well as to the Sangha of the nuns?

Thus saith the Beloved of the Gods. One copy of the above document has been deposited in your office, so that it would be accessible to you. And deposit another copy of this very document so as to make it accessible to lay followers of the Buddha. Now the lay followers should assemble near the document every fast day in order to be inspired with faith on account of this very edict. In these lithic records we have the assertion of Asoka himself that he began as a lay follower of the Buddha; that after about a year and a half of uncommitted adherence, he developed a closer association with monks and began to exert himself in the cause of the Dharma; that he admired the teachings of the Buddha and had identified his own favourite texts which he recommended to the clergy as well as to the laity; and he played a leading role, through his new administrative machinery of Dharmamahamatras, to prevent schisms in the Buddhist Sangha.

But the questions which remain yet to be solved are: when, how and by whom was Asoka converted to Buddhism? According to the Sri Lankan Pali sources, Asoka embraced Buddhism in the fourth year from his coronation. The Sanskrit sources, however, are not so specific. But both depict the early years of Asoka as rough, harsh and violent. The Pali sources speak of his wars of succession against 99 of his hundred brothers. The Sanskrit Divyavadana elaborates the ugly appearance and fierce nature of Asoka and presents a grotesque and gruesome episode of how he converted his royal pleasance into a place of terror, horror, oppression and tragic deaths of the unwary visitors and passers-by through his agent

Chandagirika. It also attributes to Asoka the beheading of 500 ministers with his own sword and the burning to death of 500 court ladies.

The Chinese Asokavadana resorts to higher levels of poetical imagination in representing Asoka as a most wicked character. These accounts of Asoka prior to his conversion had prompted Asokan scholars to consider them as the results of a tendency among Buddhist writers to "paint his character as black as possible in the days before his conversion so that he should appeal all the more powerfully to the world as a miracle of grace." The Sri Lankan Pali records, which according to Beni Madhab Barua, "cannot but appear to be comparatively more realistic and reliable, chronologically sounder and nearer the truth," have restricted the wicked past of Asoka's life to his wars of succession which must have extended for nearly four years, i.e. the interval between his succession and his coronation.

The story of Asoka's conversion according to these sources has hardly any dramatic element. The early years after his coronation are portrayed as uneventful and conservative. The only thing which seemed to have disturbed him in the humdrum life was the behaviour of the Brahmans who received his alms daily. His reaction was to look for some saintly teachers. His courtiers and officers produced their favourite teachers from among Ajivakas and Niganthas. But the emperor was unimpressed. It was by accident that he saw the young Buddhist monk, Nyagrodha, to whom he took a liking and from whom he heard a sermon on heedfulness (*appamada*).

By uttering the traditional formula of seeking refuge in the Buddha, the *Dhamma* and the *Sangha*, he became a Buddhist *upasaka*. He began to frequent the local Buddhist temple called Kukkutarama at Pataliputra and there met the learned elder, Moggaliputta Tissa. From him, the Emperor learned of the division of the Buddha's teachings into 84,000 sections and decided to construct as many Buddhist viharas in his empire- a project he completed in three years. Although he had shown utmost munificence to Buddhist institutions, he was still considered "a giver of requisites." To be an "inheritor of the religion" (sasanadayadin), one's offspring had to be ordained in the Sangha.

This, too, was delivered in the sixth year after coronation when his son Mahinda and his daughter Sanghamitta entered the Sangha. Now the problem of reconciling the dates of the Sri Lankan Pali sources with those of Asoka's own inscriptions. In Pillar Edict (PE) VI (found in five versions), which was caused to be written in the twenty-sixth year after the coronation, it is said: Twelve years after my coronation, records relating to Dharma were caused to be written by me for the first time for the welfare and happiness of the people so that, without violation thereof, there might Attain the growth of Dharma in various respects.

Though not specifically dated, the references made in the opening sentence to the period of two and a half years during which Asoka had been a lay follower of Buddhism have been relied upon to establish MRE I (found in 14 versions) to be the earliest of his inscriptions hitherto discovered. If this MRE is therefore dated 12 years after coronation, Asoka's conversion to Buddhism (or in his own words "becoming a lay follower of the Buddha"), which had taken place "a little more than two and a half years" ago, has to be dated between the eighth and ninth year after his coronation.

This date fits perfectly with the period of remorse and repentance following the Kalinga war as so eloquently and movingly described in RE XII. It also fits the two events dated in the inscriptions in the tenth year after coronation: namely, his pilgrimage to the sacred Bodhi Tree and the commencement of his role as the teacher of Dharma (MRE IV found in Greek and Aramaic near Kandahar): "Ten years having passed since his coronation, King Priyadarsi has been showing piety- eusebeia- to the people" (Greek) and "Ten years having passed, it so happened that our lord King Priyadarsi, became the institutor of Truth" (Aramaic). If we had just one source of information- either the literary sources or the inscriptions- there would have been no problem.

Nor would there be a difficulty if one accepts either one of these sources and rejects or ignores the other. It is obviously difficult to reject or ignore the inscriptions. The early Asokan scholars were quick to reject the literary sources in general. But the indispensability of the Sri Lankan Pali sources for even the identification of Asoka with Priyadarsi of the inscriptions, on the one hand, and for interpreting the names and places engraved on reliquaries of Tope No. 2 of Sanchi group and Tope No. 2 of Sonari group on the other, establishes their reliability beyond any doubt. Hence the need to delve deeper into where the two sources of information disagree.

MAJOR DISCREPANCIES IN EVENTS AND DATES

As we have seen above, the events relating to Asoka's conversion to Buddhism and his involvement in the promotion of Dharma (as he called it in his inscriptions) and Buddhadhamma (as Buddhist sources specify) have been differently described and dated in the literary sources and the inscriptions. The central issues before the historical analyst are: (1) Why was Asoka silent on Nyagrodha and Moggaliputta Tissa (or, according to Sanskrit Buddhist sources, Samudra and Upagupta), and why do the Buddhist sources make no reference whatsoever to the Kalinga war and its emotional impact on Asoka? (2) Does this mutual exclusion minimize the reliability of either or both sources? (3) Did the conversion to Buddhism precede or follow this war? One of the earliest scholars to be curious about the impression which Asoka has created to the effect that his spiritual progress was "his own doing throughout" was T.W. Rhys Davids.

His assessment of the evidence of Sri Lankan Pali sources was: "I am not prepared to say, though their evidence is so much later, there may not be some truth in their views." Thus implicitly assigning Asoka's contact with the Sangha a date anterior to the Kalinga war, he concluded: "But it is so very likely that one factor at least in the king's change of heart may have been the exhortation or conversation of one or other of the Arahats, that we may suppose both accounts to have been right." More specific was James M. Macphail. To him, the conversion of Asoka preceded the Kalinga war.

He argued as follows: It is not easy to understand why Asoka, the head of a great military empire that had been acquired in no very remote time by conquest, should have been so deeply affected and consciencestricken by his experience of what were in those days' familiar horrors of war. There must surely have been some preparation for so great a change. Possibly the teaching of the followers of Gautama had impressed him more than he himself realized, and the experience of actual bloodshed on a large scale, merely to gratify ambition and enrich the State, served to crystallize into convictions impressions that had been slowly forming in his mind.

"The issues listed above arise simply because Asoka had not stated how and when he came into contact with Buddhism. The confusion among most scholars had arisen because RE XII has been generally interpreted as an account of Asoka's conversion to Buddhism." Such an interpretation accords with the popular concept of psychological change following from a telling occurrence in a person's life (e.g. the sight of the sick, the old, the dead and the ascetic, which turned the Buddha on his way to renunciation). A very careful scrutiny of this Edict in comparison with MRE I would show that it is the latter which describes his conversion to Buddhism rather than the former.

What RE XII recounts is Asoka's intense emotional experience which prompted him to change his policy of dig-vijaya (i.e. imperialist expansion as enjoined as a major duty of a king according to the Hindu dharmasastras) to dharmavijaya or conquest through righteousness. The purpose of this Edict was specific, to dissuade his sons and grandsons from resorting to conquest by arms: "that they should regard conquest through Dharma (*dharmavijaya*) as the true conquest. Such a conquest brings happiness to all concerned both in this world and in the next."

In Asoka's own words, the effect of the Kalinga war on himself was as follows: Now that the country of the Kalingas has been conquered, the Beloved of the Gods is devoted to an intense practice of the duties relating to the Dharma, [or, according to other versions of the Edict, zealous discussion of Dharma], to a longing for Dharma and to the inculcation of Dharma among the people. This is due to the repentance of the Beloved of the Gods on having conquered the country of the Kalingas. There is an interesting drafting point which may usefully be analyzed. The timing for Asoka's involvement with Dharma is expressed in Prakrit as 'tato paca adhuna ladhesu kaligesu' (Shahbazgarhi text), or 'tato paccha adhuna ladesha kaligyesu'.

This special grammatical construction in Sanskrit, Pali and Prakrit, called the locative absolute, is used to express not merely a sequence in time (i.e. when such a thing was done...) but more emphatically a "conditioning or accompanying circumstance" (i.e. now that it has been done...). What the text with this syntactical form conveys is that the annexation of Kalinga was an obligation or even a pre-requisite which had to be fulfilled. Whether it was necessitated by royal duties as conceived at the time or by demands of national security, Asoka had to do it.

It was only after that he could devote himself to the Dharma. Of course, the miseries which his war perpetrated convinced him how wrong the pursuit of armed conquest was. Such an interpretation of the Edict on the strict analysis of Asoka's choice of words and grammatical form would certainly take away much of the dramatic effect which popular interpretations would assign to the Kalinga war. But it confirms that the information on Asoka's conversion-especially the date- as given in the Sri Lankan Pali sources could still be accurate.

HISTORICAL RELIABILITY OF ROCK EDICT XII

The third question for which an answer is sought in this chapter is: How consistent were Asoka's statements in terms of time and place? This question is raised in relation to RE XII itself, whose central theme is the conquest of Kalinga, the remorse and repentance it caused in Asoka, and the consequent change in his military or foreign policy. So far, as many as eight versions (including a condensed Greek version) have been found in such far-flung places as Afghanistan (2 copies), Pakistan (2 copies), Andhra Pradesh, Gujerat, Uttar Pradesh (near Debra Dun), Maharashtra (near Bombay) - but not a single version in or near Kalinga itself. There must be a special reason for this. This would be, on the face of it, rejected as an "argument from silence."

But that is not so in this particular case. The series of fourteen Rock Edicts (RE I – XIV) appears in exact sequence in identical words (with very minor modifications) in the eight sites mentioned above. There are two similar series of Rock Edicts ın Jaugada and Dhauli in Orissa, that is, in ancient Kalinga. They differ from the rest in one major and most significant factor. The cruc'al Rock Edict XII which expresses Asoka's heartfelt repentance on the miseries he caused to the people of Kalinga is missing, along with Rock Edicts XI and XI. If these three Edicts were simply dropped from the series, it could have been explained as an omission by the scribes.

What strikes our attention is that in their place two other Edicts have been inserted which are specifically addressed to the Mahamatras stationed at Samapa and Tosali. There is of course, the explanation which Asoka had himself given in RE XIV. By way of explaining the possible variations in text and contents, he says: In the series of records, there are texts written in a concise form or in a medium form, or in an elaborate form. And all the items of the series have not been put together in all places. There are some topics which have been repeated over and over again owing to their sweetness, so that people may act accordingly.

There may be some topics which have been written incompletely either as the particular place of a record was considered unsuitable for them or as a special reason for abridgment was believed to exist, and also owing to a fault of the scribe. According to this, the only reason for omitting RE XII could have been that Asoka considered its contents unsuitable for the people of Kalinga. Then there arises the question: Why? Was there any reason why Asoka had to keep away from his Kalingan subjects the fact that he repented the havoc he created there or that it was that war which changed his entire imperialist policy?

There is no doubt room for a sneaking suspicion that there is something very strange if Asoka considered the contents of RE XII to be unsuitable for his subjects in Kalinga at either Jaugada or Dhauli. What exactly is it that he did not want them to know the number of casualties, his repentance, or the "softening" of his militaristic policy? These are about the only sensitive matters which could have influenced his decision unless, of course, one can, even most reluctantly, conceive of an extreme case of inexactitude on the part of Asoka and conclude that the whole episode on the Kalinga war and its consequences was more imaginary than real.

It would then be only an attractive story, presented in vivid colour, to impress those who were far removed from the scene both by distance and time and hence unable to verify its truth or accuracy. That would be to say that Asoka could not possibly tell the Kalingas of a war that did not take place or whose results and extent of damage were different. In spite of the richness of details and the general historical reliability of the Buddhist literary sources in both Pali and Sanskrit, they are altogether silent on a Kalinga episode. As far as they are concerned, such a war had not been responsible for the conversion of Asoka the Wicked to Asoka the Righteous. To be more certain, one should take a closer look at the two texts which replaced RE XI - XII in Kalinga.

The text of RE XV is as follows: Thus saith the Beloved of the Gods: The following royal order has to be addressed to the Mahamatras stationed at Samapa: As regards whatever good I notice, I desire that I may carry it out by deeds and accomplish it by proper means. And I consider the following to be the principal means to this end, viz., to impart instruction to you. All men are my children. Just as, in regard to my own children, I desire that they may be provided by me with all kinds of welfare and happiness in this world and in the next, the same I desire in respect of all men. The following question may occur to the people of the unconquered territories lying beyond the border of my dominions: "What is the king's desire in respect of us?"

The following alone is my wish which should be realized by the peoples living on the borders, viz., that the king desires that they should be unworried on his account, that they should have confidence in him, and that they should expect of him only happiness and no misery. The following also should be realized by them, viz., that the king will forgive them in respect of any offence that is pardonable. My desire is that they should practise the duties associated with Dharma for my sake and that they should Attain happiness in this world as well as in the next. Now, I instruct you for the following purpose, viz., that I may free myself from the debt I owe to the people inhabiting the lands beyond the borders of my dominions by having instructed you and informed you of my will as well as my unshakeable resolution and vow.

Therefore, acting accordingly, you should perform your duties. You should also inspire the people of the bordering lands with confidence in me, so that they might realize that the king is to them even as their father, that he sympathizes with them even as he sympathizes with his own self, and that they are to the king even as his own children. Having instructed you and informed you of my will as well as my unshakeable resolution and vow, I feel that my appeal to you in this respect will be known to the people of the whole country. Indeed you are capable of inspiring them with confidence in me and securing their welfare and happiness in this world and in the next. And, by so doing, you will attain heaven and discharge the debt you owe to me.

So this record has been written here on stone for the following purpose, *viz.*, that the Mahamatras should strive to do their duty at all times in order to inspire the people living on the borders of my dominions with confidence in me and to induce them to practise the duties associated with Dharma: Therefore all of you should listen to this record read out on every Chaturmasi day as well as on the day of the Tishya constellation. You may also listen to it even on any other occasion as it presents itself. And, by so doing, you will be able to accomplish your duties.

And here is RE XVI: The Mahamatras of Tosali, who are the judicial officers of the city, have to be addressed in the following words of the Beloved of the Gods: As regards whatever good I notice, I desire that I may carry it out by deeds and accomplish it by proper means, and I consider the following to be the principal means to this end, viz., to impart instruction to you. For you are placed by me over many thousands of beings with the object that I may gain the affection of all men. All men are my children. Just as, in regard to my own children, I desire that they may be provided with all kinds of welfare and happiness in this world and in the next, the same I desire also in regard to all men. But you do not understand how far my intention goes in this respect.

A few amongst you may understand it; but even such of you understand it partly and not fully. Howsoever well-placed you may be, you have to pay attention to this matter. In the administration of justice, it sometimes happens that some persons suffer imprisonment or harsh treatment. In such cases, a person may accidentally obtain an order cancelling his imprisonment, while many other persons in the same condition continue to suffer for a long time. In such a circumstance, you should so desire as to deal with all of them impartially. But an officer fails to act impartially owing to the following dispositions, viz., jealousy, anger, and cruelty, and hastiness, wants of perseverance, laziness and fatigue.

Therefore, you should desire that these dispositions may not be yours. And the root of the complete success of an officer lies in the absence of anger and avoidance of hastiness. In the matter of administration of justice, an officer does not get up for work if he is fatigued but he has to move, to walk and to advance. Whoever amongst you pays attention to this should tell other officers:

"Pay attention to nothing except the duties assigned to you by the king. Such and such are the instructions of the Beloved of the Gods." The observance of this duty will produce great results for you; but its nonobservance will produce great harm. For, if you fail to observe this, there will be for you neither the attainment of heaven nor the attainment of the king's favour because indifferent observance of this duty on your part cannot make me excessively energetic in favouring you. If, however, you observe this duty, you will Attain heaven and also discharge the debt you owe to me, your master. And all of you should listen to this record read out on the day of the Tishya constellation. Some of you may listen to it also on other suitable occasions on any day between two days of Tishya. In case you do this, you will be able to accomplish your duty.

This record has been written here for the following purpose, viz. that the judicial officers of the city may strive to do their duty at all times and that the people within their charge suffer neither from unnecessary imprisonment nor from unnecessary harassment. Hence I shall cause my Mahamatras, who will be neither harsh nor fierce in temperament, but will be gentle in action, to set out on tours of inspection, every five years, for the following purpose, viz., to ascertain if the judicial officers have realized this object of mine and are acting according to my instructions. Similarly, from Ujjayini also, the Prince Viceroy will send officers of the same class every year for the same purpose and will not allow three years to pass without such a mission being sent out on tour.

In the same way, officers will be deputed from Takshasila also. When these Mahamatras will set out on tours of inspection every year, then without neglecting their normal duties, they will have to ascertain the following, viz., if the local judicial officers are acting according to the king's instructions. Both edicts ring an unmistakable tone of pacification; in RE XV, through persuasion and propaganda that Asoka is resolutely intent on the welfare of the people, and in RE XVI, through impartiality in judicial administration.

The people who are to be so pacified or won over are explicitly called "antanam avijitanam" (as paraphrased by Sircar, "the people of the unconquered territories lying beyond the borders of my dominions"). The location of the two inscriptions in the maritime regions of eastern Kalinga presents a further problem as to where these unconquered border areas could be. It is reasonable to assume that Samapa and Tosali were within Asoka's dominions as his Mahamatras could not have operated from them otherwise. In that case it was the littoral of Kalinga that was within his dominions. The frontier region, whose people the Emperor wanted to win over, had therefore to be located in western Kalinga (i.e. away from the sea).

What it implies is that Asoka had not annexed the whole of Kalinga to his empire and the area he calls "unconquered (avijita)" frontiers was actually the major part of Kalinga. In such a situation, the opening words of RE XII, namely, "the country of the Kalingas was conquered by King Priyadarsi"- which is repeated in modified form twice more in the text- would have been challenged in Kalinga. Even if one explains thus the omission of RE XII in the two Kalinga sites, one is faced with a further difficulty in trying to understand why RE XI and RE XI are also excluded from the series in these sites. RE XI is a straightforward declaration of the principles of moral conduct that Asoka wanted to propagate in his dominions.

But the emphasis is on the gift of Dharma (i.e. propagation of Dharma through precept and example). It runs as follows: Thus saith King Priyadarsi, Beloved of the Gods: There is no such gift as the gift of Dharma, no such act of dividing as the separation of Dharma from what is not Dharma, and no such kinship as kinship through Dharma. These comprise the following, viz., proper courtesy to slaves and servants, obedience to mother and father, liberality to friends, acquaintances and relatives as well as to the Brahmanas and sramanas, and abstention from the slaughter of living beings. In respect of this, whether one is a person's father, or son, or brother, or master, or friend, or acquaintance, one ought to say to him: "This is meritorious. This ought to be done."

If he acts in this manner, happiness in this world is attained by him and endless merit is produced for him in the next world by the said gift of Dharma." RE XI is Asoka's Magna Carta on religious tolerance. It has remained unmatched as a most enlightened statement on interreligious amity. The full text is as follows: King Priyadarsi, Beloved of the Gods, honours men of all religious communities with gifts and with honours of various kinds, irrespective of whether they are ascetics or householders. But the Beloved of the Gods does not value either the offering of gifts or the honouring of people so highly as the following, viz., that there should be a growth of the essentials of Dharma among men of all sects.

And the growth of the essentials of Dharma is possible in many ways. But its root lies in restraint in regard to speech, which means that there should be no extolment of one's own sect or disparagement of other sects on inappropriate occasions and that it should be moderate in every case even on appropriate occasions. On the contrary, other sects should be duly honoured in every way on all occasions. If a person acts in this way, he not only promotes his own sect but also benefits other sects. But if a person acts otherwise, he not only injures his own sect and disparages other sects with a view to glorifying his sect owing merely to his *Atta*chment to it; he injures his own sect very severely by acting in that way. Therefore, restraint in regard to speech is commendable, because people should learn and respect the fundamentals of one another's Dharma.

This indeed is the desire of the Beloved of the Gods, that persons of all sects become well informed about the doctrines of different religions and acquire pure knowledge. And those who are Attached to their respective sects should be informed as follows: "The Beloved of the Gods does not value either the offering of gifts or the honouring of people so highly as the following, viz., that there should be a growth of the essentials of Dharma among men of all sects." Indeed many of my officers are engaged for the realization of the said end, such as the Mahamatras in charge of the affairs relating to Dharma, the Mahamatras who are superin tendents of matters relating to the ladies of the royal household, the officers in charge of my cattle and pasture lands, and other classes of officials.

And the results of their activities, as expected by me, are the promotion of each one's sect and the glorification of Dharma. Assuming that the scribes did not make a mistake, what could reasonably explain their deletion? An in-depth analysis of the two sets of edicts (namely, RE XI - XII absent in the Kalinga series and RE XV and XVI which replace them there) raises the question whether the propagation of Dharma was not a secondary priority in Kalinga where the real priority was the pacification of the unconquered frontier people through propaganda on the Emperor's virtues on the one hand, and the impartial administration of justice on the other.

It may also be conjectured that there were no Dharma-Mahamatras at Samapa and Tosali who could be entrusted with the implementation of RE XI and XI. It is also possible, as my more recent study of Asokan edicts shows, that what is now labelled RE XI, XI and XII were actually a single edict and hence the omission as a whole in Kalinga. The doubt, however, is raised that Kalinga was really not annexed to his dominions and administered as an integral part of the empire. Thus the lithic evidence from Kalinga only deepens the mystery of the famous war which, in Asoka's own words, was the turning point not only in his life but in his attitude to war and empire building.

ASOKA IN THE PROPAGATION OF BUDDHISM IN HIS EMPIRE

The same type of discrepancy which exists between Asoka's own inscriptions and the Buddhist tradition relating to his con version to Buddhism persists as regards his role in the propagation of Buddhism. According to Buddhist literary sources, Asoka had been the ideal Buddhist ruler extending his generous and devout patronage to Buddhism in every possible way. Specifically mentioned is his initiative in both internal and foreign missionary endeavours after the Third Buddhist Council. As already stated earlier, the accuracy of especially the Sri Lankan Pali sources as regards information on these missions has been established beyond doubt on account of archaeological corroboration. But the nagging question which every Asokan scholar had to deal with has been why the inscriptions of Asoka are themselves less specific.

One of the more recent Asokan scholars, Romila Thapar, makes the following observation: More recent analyses suggest, however, that although he was personally a Buddhist, as his edicts addressed to the Buddhist *Sangha* (Order) attest, the majority of his edicts in which he attempted to define dhamma do not suggest that he was merely preaching Buddhism. In his edicts Asoka defines the main principles of dhamma as non-violence, tolerance of all sects and opinions, obedience to parents, respect to Brahmins and other religious teachers and priests, liberality toward friends, humane treatment of servants and generosity towards all. It suggests a general ethic of behaviour to which no religious or social group could object.

It also could act as a focus of loyalty to weld together the diverse strands that made up the empire. Interestingly, the Greek versions of these edicts translate dhamma as eusebeia (piety) and no mention is made anywhere of the teachings of the Buddha, as would be expected if Asoka had been propagating Buddhism.' Thapar has made two statements which need clarification: (i) that Asoka was personally a Buddhist is attested to in his edicts addressed to the Sangha; and (i) no mention is made anywhere of the teachings of the Buddha. As shown earlier, Asoka did express his affiliation to Buddhism in several lithic records and not all of them are addressed to the *Sangha*.

Certainly, MRE I which is found in thirteen locations is not an edict addressed only to the Sangha. So is RE VI, which refers to his pilgrimage to the sacred Bodhi Tree. If there is an impression created in some minds as a result of statements like Thapar's that Asoka did not broadcast his Buddhist affiliations far and wide, his lithic records would not permit such an impression to be sustained. The other statement that the teachings of the Buddha are not mentioned anywhere stands refuted by MRE II at Bairat (Bhabru) where seven identifiable discourses of the Buddha have been presented by Asoka to his co-religionists- the religious and the lay- as his recommended anthology of readings from the Buddhist Canon.

Equally significant are wordperfect direct quotations from the Tripitaka which are found in the edicts. Barua has marshalled together enough evidence in the form of no less than 270 parallels which supports his conclusion that "none was, perhaps, more steeped in the knowledge of the Buddhavacana than Asoka, that none drank deeper at that fountain of inspiration." What Thapar had in mind, quite probably, was that Asoka makes no reference to the fundamental Buddhist doctrines such as the Four Noble Truths, the three signata (*anicca-dukkha-anatta*), the twelve-point dependent causation (paticca samuppada), or even Nirvana.

The anthology of Buddhist texts which Asoka identified serves as an index to what aspect of Buddhism had attracted his attention. What we see in the edicts is nothing more than a paraphrased and condensed version of the ethical teachings of these texts. Twice in MRE II he calls these suttas "the texts of the Dharma" and "the true Dharma." It is true that the teachings of the Buddha, when shorn of the characteristic fundamental doctrines, would be in many ways similar to the contemporary religious systems of eastern India such as Jainism. Thus Asoka's Dharma could resemble any of these systems and, perhaps, Asoka had this eclectic element as one of the guiding principles in the choice of values to be inculcated. But the religious system from which Asoka's Dharma is furthest removed is Brahmanism or Hinduism founded on the authority of the Vedas.

None of the phases of pantheism, kathenotheism or monism in the development of Hindu thought is reflected in the edicts. Nor do any of the known gods of Hinduism figure by name anywhere in the hitherto discovered inscriptions. On the contrary, what they speak very lightly of are the rites and rituals which are central to Hinduism and which the dharmasastras prescribe as obligatory sacraments (*samskara*). Consider, for example, RE IX: Thus saith King Priyadarsi, Beloved of the Gods. People perform various auspicious ceremonies on the occasions of illness, the weddings of sons, the weddings of daughters, the birth of children and the setting out on journeys.

On these and similar other occasions, people perform many auspicious ceremonies. And on such occasions, the womenfolk in particular perform many and diverse ceremonies which are trivial and meaningless. Specifically prohibited by Asoka were animal sacrifices- RE I. Yet the Brahmins were held in high regard and his injunction on showing reverence to religious persons always grouped Sramanas and Brahmanas together. One conclusion which emerges from all this internal evidence of Asoka's own lithic records is that the Dharma he taught was none other than the code of ethics of Buddhism as the Buddha himself preached it in such suttas as Sigalovada, Dhammika, Vyagghapajja, Parabhava, etc., each of which is as devoid of references to characteristic Buddhist doctrines as Asoka's inscriptions are.

So when, as a minimum message, the Rajjukas and Pradesikas were ordered to convey the following to his subjects, Asoka was presenting the quintessence of practical Buddhism: Meritorious is obedience to mother and father. Meritorious is liberality to friends, acquaintances and relatives and to the Brahmanas and Sramanas. Meritorious is abstention from the silaughter of living beings. Meritorious is to spend little and store little. One should obey one's mother and father and likewise one's elders. One should be steadfast in one's kindness towards living beings. One should speak the truth. In this way, one should propound these attributes of Dharma. In the same way, the pupil should honour his teacher and this practice should be established by one in the proper manner among one's relations. This is an ancient rule and the principle is long standing. One should act in this way.

Thus saith King Priyadarsi, Beloved of the Gods: A person has an eye on his good deed only and says to himself: "This good deed has I done." Not in the least does he notice his sin (papa), saying to himself: "This sinful act have I perpetrated," or "This indeed is what is called sin." But this is certainly difficult to scrutinize. Nevertheless, one should verily look into the matter thus: "These passions surely lead to sin, such as violence, cruelty, anger, vanity and jealousy. Let me not ruin myself by reason of these very passions." One should seriously reflect on the following: "This one is for my good only in this world and the other one is for my good also in the next world". These teachings, in fact, are the very ones which are elaborated in the seven Buddhist texts he recommended in the Bairat (Bhabru) Edict.

Once again the Sri Lankan Pali sources provide further evidence on the kind of Buddhist teachings Asoka must have underscored. The first sermon which each of the teams of Buddhist missionaries preached is recorded as follows: Majjhantika in Kashmir and Gandhara: Asivisûpama Sutta-either Asivisa Sutta of the Samyutta Nikaya, which is an allegory on evil forces a person, has to be conscious of, or Asivisa Sutta of the Anguttara Nikaya, on anger. Rakkhita in Vanavasa: Anamatagga Samyutta, which concentrates on the evils of ignorance and craving. Dharmarakkhita, the Greek, in Aparanta: Aggikkhandhopama Sutta (also preached by Mahinda in Sri Lanka), which emphasizes moral conduct.

Mahadhammarakkhita in Maharashtra: Mahanarada-kassapa Jataka, which upholds goodness, generosity and charity as opposed to hedonistic pleasures. Maharakkhita in the Greek country: Kalakarama Sutta, on the Buddha's comprehension of the world without being subject to it. Majjhima in Himalaya: Dhammacakkappav*Atta*na Sutta, the first sermon outlining the Four Noble Truths and the Noble Eightfold Path. Uttara in Suvannabhûmi: Brahmajala Sutta, which analyses different philosophical speculations and underscores moral conduct. Mahinda in Sri Lanka: Cûlahatthipadopama Sutta, which stresses the life of a real devotee.

With the exception of the Dhammacakkappavattana Sutta, all these sermons could be described as not highlighting characteristic Buddhist teachings, just like Asoka's inscriptions.

But none could deny that these suttas do constitute the teachings of the Buddha. It is also evident that the foundation for the code of moral conduct which Asoka expounded in his edicts and inscriptions is identical with that of popular Buddhism, that is, Buddhism as a popular mass religion founded on the principle of reward or retribution for action not only in this very life but also in the next.

Taught through a vast array of interesting narratives presented in the Jatakas, Vimanavatthu, Petavatthu, Apadana, Buddhavamsa and Cariyapitaka in the Tripitaka itself and elaborated an extensive literature in all Buddhist countries, this form of popular Buddhism promoted happiness in the next birth- usually in one of the heavens- as the immediate goal of liberality and good conduct. This message has been conveyed in Buddhist circles not only through verbal communication, but more importantly through visual aid in sculpture and painting. RE V – IV underlines Asoka's adoption of similar means for the propagation of *Dhamma*.

He says: Abstention from slaughter of life, absence of cruelty to living creatures, seemly behaviour to relatives, seemly behaviour to the Brahmanas and Sramanas, obedience to mother and father, and obedience to the aged have increased now owing to the instruction in Dharma imparted by King Priyadarsi, Beloved of the Gods, to such a degree as was not possible to achieve for many hundreds of years in the past by means of showing to the people the representations of celestial cars and celestial elephants, masses of hellfire as well as many other heavenly forms. The practices of Dharma of the above kind as also of various other kinds have increased and King Priyadarsi Beloved of the Gods will cause such practices of Dharma to increase still more.

If Asoka was responsible for this innovation, as the edict suggests, the fact that the practice of illustrating happiness in heavens and suffering in hells has remained a significant aspect of Buddhist art would imply its original association with the propagation of Buddhism. Taking all these clues into consideration, it is reasonable to conclude that Asoka's claim that "every proclamation by beating of drums has become the proclamation of Dharma" applies to the propagation of popular Buddhism through both administrative mechanisms (which the edicts and inscriptions outline) and missionary operations (of which detailed and accurate records have been preserved by the Sri Lankan Sangha).

7

Carvaka, Lokayata and Nastika

CÂRVÂKA

Cârvâka is a system of Indian philosophy that assumes various forms of philosophical skepticism and religious indifference. It is also known as Lokâyata. It is named after its founder, Cârvâka, author of the Bârhaspatya-sûtras. In overviews of Indian philosophy, Cârvâka is classified as a "heterodox" (*nâstika*) system, the same classification as is given to Buddhism and Jainism. It is characterized as a materialistic and atheistic school of thought. While this branch of Indian philosophy is not considered to be part of the six orthodox schools of Hindu philosophy, it is noteworthy as evidence of a materialistic movement within Hinduism.

NAME AND ORIGINS

The name Lokâyata can be traced to Kautilya's Arthashastra, which refers to three ânvîkcikîs (logical philosophies), Yoga, Samkhya and Lokayata. Lokayata here still refers to logical debate (disputatio, "criticism") in general and not to a materialist doctrine in particular. Similarly, Saddaniti and Buddhaghosa in the 5th century connect the "Lokayatas" with the Vitandas (sophists). Only from about the 6th century is the term restricted to the school of the Lokyâtikas. The name Cârvâka is first used in the 7th century by the philosopher Purandara, who refers to his fellow materialists as "the Cârvâkas", and it is used by the 8th century philosophers Kamalaúîla and Haribhadra. Shankara, on the other hand, always uses Lokâyata, not Cârvâka.

E. W. Hopkins, in his The Ethics of India (1924) assumes that Cârvâka philosophy is co-eval with Buddhism, mentioning "the old Cârvâka or materialist of the 6th century BC"; Rhys Davids assumes that lokayata in ca. 500 BC came to mean "scepticism" in general without yet being organized as a philosophical school, and that the name of a villain of the Mahabharata, Cârvâka, was Attached to the position in order to disparage it. The earliest positive statement of skepticism is preserved from the epic period, in the Ramayana-

Regard only that which is an object of perception, and cast behind your back whatever is beyond the reach of your senses (2.108)

The Cârvâka School thus appears to have gradually grown out of generic skepticism in the Mauryan period, but its existence as an organized body cannot be ascertained for times predating the 6th century. The Barhaspatya sutras were likely also composed in Mauryan times, predating 150 BC, based on a reference in the Mahabhasya of Patanjali (7.3.45).

LOSS OF ORIGINAL WORKS

Chatterjee and Datta explain that our understanding of Cârvâka philosophy is fragmentary, based largely on criticism of the ideas by other schools, and that it is not a living tradition:

"Though materialism in some form or other has always been present in India, and occasional references are found in the Vedas, the Buddhistic literature, the Epics, as well as in the later philosophical works we do not find any systematic work on materialism, nor any organised school of followers as the other philosophical schools possess. But almost every work of the other schools states, for refutation, the materialistic views. Our knowledge of Indian materialism is chiefly based on these."

Available evidence suggests that Cârvâka philosophy was set out in the Barhaspatya sutras, probably in Mauryan times.

Neither this text nor any other original text of the Cârvâka School of philosophy has been preserved. Its principal works are known only from fragments cited by its Hindu and Buddhist opponents. Cârvâka philosophy appears to have died out some time in the 15th century. Countering the argument that the Cârvâkas opposed all that was good in the Vedic tradition, Dale Riepe says, "It may be said from the available material that Cârvâkas hold truth, integrity, consistency, and freedom of thought in the highest esteem."

MADHAVACHARYA AND CÂRVÂKA

Madhavacharya, the 13th & 14th-century Vedantic philosopher from South India starts his famous work The Sarva-darsana-sangraha with a chapter on the Cârvâka system with the intention of refuting it. After invoking, in the Prologue of the book, the Hindu gods Shiva and Vishnu, ("by whom the earth and rest were produced"), Madhavacharya asks, in the first chapter:

...but how can we attribute to the Divine Being the giving of supreme felicity, when such a notion has been utterly abolished by Charvaka, the crest-gem of the atheistic school, the follower of the doctrine of Brihaspati? The efforts of Charvaka are indeed hard to be eradicated, for the majority of living beings hold by the current refrain:

While life is yours, live joyously; none can escape Death's searching eye:

When once this frame of ours they burn, how shall it e'er again return?

Quotations attributed to Cârvâka from Sarva-Darsana-Sangraha:

The Agnihotra, the three Vedas, the ascetic's three staves, and smearing oneself with ashes- Brihaspati says, these are but means of livelihood for those who have no manliness nor sense. In this school there are four elements, earth, water, fire and air; and from these four elements alone is intelligence produced - just like the intoxicating power from kinwa &c,

mixed together; since in "I am fat", "I am lean", these attributes abide in the same subject, and since fatness, and leanness, reside only in the body, it alone is the soul and no other, and such phrases as "my body" are only significant metaphorically.

If a beast silain in the Jyothishtoma rite will itself go to heaven, why then does not the sacrificer forthwith offer his own father? If the Sraddha produces gratification to beings that are dead, then why not give food down below to those who are standing on the house-top? If he who departs from the body goes to another world, how is it that he comes not back again, restless for love of his kindred?

Hence it is only as a means of livelihood that Brahmans have established here all these ceremonies for the dead; there is no other fruit anywhere. The three authors of the Vedas were buffoons, knaves, and demons. All the well-known formulae of the pandits, jarphari, turphari, etc and all the obscene rites for the queen commanded in Aswamedha, these were invented by buffoons, and so all the various kinds of presents to the priests, while the eating of flesh was similarly commanded by night-prowling demons. Those parts which survive indicate a strong anti-clerical bias, accusing Brahmins of fostering religious beliefs only so they could obtain a livelihood. The proper aim of a Charvakan or Charvaka, according to these sources, was to live a prosperous, happy, and productive life in this world.

TATTVOPAPLAVASIMHA OF JAYARASI BHATTA

The Tattvopaplavasimha of Jayarashi Bhatta (ca. 8th century) is often cited as the only extant authentic Cârvâka text, but which also shows Madhyamaka influence. It is, in any case, among the most important documents for the study of the Cârvâka School.

ASTIKA SCHOOLS, BUDDHISM, AND JAINISM VERSUS CÂRVÂKA

Cârvâkas cultivated a philosophy wherein theology and what they called "speculative metaphysics" were to be avoided. The Cârvâkas accepted direct perception as the surest method to prove the truth of anything. Though their opponents tried to caricature the Lokayatikas' arguments, the latter did not completely reject the method of inference. Debiprasad Chattopadhyaya quotes S. N. Dasgupta:

"Purandara (a Lokâyata philosopher) [...] admits the usefulness of inference in determining the nature of all worldly things where perceptual experience is available; but inference cannot be employed for establishing any dogma regarding the transcendental world, or life after death or the law of karma which cannot be available to ordinary perceptual experience."

While a Cârvâka's thought is characterized by an insistence on joyful living on one hand and Jainism is known to emphasize penance on the other, Buddhism is said to stand for a "middle way", avoiding indulgence in sensual pleasures and penance alike. Temperance - the enjoyment of life's pleasures in a moderate manner, rather than total abstinence - was the Cârvâkas' primary modus operandi. In this respect, they much resemble the Epicureans of Greece.

The Cârvâkas did not deny the difference between the dead and the living and recognized both as realities. A person lives, the same person dies: that is a perceived, and hence the only provable, fact. In this regard, the Cârvâkas found themselves at odds with all the other religions of the time. Of the five fundamental elements, the *Panchamahabhutas*, *prithvi* (earth or solidity), *jal* (water or liquidity), *agni* (fire or fieriness or brightness), vayu (wind or movement), and *akasha* (lit.space - aether or emptiness), the Cârvâkas recognised the validity of only the first four and thought that a combination of these four elements produced a certain vitality called life.

Rejection of the soul as separate from the body led the Cârvâkas to confine their thinking to this world only. This does not mean that they denied the cause-effect relationship. They accepted the "like causes like result" (*Karmavipaka*) rule, restricted it to this life and this world and admitted exceptions to that rule. Whereas most systems of Astika philosophy advocated a caste system, the Cârvâkas denounced the caste system, calling it artificial, unreal and hence unacceptable. "What is this senseless humbug about the castes and the high and low among them when the organs like the mouth, etc in the human body are the same?"

ABUL FAZL ON LOKÂYATA

Ain-i-Akbari, written by Abul Fazl, the famous historian of Akbar's court, mentions a symposium of philosophers of all faiths held in 1578 at Akbar's insistence. Some Cârvâka thinkers are said to have participated in this symposium. Under the heading "Nastika," Abul Fazl has referred to the good work, judicious administration, and welfare schemes that were emphasized by the Cârvâka lawmakers. Somadeva has also mentioned the Cârvâka method of defeating the enemies of the nation.

Contrary to popular opinion, these so-called "peasant religions(or opinions)" - the direct transilation of the word "Lokayata" - never demanded that the practitioner give up happiness; all they said was that that the means of happiness is giving up that which contradicts carvaka, who claimed that (material) pleasures suffice to give happiness to the (material) body.

ÂSTIKA AND NÂSTIKA

Astika and Nastika are technical terms in Hinduism used to classify philosophical schools and persons, according to whether they accept the authority of the Vedas as supreme revealed scriptures, or not. By this definition, Nyaya, Vaisheshika, Samkhya, Yoga, Purva Mimamsa and Vedanta are classified as astika schools; while Charvaka, Jainism and Buddhism are considered nastika schools. The distinction is similar to the orthodox/heterodox distinction in the West.

In non-technical usage, the term astika is sometimes loosely translated as "theist" while nastika is translated as "atheist". However this interpretation is distinct from the use of the term in Hindu philosophy. Notably even among the astika schools, samkhy and the early mimamsa school do not accept a God while accepting the authority of the Vedas; they thus are "atheistic astika schools".

The different usages of these terms are explained by Chatterjee and Datta as follows:

> In modern Indian languages, 'âstika' and 'nâstika' generally mean 'theist' and 'atheist', respectively. But in Sanskrit philosophical literature, 'âstika' means 'one who believes in the authority of the Vedas' or 'one who believes in life after death'. The word is used here in the first sense. In the second sense, even the Jaina and Buddha schools are 'âstika', as they believe in life after death. The six orthodox schools are 'âstika', and the Cârvâka is 'nâstika' in both the senses.

Astika is a Sanskrit adjective (and noun) that is derived from asti ("it is or exists") meaning "believing" or "pious"; or "one who believes in the existence (of God, of another world, etc.)." Nastika (na (not) + âstika) is its negative, literally meaning "not believing" or "not pious". As used in Hindu philosophy the differentiation between astika and nastika refers to belief in Vedic authority, not belief or lack of belief in theism. As N. N. Bhattacharyya writes:

> The followers of Tantra are often branded as Nâstika by the upholders of the Vedic tradition. The term Nâstika does not denote an atheist. It is applied only to those who do not believe in the Vedas. The Sankhyas and Mîmamsakas do not believe in God, but they believe in the Vedas and hence they are not Nâstikas. The Buddhists, Jains, and Cârvâkas do not believe in the Vedas; hence they are Nâstikas.

CLASSIFICATION OF SCHOOLS

Many Indian intellectual traditions were codified during the medieval period into a standard list of six orthodox systems, the shaddarshanas (*°addarœana*), all of which cite Vedic authority as their source:

- Nyaya, the school of logic
- Vaisheshika, the atomist school
- Samkhya, the enumeration school

- Yoga, the school of Patanjali (which assumes the metaphysics of Samkhya)
- Purva Mimamsa (or simply Mimamsa), the tradition of Vedic exegesis, and
- Vedanta (also called Uttara Mimamsa), the Upanishadic tradition.

These are often coupled into three groups for both historical and conceptual reasons: Nyaya-Vaishesika, Samkhya-Yoga, and Mimamsa-Vedanta.

The three main schools of Indian philosophy that do not base their beliefs on the Vedas were regarded as heterodox by Brahmans:

- Buddhism
- Jainism
- Cârvâka

The use of the term nastika to describe Buddhism and Jainism in India is explained by Gavin Flood as follows:

At an early period, during the formation of the Upani°ads and the rise of Buddhism and Jainism, we must envisage a common heritage of meditation and mental discipline practiced by renouncers with varying affiliations to non-orthodox (Veda-rejecting) and orthodox (Veda-accepting) traditions.... These schools [such as Buddhism and Jainism] are understandably regarded as heterodox (nâstika) by orthodox (âstika) Brahmanism.

The Tantric traditions in Hinduism have both astika and nastika lines; as Banerji writes in "Tantra in Bengal":

Tantras are... also divided as âstika or Vedic and nâstika or non-Vedic. In accordance with the predominance of the deity the âstika works are again divided as Úâkta, Saiva, Saura, Ganapatya and Vaisnava.

LOKAYATA

"Atheism is a necessary protest against the wickedness of the churches and the narrowness of the creeds. God uses it as stone to smash these soiled card-houses."- Sri Aurobindo of the numerous schools of thought that gained prominence during the epic period as a reaction against the excessive ritualism and empty dogmatism of vedic religion or perhaps the increasing rigidity of caste system, one school of thought attracts the attention of present day scholars not only for its radical approach to the problems of blind belief but also for its similarities with the modern day rationalism and materialism of the west. It was the lokayata school of thought, believed to have been founded by Charvaka, whose history is shrouded in great mystery and myth. The world lokayata was used to refer to the person who believed in the reality of this world and the physical existence of man and of other beings on earth and nothing else.

'Loka' means the world and 'lokayata' means he who is centered around or relies upon this world only. The lokayatas believed in the existence of this world only, neither in heaven nor in hell, neither in vice nor virtue. They accepted only that reality which they could subjectively perceive and interact with, not in any imaginary world or some kind of ideal world. Practical and down to the earth, they believed in the existence of four elements only, namely the earth, water, fire, and air instead of the five elements of the vedic scriptures of which space or ether was the fifth element. The Charvaka system of thought believed neither in God nor in the after life of man. Their doctrines are traced to an ancient scripture called the Charvaka Dharma probably written by an author of the name of Charvaka.

Reference to the Charvakas or the Lokayatas was found in some ancient Hindu and Buddhist Scriptures such as the Prabhodha Chandrodaya, an allegorical play in which a character sums up the beliefs of this school, and also the epics, the Ramayana and the Mahabharata. One of the chief protagonists of this school existed during the time of the Buddha and his name was Ajita Kesakamabali. He recognized only four elements and declared that a combination of these four elements produced certain vitality called life, which is very much in tune with the modern theories of creation of life on earth. At the time of death these four elements would return to their respective sources, earth to earth, air to air and so on. There was no mystery of life beyond this. "When the body dies both fool and wise alike are cut off and perish. They do not survive after death."

According to the Charvakas there was no soul. Death was the end of all existence. The body itself was *Atman* and enjoyment of this life in the bodily form should be the chief purpose of life. Whatever was within the field of perception was true and it alone existed. Anything beyond the senses was false, a mere illusion or self induced delusion. Inference by itself could not be the basis of truth and therefore it was invalid. We should not depend upon the experience of others to know the truth. We should not base our belief upon the teachings of others as long as they were not confirmed by our own personal experience. Subjective experience was therefore the basis of all truth and of ones conduct in this world.

The Charvakas did not accept the Vedas, or the Vedic rites prescribed by the Vedas. They contended that one should not practice these religious rites, whose results no one could verify with certainty. They did not believe in karma or the concept of sacrifice. What was the use of sacrificing something today, in the hope of getting some future benefit whose arrival was never certain? Earthly enjoyment was the highest ideal and it should not be sacrificed in the hope of some better after life. Since matter was the only thing that was perceivable by the senses, matter alone was real. Intelligence was also a form of matter, like the body, because it was produced by the modification of the four elements and was destroyed the way the body was destroyed when these elements were dissolved. The physical self alone was real and the mind and the body were part of this physical self.

Two interpretations are given for the word Charvaka. According to one interpretation, the word 'char' means 'charming and alluring and the word 'vak' means speech. Probably the Charvakas were good orators and their words were instantly appealing to the audience as they appealed to the senses directly and required no blind faith to sustain themselves. According to another interpretation, the word 'charva' means grinding and chewing and the world 'Charvaka' means he who grinds both vice and virtue. The Charvakas are also known as Brihaspatayas because it is believed that Brihaspathi was the author of this doctrine. Another sect which was close to the lokayatas in their thinking was the sect of the kapalikas, who believed in the practice of sex and gory rituals to gain siddhis or spiritual powers.

Probably the Charvaka School must have provided some background from which the later schools of Tantricism emerged both in Hinduism and Buddhism as a way of compromise between materialism and spiritualism. The disbelief and atheism of ancient India is summed up in the following lines from the *Savradarshana Samgraha*.

"There is no heaven, no final liberation, nor any soul in another world,

Nor do the actions of the four castes, etc., produce any real effect.

The Agnihotra, the three Vedas, the ascetic's three staves, and smearing one's self with ashes,

We're made by Nature as the livelihood or those destitute of knowledge and manliness."

The Charvaka School of thinking had many draw backs. Its chief weakness was its excessive reliance upon subjective experience and upon sensory perceptions, as the basis of truth. These two are not perfect and reliable instruments of truth and they would not always guarantee complete wisdom. The Charvakas ignore the fundamental fact that our perceptions can be very misleading and that they are colored by our own prejudices, fears, anxieties, expectations, desires, thoughts and most important of all by our own ignorance. They also fail to explain the role of Nature, the rationale for good social conduct or the need for social harmony. The Charvakas provide very simplistic solutions to the complex problems of pain and suffering, and fall short of providing lasting solutions to the real problems of human life and society. In short they fail to explain such human needs and aspirations that are not purely physical or mental but spiritual and the importance of such morals and social values in human life that distinguishes us from the world of the animals.

"Truth" for the exponents of this tradition was that which could be perceived by human senses of sight, hearing, smell, taste or touch.

This kind of down-to-earth approach necessitated to the recognition of the limits to human knowledge and capacity. But it also tethered the exponents of Lokayata to a realistic and convincing approach. Nothing was accepted as a matter of faith and the quest to know more about the unknown was the driving force of this school. According to the Lokayata doctrine, the universe was made up of active physical forces (like gravitation) which activated and stimulated each other. But these physical forces although active were not alive as they did not move about consciously towards any set purpose.

This is where the Lokayata School differed from other philosophies which interpreted the "active" quality of these forces as proof of their being "alive". The idea that the active powers of the physical universe like thunder, lightning, rain and storms were alive and moved about consciously to achieve a set purpose was the foundation of most philosophies. The exponents of Lokayata did not believe in concepts such as life after death or rebirth.

A charge that was made against adherents of this philosophy was that they emphasized only the material aspects while disregarding spiritual ones. But this was natural in a school which looked upon only the perceptible as real.

According to the Lokayata doctrine, the universe was made up of active physical forces (like gravitation) which activated and stimulated each other. But these physical forces although active were not alive as they did not move about consciously towards any set purpose. This is where the Lokayata School differed from other philosophies which interpreted the "active" quality of these forces as proof of their being "alive". The idea that the active powers of the physical universe like thunder, lightning, rain and storms were alive and moved about consciously to achieve a set purpose was the foundation of most other philosophies.

But it was the Lokayata outlook that was reflected in the advances made by ancient Indian Astronomers like Aryabhatta and Varahamihira who tried to understand and interpret the physical universe around them in physical terms.

Seen here are views of the Jantar-Mantar (Yantra-Mantra) which are astronomical observatories built by Raja Jai Singh of Jaipur. This observatory at Delhi, built in the 18th century on principles of creating tools for astronomical observations and measurements is based on the techniques enunciated in ancient Hindu astronomical texts like the Aryabhattiya and Pancha-siddhanka which date back to the 5th century C.E.

Lokayata looked upon Man and his psyche a result of the material conditions around him. In this respect this school came close to modern interpretations which look upon man to be ultimately a result of physical evolution of the universe, and religion together with all aspects of the human psyche a result of Man's intellectual and emotional evolution. Thus the Lokayata philosophy which seems closest to the modern Rationalism seems to have been popular at some stage in history in ancient India.

The term Lokayata itself can be translated as 'widespread among the people'. Its principle exponent is considered to be a philosopher named Charavaka who is said to be a contemporary of Sri Krishna and if legend is to be believed, he was burned at the orders of Yudhisthira after the Mahabharat war. His crime was apostasy in declaring that the Vedas are not the ultimate in human knowledge.

Modern philosophers who have propounded this philosophy include like Dharmanand Kosambi, Rahul Sankrutyan and Devi Prasad Chattopadhyay. There existed other philosophical schools like Nyaya, Vaisheshika, Yoga and

Mimansa, but the three schools discussed here represented the major under-currents of Indian philosophical thought.

As mentioned earlier, philosophies interacted closely with religions and Hinduism, Buddhism, Jainism all show traces of ideas borrowed from the different philosophical schools which strictly speaking were part of no religion.

8

Philosophy of Early History Buddhist Schools

The Early Buddhist schools are those schools into which, according to most scholars, the Buddhist monastic Sangha initially split, due originally to differences in Vinaya, and later also due to doctrinal differences and geographical separateness of groups of monks. The original Sangha split into the first early schools (commonly believed to be the Sthaviravadins and the Mahasanghikas) a significant number of years (at least 100) after the death of Gautama Buddha. Later, these first early schools split into further divisions such as the Sarvastivadins and the Dharmaguptakas, and ended up numbering, traditionally, about 18 or 20 schools. In fact, there are several overlapping lists of 18 schools preserved in the Buddhist tradition, totalling about twice as many, though some may be alternative names. It is thought likely that the number is merely conventional.

The arising of the Mahayana school of Buddhism (1st / 2nd century CE) went together with the writing of the new Mahayana Sutras. The supposed philosophy or attitude that according to the Mahayana unites the separate early schools was called Hinayana, a term many consider to be derogatory and offensive. The schools sometimes split over ideological differences concerning the 'real' meaning of teachings in the Suttapitaka, and sometimes over disagreement concerning the proper observance of vinaya. These ideologies became embedded in large works such as the Abhidhammas and commentaries. When comparing the existing versions of the Suttapitakas of various sects, there is some evidence that ideologies from the Abhidhammas sometimes found their way back into the Suttapitakas, to support the statements made in those Abhidhammas.

THE FIRST COUNCIL

Three months after the passing of Gautama Buddha, according to the scriptures, the First Council was held at Rajagaha by some of his disciples who had Attained Arahantship (Enlightenment). At this point, Theravada tradition maintains that no conflict about what the Buddha taught is to have occurred, and the teachings were divided into various parts and each was assigned to an elder and his pupils to commit to memory. The accounts of the Council in the scriptures of different schools differ as to what was actually recited at the Council. Venerable PurâGa is recorded as having said: "Your reverences, well chanted by the elders are the Dhamma and Vinaya, but in that way that I heard it in the Lord's presence, that I received it in his presence, in that same way will I bear it in mind."

Many scholars deny that the First Council actually took place. Some scholars consider this council fictitious. The First Buddhist council was convened in the year following the Buddha's Parinibbana, which would be 499/8 BCE according to Theravada tradition, at various earlier dates according to various Mahayana traditions, and various later dates according to various Western estimates. According to late commentarial accounts, King Ajatashatru sponsored the council. Tradition holds that the Council was held in a hall erected by Ajatasattu outside the Sattaparnaguha Cave (Pali: Sattapanniguha) in Rajgir, three months after the Buddha had died. Detailed accounts of the council can be found in the Khandhaka sections of the canonical Vinayas.

According to this record the incident which prompted the Elder Mahakassapa to call this meeting was his hearing a disparaging remark about the strict rule of life for monks. This is what allegedly happened. The monk Subhadda, who had ordained late in life, upon hearing that the Buddha had expired, voiced his resentment at having to abide by all the rules for monks laid down by the Buddha. Many monks lamented the passing of the Buddha and were deeply grieved. However, the Elder Mahakassapa heard Subhadda say: "Enough your Reverences do not grieve do not lament. We are well rid of this great recluse (the Buddha). We were tormented when he said, 'this is allowable to you, this is not allowable to you' but now we will be able to do as we like and we will not have to do what we do not like."

Mahakassapa was alarmed by his remark and feared that the Dhamma and the Vinaya might be corrupted and not survive intact if other monks were to behave like Subhadda and interpret the Dhamma and the Vinaya rules as they pleased. To avoid this he decided that the Dhamma must be preserved and protected. To this end after gaining the Sangha's approval he called to council five hundred Arahants. Ananda was to be included in this provided he attained Arahanthood by the time the council convened. With the Elder Mahakassapa presiding, the five-hundred Arahant monks met in council during the rainy season.

The first thing Mahakassapa did was to question the foremost expert on the Vinaya of the day, Venerable Upali on particulars of the monastic rule. This monk was well qualified for the task as the Buddha had taught him the whole of the Vinaya himself. The Elder Mahakassapa asked him specifically about the ruling on the first offense parajika, with regard to the subject, the occasion, the individual introduced, and the proclamation, the repetition of the proclamation, the offense and the case of non-offense. Upali gave knowledgeable and adequate answers and his remarks met with the unanimous approval of the presiding Sangha. Thus, the Vinaya was formally approved. The Elder Mahakassapa then turned his attention to Ananda in virtue of his reputable expertise in all matters connected with the Dhamma.

Happily, the night before the Council was to meet, Ananda had Attained Arahantship and joined the Council. The Elder Mahakassapa, therefore, was able to question him at length with complete confidence about the Dhamma with specific reference to the Buddha's sermons. This interrogation on the Dhamma sought to verify the place where all the discourses were first preached and the person to whom they had been addressed. Ananda aided by his word-perfect memory was able to answer accurately and so the Discourses met with the unanimous approval of the Sangha. The First Council also gave its official seal of approval for the closure of the chapter on the minor and lesser rules, and approval for their observance. It took the monks seven months to recite the whole of the Vinaya and the Dhamma and those monks sufficiently endowed with good memories retained all that had been recited.

This historic first council came to be known as the Pancasatika because five-hundred fully enlightened Arahants had taken part in it. Some scholars deny that the First Council actually took place. According to the Macmillan *Encyclopedia of Buddhism* (2004), "... its historicity is questioned by virtually all Buddhist scholars. They argue that while it was not unlikely that a small group of Buddha's intimate disciples gathered after his death, a council held in the grand style described in the scriptures is almost certainly a fiction."

THE SECOND COUNCIL

The Second Council did not cause a split in the Sangha, as is sometimes believed to be the case. The Second Council was strictly about the misbehavior of a group of monks, who changed their behaviors after the council. The Second Buddhist council took place in Vesali, about one hundred years after the Buddha's Parinibbâna, in order to settle a serious dispute on Vinaya. The orthodox monks were able to convince the monks whose behaviour was under question. Accounts of the dispute are preserved in the Vinaya texts of several of the early Buddhist schools. Virtually all scholars agree that this second council was a historical event.

Some time after the Second Council, schisms occurred within the monastic Sangha, which resulted in the formation of several subgroups such as Sthaviravada, Mahasanghika and Sarvastivada.

The dispute arose over the 'Ten Points.' This is a reference to claims of some monks breaking ten rules, some of which were considered major. The specific ten points were:

1. Storing salt in a horn.
2. Eating after midday.
3. Eating once and then going again to a village for alms.
4. Holding the Uposatha Ceremony with monks dwelling in the same locality.
5. Carrying out official acts when the assembly was incomplete.
6. Following a certain practice because it was done by one's tutor or teacher.
7. Eating sour milk after one had his midday meal.
8. Consuming strong drink before it had been fermented.
9. Using a rug which was not the proper size.
10. Using gold and silver.

The key issue was the use of 'gold and silver', which is an Indic idiom that includes any kind of money. The monks of Vesali had taken to wandering for alms with the specific goal of collecting money, to which the visiting monk Yasa objected. Some of the other points are also important, for example point 6, which would allow monks to not follow the Vinaya on any point which their teacher did not follow or practice. This behaviour was noted, became an issue and caused a major controversy. The monastic Sangha is structured so that all actions and decisions must be unanimously agreed upon through consensus. Since the monks accused of breaking these ten rules refused to be reprimanded or acknowledge fault, the Sangha was unable to resolve this dispute in any other way than by convening the Second Buddhist Council.

Some of the 'Ten Points' were against minor (*dukkata* or *sekhiya*) rules. Before the Buddha's Parinibbâna he told Ven. Ananda that the community may (unanimously) relinquish the minor rules of the Vinaya but at the First Buddhist Council there was uncertainty about which rules he was referring to and it was unanimously decided to keep the Vinaya as it was during the Buddha's lifetime. However, 100 years later some monks felt that certain rules could be relaxed. The Second Buddhist Council made the unanimous decision not to relax any of the rules, and censured the behaviour of the monks who were accused of violating the 'Ten Points'.

PERIOD BETWEEN THE SECOND AND THIRD COUNCIL

Most scholars believe that the first split occurred between the second and third council, and was probably about monastic discipline. Generally, it is believed that the first split was between the Sthaviravada and the Mahasanghika. However, after this initial division, more were to follow.

THIRD COUNCIL UNDER ASOKA

Tradition mostly says Buddhism split into 18 schools, but different sources give different lists, and scholars conclude that the number is merely conventional. In the 3rd century BCE, Theravadin sources state that a Third Council was convened under the patronage of Emperor Ashoka, but no mention of this council is found in other sources. Some scholars argue that there are certain implausible features of the Theravada account which imply that the Third Council was ahistorical. The remainder considers it a purely Theravada/Vibhajjavada council. It is generally accepted, however, that one or several disputes did occur during Asoka's reign, involving both doctrinal and vinaya matters, although these may have been too informal to be called a Council. The Sthavira School had, by the time of King Ashoka divided into three sub-schools, doctrinally speaking, but these did not become separate monastic orders until later.

According to the Theravadin account, this Council was convened primarily for the purpose of establishing an official orthodoxy. At the council, small groups raised questions about the specifics of the vinaya and the interpretation of doctrine. The chairman of the council, Moggaliputta Tissa, compiled a book called the Kathavatthu, which was meant to refute these arguments. The council sided with Moggaliputta and his version of Buddhism as orthodox; it was then adopted by Emperor Ashoka as his empire's official religion. This school of thought was termed Vibhajjavada (Pali), literally "thesis of [those who make] a distinction" as to the existence of dhammas in the past, future and / or present.

The version of the scriptures that had been established at the Third Council, including the vinaya, sutta and the abhidhamma (collectively known as Tripitaka), was taken to Sri Lanka by Emperor Ashoka's son, the Venerable Mahinda. There it was eventually committed to writing in the Pali language. The Pali Canon remains the most complete set of Nikaya scriptures to survive, although the greater part of the Sarvâstivâdin canon survives in Chinese translation, some parts exist in Tibetan translations, and some fragments exist in Sanskrit manuscripts, while parts of various canons (sometimes unidentified), exist in Chinese and fragments in other Indian dialects.

The Third Buddhist council was convened in about 250 BCE at Asokarama in Patiliputta, supposedly under the patronage of Emperor Asoka. The reason for convening the Third Buddhist Council is reported to have been to rid the Sangha of corruption and bogus monks who held heretical views. It was presided over by the Elder Moggaliputta Tissa and one thousand monks participated in the Council. However, the council is unrecognized and unknown to all Buddhist sources outside of the Theravada school, and its importance to these other schools is therefore debatable. Tradition has it that Asoka had won his throne through shedding the blood of his father's entire son's except his own brother, Tissa Kumara, who eventually got ordained and achieved Arahantship.

The Theravadin account of the background to the Third Council is as follows: Emperor Asoka was crowned in the two hundred and eighteenth year after the Buddha's Mahaparinibbâna. At first he paid only token homage to the *Dhamma* and the *Sangha* and also supported members of other religious sects as his father had done before him. However, all this changed when he met the pious novice-monk Nigrodha who preached him the Appamada-vagga. Thereafter he ceased supporting other religious groups and his interest in and devotion to the *Dhamma* deepened. He used his enormous wealth to build, it is said, eighty-four thousand pagodas and viharas and to lavishly support the bhikkhus with the four requisites. His son Mahinda and his daughter Sanghamitta were ordained and admitted to the *Sangha.*

Eventually, his generosity was to cause serious problems within the Sangha. In time the order was infiltrated by many unworthy men, holding heretical views and who were attracted to the order because of the Emperor's generous support and costly offerings of food, clothing, shelter and medicine. Large numbers of faithless, greedy men espousing wrong views tried to join the order but were deemed unfit for ordination. Despite this they seized the chance to exploit the Emperor's generosity for their own ends and donned robes and joined the order without having been ordained properly. Consequently, respect for the Sangha diminished.

When this came to light, some of the genuine monks refused to hold the prescribed purification or Uposatha ceremony in the company of the corrupt, heretical monks. When the Emperor heard about this he sought to rectify the situation and dispatched one of his ministers to the monks with the command that they perform the ceremony. However, the Emperor had given the minister no specific orders as to what means were to be used to carry out his command. The monks refused to obey and hold the ceremony in the company of their false and 'thieving' companions (Pali, *theyya-sinivâsaka*).

In desperation the angry minister advanced down the line of seated monks and drawing his sword, beheaded all of them one after the other until he came to the King's brother, Tissa who had been ordained. The horrified minister stopped the silaughter and fled the hall and reported back to the Emperor. Asoka was deeply grieved and upset by what had happened and blamed him for the killings. He sought Thera Moggaliputta Tissa's counsel. He proposed that the heretical monks be expelled from the order and a third Council be convened immediately.

COUNCIL

So it was that in the seventeenth year of the Emperor's reign the Third Council was called. Thera Moggaliputta Tissa headed the proceedings and chose one thousand monks from the sixty thousand participants for the traditional recitation of the *Dhamma* and the Vinaya, which went on for nine months. The Emperor, himself questioned monks from a number of monasteries about the teachings of the Buddha. Those who held wrong views were exposed and expelled from the Sangha immediately. In this way the Bhikkhu Sangha was purged of heretics and bogus *bhikkhus*. According to the Pali account, the Elder Moggaliputta Tissa, in order to refute a number of heresies and ensure the *Dhamma* was kept pure, complied a book during the council called the *Kathavatthu*.

This book consists of twenty-three chapters, and is a collection of discussions on the points of controversy. It gives refutations of the 'heretical' views held by various Buddhist sects on matters philosophical. The Kathavatthu is the fifth of the seven books of the Abhidhamma Pitaka. However, the historicity of this has been questioned, as the account preserved in the San Jian Lu Pi Po Sho (Sudassanavinayavibhasha), although otherwise almost identical, does not mention the Kathavatthu. Moggaliputtatissa told Ashoka that the doctrine taught by the Buddha was the Vibhajjavada, the Doctrine of Analysis. This term is used in various senses, and it is not clear exactly what it meant in this context. Traditionally, however, the Sri Lankan Theravadins and other mainland schools of Early Buddhism identified themselves as Vibhajjavada.

EMISSARIES

One of the most significant achievements ascribed by Theravada tradition to this Dhamma assembly and one which was to bear fruit for centuries to come, was the Emperor's sending forth of monks, well versed in the Buddha's Dhamma and Vinaya who could recite all of it by heart, to teach it in nine different countries.

RESULTS OF MISSIONS

The Dhamma missions to Sri Lanka and Kashmir and Gandhara were very successful, leading to a long-term presence and dominance of Buddhism in those areas. It is not clear exacly how influential the interactions to Egypt and Greece may have been, but some authors have commented that some level of syncretism between Hellenist thought and Buddhism may have started in Hellenic lands at that time. They have pointed to the presence of Buddhist communities in the Hellenistic world around that period, in particular in Alexandria (mentioned by Clement of Alexandria), and to the pre-Christian monastic order of the Therapeutae (possibly a deformation of the Pali word "Theravada"), who may have "almost entirely drawn (its) inspiration from the teaching and practices of Buddhist asceticism" (Robert Linssen).

Possibly Buddhist gravestones from the Ptolemaic period have also been found in Alexandria, decorated with what may be depictions of the Dharma wheel (Tarn, "The Greeks in Bactria and India"). Commenting on the presence of Buddhists in Alexandria, some scholars have even pointed out that "It was later in this very place that some of the most active centers of Christianity were established" (Robert Linssen "Zen Living"). In the 2nd century CE, the Christian theologian Clement of Alexandria recognized Bactrian Buddhists (Sramanas) and Indian Gymnosophists for their influence on Greek thought:

"Thus philosophy, a thing of the highest utility, flourished in antiquity among the barbarians, shedding its light over the nations. And afterwards it came to Greece. First in its ranks were the prophets of the Egyptians; and the Chaldeans among the Assyrians; and the Druids among the Gauls; and the Sramanas among the Bactrians; and the philosophers of the Celts; and the Magi of the Persians, who foretold the Saviour's birth, and came into the land of Judaea guided by a star. The Indian gymnosophists are also in the number, and the other barbarian philosophers. And of these there are two classes, some of them called Sramanas, and others Brahmins" - Clement of Alexandria "The Stromata, or Miscellanies" Book I, Chapter XV

DEVELOPMENTS DURING AND AFTER THE THIRD COUNCIL

Whatever might be the truth behind the Theravâdin account, it was around the time of Asoka that further divisions began to occur within the Buddhist movement and a number of additional schools emerged, including the Sarvâstivâda and the Sammitîya. All of these early schools of Nikayan Buddhism eventually came to be known collectively as the Eighteen Schools in later sources. Unfortunately, with the exception of the Theravâda, none of early these schools survived beyond the late medieval period by which time several were already long extinct, although a considerable amount of the canonical literature of some of these schools has survived, mainly in Chinese translation. Moreover, the origins of specifically Mahâyâna doctrines may be discerned in the teachings of some of these early schools, in particular in the Mahâsânghika and the Sarvâstivâda.

During and after the Third Council, elements of the Sthavira group called themselves Vibhajjavadins. One part of this group was transmitted to Sri Lanka and to certain areas of southern India, such as Vanavasi in the south-west and the Kañci region in the south-east. This group later ceased to refer to themselves specifically as Vibhajjavadins, but reverted to calling themselves Theriyas, after the earlier Theras or Sthaviras. Still later, at some point prior to the *Dipavamsa* (4th century), the Pali name Theravâda was adopted and has remained in use ever since for this group. The Pudgalavâdins were also known as Vatsiputrîyas after their putative founder, though this group later became known as the Sammitîya school, after one of its subdivisions, though it died out around the 9th or 10th century CE.

Nevertheless, during most of the early medieval period, the Sammitîya School was numerically the largest Buddhist group in India, with more followers than all the other schools combined. The Sarvâstivâdin School was most prominent in the north-west of India and provided some of the doctrines that would later be adopted by the Mahâyana. Another group linked to Sarvâstivâda was the Sautrântika School, which only recognized the authority of the sutras and rejected the Abhidharma transmitted and taught by the Vaibhâsika wing of Sarvâstivâda. Based on textual considerations, it has been suggested that the Sautrântikas were actually adherents of Mûla-Sarvâstivâda. The relation between Sarvâstivâda and Mûla-Sarvâstivâda is unclear. Between the 1st century BCE and the 1st century CE, the terms Mahayana and Hinayana were first used in writing, in, for example, the *Lotus Sutra*.

THE CHINESE PILGRIMS

During the first millennium, monks from China such as Faxian, Yijing and Xuanzang made pilgrimages to India and wrote accounts of their travels when they returned home. These Chinese travel records constitute extremely valuable sources for information concerning the state of Buddhism in India during the early medieval period. By the time the Chinese Pilgrims Xuanzang and Yi Jing visited India in the medieval period there were five early Buddhist schools that they mention far more frequently than others.

EARLY SECTARIAN DIVISIONS

Some of the lists that are available concerning the early Buddhist schools are mentioned below.

EIGHTEEN SCHOOLS

The exact lineages of the different schools are complex. Different traditions and scholarship hold to different views. Sometimes the same school may be referred to under different names; or different schools might bear the same name. In many cases, the different 'schools' may be just regional variants without serious doctrinal divergences.

LEGACY

The Theravâda School of Sri Lanka, Burma, and Thailand is descended from the Sthaviravâdin and (more specifically) the Vibhajjavada School. It underwent two more changes of name in the mean time. In the Indian accounts it is sometimes called the Tâmraparnîya (translation: Sri Lankan lineage), but there is no indication that this referred to any change in doctrine or scripture, while it is very obvious that it refers to geographical location. At some point prior to the *Dipavamsa* (4th century) the name was changed to Theravada, probably to reemphasize the relationship to the original Sthaviravada, which is the Sanskrit version of the Pali term Theravada.

The Theravada school is the only remaining school which is exclusively aligned with the philosophic outlook of the early schools. However, significant variation is found between the various Theravadin communities, usually concerning the strictness of practice of Vinaya and the attitude one has towards Abhidhamma.

Both these, however, are aspects of the Vibhajjavadin recension of the Tipitaka, and the variation between current Theravada groups is mainly a reflection of accent or emphasis, not content of the Tipitaka or the commentaries. The Tipitaka of the Theravada and the main body of its commentaries are believed to come from (or be heavily influenced by) the Sthaviravadins and especially the subsequent Vibhajjavadins.

Most of the early schools of Buddhism have been lost. Therevada, the tradition of 'The Elders' is one surviving model. Schools such as Zen trace their roots through, Ch'an and the Indian monk Bodhidharma, who was a patriarch of the Dhyana School of direct meditation. Tantra and other forms of Esoteric Buddhism trace their heritage to earlier or other lineages of enlightened Buddhas.

THERAVADA

Theravada (pronounced - more or less - "tay-rah-vah-dah"), the "Doctrine of the Elders," is the school of Buddhism that draws its scriptural inspiration from the texts of the Pali Canon, or Tipitaka, which scholars generally accept as containing the earliest surviving record of the Buddha's teachings. For many centuries, Theravada has been the predominant religion of continental Southeast Asia (Thailand, Myanamar/Burma, Cambodia, and Laos) and Sri Lanka; today Theravada Buddhists number over 100 million worldwide. In recent decades Theravada has begun to take root in the West.

DEFINITION FROM ACCESS TO INSIGHT

CH'AN AND ZEN

Started from the Dhyana School by the conglomerate, legendary Bodhidharma whose attributed works include:

1. The Outline of Practice
2. The Bloodstream Sermon
3. The Wake-Up Sermon
4. The Breakthrough Sermon

The lineage of this school comes from a legendary sermon of the Buddhas which consisted of raising a flower, leading to the instant understanding of one attendee who then founded what was to become Zen.

SHINGON

Japanese school of esoteric Buddhism started by Kukai who studied esoteric Buddhism in China from 804 to 806. He developed his own synthesis of esoteric practice and doctrine, centred on the cosmic Buddha Vairocana, held to be identical with the Shinto sun goddess Amaterasu. Kukai combined the cosmic Buddha Vairocana with the Ultimate Reality, thus producing a composite figure embodying all being.

Most notable treatise is the Sokushin-jobutsugi (The Doctrine of Becoming a Buddha with One's Body during One's

Earthly Existence). Two sacred mandalas presenting diagramatically the two aspects of Vairocana, the Diamond World (kongo-kai) and Womb World (taizo-kai) are placed on Shingon altars.

PURE LAND

Pure Land Buddhism is based upon the Pure Land sutras first brought to China circa 150, which describe Amitabha, an ancient Buddha. This concept personified or otherwise can be translated variously but is usually shortened to "Amituo" or "Amitofo" in Chinese, "Amida" in Japanese and "Amito" in Korean. Although the Infinite Life Sutra, or Longer Pure Land Sutra, was translated into Chinese by the royal Kuchean monk Po-Yen as early as 258, the Pure Land school first became prominent with the founding of a monastery upon the top of Mount Lushan by Hui-yuan in 402. It spread throughout China quickly and was systematized by Shan-tao (613-681). The philosophy spread to Japan and slowly grew in prominence.

Honen Shonin (1133-1212) established Pure Land Buddhism as an independent sect in Japan, known as Jodo Shu. Today Pure Land is the dominant form of Buddhism in Japan. Contemporary Pure Land traditions see the Buddha Amitabha preaching the Dharma in his buddha-field (sa. buddhakchetra), called the "Pure Land" or "Western heaven", a region offering respite from karmic transmigration. In such traditions, entering the Pure Land is popularly perceived as equivalent to the Attainment of Nirvana. In fact, the main idea behind Pure Land Buddhism is that Nirvana is no longer practical or possible to Attain in our present day.

Instead, devotion to Amitabha will gain one enough karmic merit to go to the Pure Land (reminiscent of Heaven) from which Nirvana will be easier to attain, because in this paradise there are no negative experiences so no new negative karma is created. Existing negative karma would disappear. Some Pure Land Buddhists have taught that in order for a devotee to be reborn in Amitabha's Western Paradise, they should chant or repeat a mantra or prayer to Amitabha as often as possible to reinforce a proper and sincere state of mind (ex:

J. Namu Amida butsu). This fairly simple form of veneration has contributed greatly to its popularity, especially in Japan.

Yogacara (also known as *Cittamatra*) is a philosophical school that has its origins in India with the monk Asanga who worked alongside his brother, arya Vasubandhu to compile a set of texts on teachings passed to him from the Bodhisattva Maitreya. The teachings have several important elements to them that have influenced many schools of practice, especially the Zen schools and the Nyingma lineage of Tibetan Buddhism.

The first important aspect of Yogacara, which lead to its alternative name Cittamatra ("mind only"), is the relation of phenomena (dharmas) to the mind. The Yogacarins point out that the only way we know of the existence of phenomena is from a subjective perception of them. It is only through the six senses (sight, hearing, smell, taste, touch and thought) that a human is aware of anything. In a similar way to the Idealists such as Bishop Berkeley, the Yogacarins ask "how do we know there's actually an objective world 'out there'? What is its relation to the mind?"

Buddhist philosophy of the mind normally breaks the mind and body into eighteen parts, called the *dhatus*. We are aware of six different kinds of phenomena. These are objects of sight, hearing, smell, taste, touch and thought. Objects of thought include discursive thoughts, emotions etc. The mind that percieves these can therefore be broken down into six 'sense-minds', one for each sense object. In addition, there are six organs of perception; the eyes, ears, nose, tongue, body and mind-organ. The yogacarins state that the object sensed and the respective sense-organs are intimately linked, and in fact arise from the same cause.

The analysis of how they arise is linked to another important concept the Yogacara introduced; the storehouse consciousness (*alayavijnana*). This answers the question of 'where are karmic seeds (*bija*) stored before coming into fruition?' Since there is a delay between most actions and their corresponding results, the mental karmic seed that will produce a result in the future must reside somewhere. The storehouse consciousness is the Yogacarin's answer to this. The *alayavijnana* is where the collection of seeds resides, and also answers the questions relating to the eighteen dhatus. A single karmic seed that comes into fruition grows from where it is stored in the mind-stream's alaya, and produces "both" the sense consciousness and the object it is consciousness. In this way the eighteen dhatus grow from the alaya and therefore all parts of being arises from their own storehouse consciousness under the influence of the karma they have accrued.

In addition to the seven parts of the mind (six senses, plus *alaya*) the Yogacarins posit another part of the mind, the conceptual mind: the "manas". This is the parts of the mind-stream that intellectualise and discriminate phenomena in an incorrect, ignorant way, and sees phenomena as being objectively real and separate from the being that perceives them. One more important concept taught by the Yogacara is the three levels of truth. There can be said to be three levels of understanding. The first is the completely erroneous view of phenomena having self nature - an objective, permanent nature that is not dependent. The second view, which is correct according to the relative truth of how things function, is that phenomena are subject to dependent origination.

All phenomena arise from causes; the mechanism by which this happens is therefore the fruition of the seeds held in the alayavijnana. Then there is the third level of truth, which is the ultimate nature of reality according to the Yogacara. This is that consciousness is the ultimate nature of things, since it is consciousness that gives rise to them. There is nothing that does not ultimately come from consciousness. This is the Yogacara interpretation of emptiness. There are several misconceptions about the Yogacara School. The first is that all things exist in some kind of cosmic consciousness. This is the view of some Hindu schools, for example, but it is not the Yogacara view. Each mind-stream has its own separate alaya, and the extent to which the experiences of any two beings overlap (which is an important question with relation to the six realms of existence) is due to the extent that the karma of those two beings. Similar karmic patterns in the mind produce an experience that is similar.

The second is that the school is a completely idealistic one; that physical reality doesn't exit at all. This is incorrect, since on the relative level they do exist. It is their origin that is tied to the mind; as no object arises without the storehouse consciousness producing it alongside the sense organs and sense consciousnesses to perceive it. Buddhist philosophy is the branch of Eastern philosophy based on the teachings of Gautama Buddha (c. 563 BCE- c. 483 BCE). Buddhist philosophy deals extensively with problems in metaphysics, phenomenology, ethics, and epistemology. From its inception, Buddhism has had a strong philosophical component. Buddhism is founded on the rejection of certain orthodox philosophical concepts, in which the Buddha had been instructed by various teachers. Buddhism rejects atheism, theism, monism, and dualism alike.

The Buddha criticized all concepts of metaphysical being and non-being, and this critique is inextricable from the founding of Buddhism. Particular points of Buddhist philosophizing have often been the subject of disputes between different schools of Buddhism. Metaphysical questions such as "Is there a god?" and "Does the soul (*Atman*) really exist?" have divided the Buddha's followers even during his own lifetime, and epistemological debates over the proper modes of evidence have always been lively in Buddhism. Readers should note that theory for its own sake is not valued in Buddhism, but theory pursued in the interest of enlightenment for oneself or others is fully consistent with Buddhist values and ethics.

BUDDHISM AS PHILOSOPHY

Some have asserted that Buddhism as a whole is a philosophy rather than a religion. Proponents of such a view may argue that (a) Buddhism is non-theistic (i.e., it has no special use for the existence or nonexistence of a god or gods) or atheistic and (b) religions necessarily involve some form of theism. Others might contest either part of such an argument.

Other arguments for Buddhism "as" philosophy may claim that Buddhism does not have doctrines in the same sense as other religions; the Buddha himself taught that a person should accept a teaching only if one's own experience verifies it.

Arguments against Buddhism as a philosophy might call attention to the way Buddhism's pervasive inclusion of supernatural entities (not "gods" in the sense of Western monotheism, of course), to what most scholars identify as worship practices (ceremonial reverence of saints, etc.), to Buddhism's thoroughly developed hierarchies of clergy (not usually characteristic of a "philosophy"), and its overall religious organization. A third perspective might take the position that Buddhism can be practiced either as a religion or as a philosophy. A similar distinction is often made with reference to Taoism.

Lama Anagorika Govinda expressed it as follows in the book *A Living Buddhism for the West*:

"Thus we could say that the Buddha's Dharma is, as experience and as a way to practical realization, a religion; as the intellectual formulation of this experience, a philosophy; and as a result of self-observation and analysis, a psychology.

Whoever treads this path acquires a norm of behavior that is not dictated from without, but is the result of an inner process of maturation and that we - regarding it from without - can call morality."

It should also be noted that in the South and East Asian cultures in which Buddhism achieved most of its development, the distinction between philosophy and religion is somewhat unclear and possibly quite spurious, so this may be a semantic problem arising in the West alone.

PHILOSOPHICAL AREAS ADDRESSED IN BUDDHISM

Decisive in distinguishing Buddhism from what is commonly called Hinduism is the issue of epistemological justification. The schools of Indian logic recognize a certain set of valid justifications for knowledge, while Buddhism recognizes a smaller set. Both accept perception and argument, for example, but for the orthodox schools (of Hinduism), the received textual tradition (e.g., the Vedas) is in itself an epistemological category equal to perception and argument (although this is not necessarily true for some of the non-orthodox schools, like Vedanta). Thus, in the orthodox schools, if a claim was made that could not be substantiated by appeal to the textual canon, it would be viewed as ridiculous as a claim that the sky was green.

Buddhism, on the other hand, rejected an inflexible reverence of accepted doctrine. As the Buddha said:

Do not accept anything by mere tradition... Do not accept anything just because it accords with your scriptures... Do not accept anything merely because it agrees with your pre-conceived notions... But when you know for yourselves - these things are moral, these things are blameless, these things are praised by the wise, these things, when performed and undertaken, conduce to well-being and happiness - then do you live acting accordingly -The Kalama Sutta, *Anguttara Nikaya* II.65

METAPHYSICS AND PHENOMENOLOGY

Issues Arising from the Doctrine of Anatta

In earliest Buddhism and today still in Theravâda and the Madhyamaka, any metaphysical essence or being underlying the play of phenomenal experience is rejected. No "soul" or permanent self was recognized, and the perception of a continuous identity was held to be an illusion. Any feeling whatsoever, any perception whatsoever, any mental processes whatsoever, any consciousness whatsoever - past, future, or present; internal or external; blatant or subtle, common or sublime, far or near; every consciousness - is to be seen as it actually is with right discernment as "This is not mine. This is not my self. This is not what I am." - The Anattalakkhana Sutta, Samyutta Nikaya XXI.59

From within the context of the Madhyamaka, we find Candrakirti:

"Self is an essence of things that does not depend on

others; it is an intrinsic nature. The non-existence of that is selflessness". - Bodhisattvayogacaryâcatuhúatakatikâ, 256.1.7

This anti-essentialist teaching, known as *Anatta*, brought up many questions. If there is no *Atman* or Brahmana underlying the objects and events of the universe, how could they be explained? What gave them their existence? And if there was no "self", who makes the decisions we think we make, and what gets reincarnated? Early Buddhist philosophers and exegetes created a pluralist metaphysical and phenomenological system in which all experiences of people, things, and events, can be broken down into smaller and smaller perceptual or perceptual-ontological units called dharmas.

These dharmas (roughly synonymous with "phenomena") were interpreted differently by different schools: some held they were real, some held only some were real, some held all were illusory, some held they were empty; some held they were intrinsically associated with suffering, etc.

Other debates in metaphysics and phenomenology include the issue of the Pudgala, or "person", which was inserted by the Pudgalavada School to replace the *Atman* as that which transmigrates and that which carries the burden of karma from one life to another. Other schools made unsurprising objection to this. There were further sub-debates regarding whether the *pudgala* was real or illusory or something in between.

The Yogacara School, somewhat later, would later elevate the mind to act as a substitute for Brahmana, much as the Pudgala replaces the *Atman*. In many or all of these debates, some would point out the irony of pursuing questions which the Buddha was often prone to refuse to answer, on the grounds that they were non-conducive to enlightenment.

DEPENDENT ORIGINATION

The original positive Buddhist contribution to the field of metaphysics is pratîtyasamutpâda, which arises from the

Buddhist critique of Indian theories of causality. It states that events are not predetermined, nor are they random, and it rejects notions of direct causation owing to the need for such theories in the Indian context to be undergirded by substantialist metaphysics. Instead, it posits the arising of events under certain conditions which are inextricable, such that the units in question at no time have independent existence.

This being, that becomes.

From the arising of this, that arises.

This not being, that does not become.

From the ceasing of this, that ceases. -*Samyutta Nikaya* i.28

Pratityasamutpada goes on to posit that certain specific events, concepts, or realities are always dependent on other specific things. Craving, for example, is always dependent on, and caused by, emotion. Emotion is always dependent on contact with our surroundings.

This chain of causation purports to show that the cessation of decay, death, and sorrow is indirectly dependent on the cessation of craving, and ultimately dependent on an all-encompassing stillness.

Nâgârjuna, one of the most influential Buddhist philosophers, asserted a direct connection between, even identity of, dependent origination, *Anatta*, and *úûnyatâ*. He pointed out that implicit in the early Buddhist concept of dependent origination is the lack of any substantial being (*Anatta*) underlying the participants in origination, so that they have no independent existence, a state identified as emptiness (*úûnyatâ*), or emptiness of a nature or essence (*sva-bhâva*). This element of Nâgârjuna's thought is relatively uncontroversial, but it opens the way for his identification of *samsâra* and Nirvana, which was revolutionary.

INTERPENETRATION

This doctrine comes from the Avatamsaka Sutra and its associated schools. It holds that all phenomena are intimately connected. Two images are used to convey this idea. The first is known as Indra's net. The net is set with jewels which have the extraordinary property that they reflect all of the other jewels. The second image is that of the world text.

This image portrays the world as consisting of an enormous text which is as large as the universe itself. The 'words' of the text are composed of the phenomena that make up the world. However, every atom of the world contains the whole text within it. It is the work of a Buddha to let out the text so that beings can be liberated from suffering. This idea was enormously influential on the Japanese monk Kûkai in founding the Shingon school of Buddhism.

ETHICS

Although there are many ethical tenets in Buddhism that differ depending on whether one is a monk or a layman, and depending on individual schools, the Buddhist system of ethics can always be summed up in the Eightfold Path. And this, monks, is the noble truth of the way of practice leading to the cessation of suffering - precisely this Noble Eightfold Path - right view, right resolve, right speech, right action, right livelihood, right effort, right mindfulness, and right concentration. -Samyutta Nikaya LVI.11

The purpose of living an ethical life is to escape the suffering inherent in (unenlightened) worldly life. Although early Buddhism (Hinayana) is contrasted with later Buddhism (Mahayana) in that the latter emphasizes striving for the enlightenment of all (apparent) beings rather than simply oneself, in neither case can the motivation for ethical living be called 'selfish', because Buddhist doctrine holds the notion of a 'self' to be illusory. Buddhist teachings claim that there is no real difference between us and others; therefore one should attempt to increase the happiness of all living things as eagerly as one's own. This is why many Buddhists choose to be vegetarians.

DEVELOPMENT OF BUDDHIST PHILOSOPHY

The philosophical outlook of Earliest Buddhism was primarily negative, in the sense that it focused on what doctrines to reject more than on what doctrines to accept. This dimension has been preserved by the Madhyamaka School. It includes critical rejections of all views, which is a form of philosophy, but it is reluctant to posit its own. Only knowledge that is useful in achieving enlightenment is valued. The cycle of philosophical upheavals that in part drove the diversification of Buddhism into its many schools and sects only began once Buddhists began attempting to make explicit the implicit philosophy of the Buddha and the early Suttas.

After the death of the Buddha, attempts were made to gather his teachings and transmit them in a commonly agreed form, first orally, then also in writing (The Tripitaka). In addition to collecting the Buddha's speeches and rules for monastic life (Vinaya), monks soon undertook to condense what they considered the essential elements of Buddhist doctrine into lists of categories, provided with extensive commentary. This process took shape from about the 2nd century BCE to probably the 2nd century CE.

LATER DEVELOPMENTS

Very soon after, additional teachings began to be added to the list of important Buddhist texts and many of these altered and refined Buddhist philosophy.

COMPARISON WITH OTHER PHILOSOPHIES

Arthur Schopenhauer in his "World as Will and Idea" presented a description of suffering and its cause in a Western garb. Baruch Spinoza, though he argued for the existence of a permanent reality, asserts that all phenomenal existence is transitory. In his opinion sorrow is conquered "by finding an object of knowledge which is not transient, not ephemeral, but is immutable, permanent, and everlasting." Buddhism teaches that such a quest is bound to fail. David Hume, after a relentless analysis of the mind, concluded that consciousness consists of fleeting mental states. Hume's Bundle theory is a very similar concept to *Anatta*.

9

Philosophy of Mahayana Buddhist School

According to tradition three Buddhist Councils were held to resolve the doctrinal differences among Buddhist leaders. Only regarding the fourth that was held in Kashmir there is historical evidence. From then nowadays Buddhism came to be divided into the Mahayana and Hinayana schools. The Brahmins and their lay supporters had by now largely turned away from the older gods. In north-western India the rule of Greeks, Sakas and Kushans in turn threw open the gates to the west. It was these new elements that sought a new outlook in Buddhism. Thus the claim arose that a new Great Vehicles (Mahayana) was found would carry many souls to salvation.

Mahayana soon became popular in many parts of India as it fitted with the mood of the times and the needs of many simple people better than did the lesser Vehicle (Hinayana). The lesser Vehicle remained intact in ceyton and soon in Thailand and other parts of South-East Asia it became the national religion. Mahayana on the other hand it self (soon divided by various schisms) was carried by successior of Indian monks to China and thence to Japan. Regarding Mahayana's chronological authenticity it is generally held that it originated around the first century B.C. in Andhra. Soon it was expounded by a group of Buddhist philosophers.

The outstanding among them was nagarjuna. It was he who conceived the doctrine of the void (Sunyata) meaning that every thing which is around us is emptiness and whatever we perceive is mere illusion. This void is in fact the Nirvana or end to the cycle of birth and rebirth which every Buddhist secks.

A new feature of the Manayana Buddhism is the concept of the future Buddha. The Buddha himself probably taught that he was the last of the long succession of earlier Buddhas. The carvings on the stupas of Barhut and Sanchi depict crowds of worshippers before the symbols of the Buddha. Little later sculptors began to carve images of the Buddha himself. Soon the Buddhist sects took to worshipping images under the new (foreign) rulers of north-western India. Zoroastrianism and Buddhism came in contact and probably through this the idea of future Buddha became part of the orthodox Buddhists. Thus the cult of Maitreya or the future Buddha was widespread among al Buddhist sects by the time Menander came to Patliputra.

Romila Thapar holds the view that this aspect of Maitreya Buddha had its origin out side India. The Maitreya Buddha saves the world. This idea is further linked to the concept of the suffering saviour of the Bodhisattva who redeems humanity through his own suffering. In these twin concepts we clearly see the beliefs that were current in Palestine of the day. These belief reappear in later day Christianity as Jesus Christ the son of God, who was born to redeem the suffering of man and the future promise of second coming. The concept of the Maitreya Buddha came to be linked with the older conception of Buddhism, the previous incarnations of Buddha known as *Bodhisattavas*. The *Bodhisattava* concept reached its consummation with the final birth of Gautama in the Sakyas. However as Maitreya and other unnamed Buddhas after him are yet to come there must be *Bodhisattavas* existing in the universe.

These *Bodhisattavas* might be adored and prayed with out any misgiving. Thus the *Bodhisattava* doctrine believed in theheavens filled with mighty forces of goodness and presented Buddhism with a new my theology. It was this development that constituted the hall mark of Mahayana the

Great vehicle. The universe of the Great vehicle contains numerous *Bodhisattava*. The chief of them from the earthly point of view is avalokitesvara padmapani. His special attribute is compassion. Vajrapani a sterner *Bodhisattava* is for the sin and evil. The great Maitreya the future Buddha is worshipped as *Bodhisattava*. Every thing from the humblest worm onwards is in a sense a *Bodhisattava* since all beings will attain Nirvana and become the Buddha.

The great Vehicle was not content with creating this pantheon of noble and beneficent *Bodhisattavas*. It was claimed that Gautam Buddha was not a mere man but the earthly expression of a mighty spiritual being. The Buddha's Body of bliss is the presiding deity on the most important Mahayana heaven Sukhavati where they are reborn in the buds of lotuses which rise from a lively lake before the Buddha's throne. This divine Buddha is usually called Amitabha or Amitayus. He too shares the compassion of the *Bodhisattava*. The Mahayana sect produced soon new versions of the Pitakas of scriptural texts of Buddhism they are all writings in Samskrit which became the official language of Mahayana. Many of these texts are ostensibly sermons of the Buddha.

The new Buddhist philosophical school of Mahayana came into existence during the 200 B.C. 300 A.D. period. Asvaghosha's name is associated with the school. Some of his famous works contain the philosophy of Mahayana. The book called Sraddhotpada-Sastra is attributed to him. Mahayana doctrine has two philosophical schools Madhamika and Yogachara. For quite some time Buddhism began to slowly develop into a theistic religion with the Buddha as the object of the cult. Exponents of the Madhyamika were Nagarjuna and his disciple Aryadeva. It was with Nagarjuna that Mahayana developed its own system of philosophy. Later aryadeva write a commentary on the work. It appears from evidence that the Satavahanas were great patrons of Buddhism.

The philosophy of Madhyamika is commonly characterized as Sunyavada-the philosophy of relativism. According to this the phenomenal world is a mere illusion from the view-point of ultimate truth. The second school called Yogacara is of later origin two brothers Asanga and Vasubandhu are generally believed to have been the first exponents of this system. This school also formulates two kinds of Truths-the Ultimate and the Relative and looks upon phenomenal world as an illustion. It asserts however that this illusion is mental illusion and therefore considers consciousness as real.

There is nothing strange about the emergence of Mahayana. The earlier form of Buddhism was rather arid unlike the Mahayana. The Mahayana requires us to take part in the world and evolve new social and religious ideals. The Mahayana happens to be more emotional and filling than Hinayana which reduces Nirvana and ethical life to great aridity. The Mahayana Buddhism is theistic similar to the theistic beliefs of Shaivism and Vaishnavism preaching loving devotion to personal God whom the devotee loves with all his heart and easy spontaneous grace. On the metaphysical side it led to a school of thought similar to the conception of an absolute with regard to which all determination would prove to be negation. Reason and language only applied to finite and nothing can be said of the infinite.

The different forms of Buddhism can be understood by becoming familiar with the two major schools that arose out of the Buddha's basic teachings:

The two major schools of Buddhism, Theravada and the Mahayana, are to be understood as different expressions of the same teaching of the historical Buddha. Because, in fact, they agree upon and practicing the core teachings of the Buddha's Dharma. And while there was a schism after the first council on the death of the Buddha, it was largely over the monastic rules and academic points such as whether an enlightened person could lapse or not. Time, culture and customs in the countries in Asia which adopted the Buddha-dharma have more to do with the apparent differences, as you will not find any animosity between the two major schools, other than that created by healthy debate on the expression of and the implementation of the Buddha's Teachings.

THERAVADA (THE TEACHINGS OF THE ELDERS)

In the Buddhist countries of southern Asia, there never arose any serious differences on the fundamentals of Buddhism. All these countries - Sri Lanka, Cambodia, Laos, Burma, Thailand, have accepted the principles of the Theravada school and any differences there might be between the various schools is restricted to minor matters. The earliest available teachings of the Buddha are to be found in Pali literature and belong to the school of the Theravadins, who may be called the most orthodox school of Buddhism. This school admits the human characteristics of the Buddha, and is characterised by a psychological understanding of human nature; and emphasises a meditative approach to the transformation of consciousness.

The teaching of the Buddha according to this school is very plain. He asks us to 'abstain from all kinds of evil, to accumulate all that is good and to purify our mind'. These can be accomplished by The Three Trainings: the development of ethical conduct, meditation and insight-wisdom. The philosophy of this school is straight forward. All worldly phenomena are subject to three characteristics - they are impermanent and transient; unsatisfactory and that there is nothing in them which can be called one's own, nothing substantial, nothing permanent. All compounded things are made up of two elements - the non-material part, the material part. They are further described as consisting of nothing but five constituent groups, namely the material quality, and the four non-material qualities - sensations, perception, mental formatives and lastly consciousness.

When an individual thus understands the true nature of things, she/he finds nothing substantial in the world. Through this understanding, there is neither indulgence in the pleasures of senses or self-mortification, following the Middle Path the practitioner lives according to the Noble Eightfold Path which consists of Right View, Right Resolve, Right Speech, Right Actions, Right Occupation, Right Effort, Right Mindfulness and Right Concentration. She/he realises that all worldly suffering is caused by craving and that it is possible to bring suffering to an end by following the Noble Eight Fold Path. When that perfected state of insight is reached, i.e.Nibanna, that person is a 'worthy person' an Arhat. The life of the Arhat is the ideal of the followers of this school, 'a life where all (future) birth is at an end, where the holy life is fully achieved, where all that has to be done has been done, and there is no more returning to the worldly life'.

MAHAYANA (THE GREAT VEHICLE)

The Mahayana is more of an umbrella body for a great variety of schools, from the Tantra school (the secret teaching of Yoga) well represented in Tibet and Nepal to the Pure Land sect, whose essential teaching is that salvation can be attained only through absolute trust in the saving power of Amitabha, longing to be reborn in his paradise through his grace, which are found in China, Korea and Japan. Ch'an and Zen Buddhism, of China and Japan, are meditation schools. According to these schools, to look inward and not to look outwards is the only way to achieve enlightenment, which to the human mind is ultimately the same as Buddhahood. In this system, the emphasis is upon 'intuition', its peculiarity being that it has no words in which to express it at all, so it does this in symbols and images. In the course of time this system developed its philosophy of intuition to such a degree that it remains unique to this day.

It is generally accepted, that what we know today as the Mahayana arose from the Mahasanghikas sect who were the earliest seceders, and the forerunners of the Mahayana. They took up the cause of their new sect with zeal and enthusiasm and in a few decades grew remarkably in power and popularity. They adapted the existing monastic rules and thus revolutionised the Buddhist Order of Monks. Moreover, they made alterations in the arrangements and interpretation of the Sutra (Discourses) and the Vinaya (Rules) texts. And they rejected certain portions of the canon which had been accepted in the First Council. According to it, the Buddhas are lokottara (supramundane) and are connected only externally with the worldly life. This conception of the Buddha contributed much to the growth of the Mahayana philosophy.

Mahayana Buddhism is divided into two systems of thought: the Madhyamika and the Yogacara. The Madhyamikas were so called on account of the emphasis they laid on the middle view. Here, the middle path stands for the non-acceptance of the two views concerning existence and nonexistence, eternity and non eternity, self and non-self. In short, it advocates neither the theory of reality nor that of the unreality of the world, but merely of relativity. It is, however, to be noted that the Middle Path propounded at Sarnath by the Buddha had an ethical meaning, while that of the Madhyamikas is a metaphysical concept.

The Yogacara School is another important branch of the Mahayana. It was so called because it emphasised the practice of yoga (meditation) as the most effective method for the attainment of the highest truth (Bodhi). All the ten stages of spiritual progress of Bodhisattvahood have to be passed through before Bodhi can be attained. The ideal of the Mahayana school, therefore, is that of the Bodhisattva, a person who delays his or her own enlightenment in order to compassionately assist all other beings and ultimately attains to the highest Bodhi.

The origins of the second major division within Buddhism are shrouded in uncertainty. What was to be called Mahayana, or the "Great Vehicle," did not originate with any one reforming individual or emerge at any specific time. It at least partially had its roots in a pan-Indian devotional movement (bhakti) that also had a dramatic impact on the Hindu traditions of India around 150 B.C.E. and in the centuries following. Mahayana is also sometimes traced back to the "Great Assemblists," or Mahasanghikas, but it seems that for many years, even centuries, monks who eventually became Mahayana lived and studied in the same monasteries as others.

Perhaps the best way to envision Mahayana Buddhism in its earliest years was as a set of new texts that introduced new doctrinal elements into Buddhism. Those who accepted the canonical legitimacy of these new texts were Mahayana. The doctrines put forward in these new texts were not, however, represented as new. Rather, they too were supposed to originate with the Buddha; they were regarded as "turnings of the wheel of dharma" that taught the deeper meanings of the Buddha's message for disciples who were more capable.

Chief among the distinctive teachings of Mahayana was a new conceptualization of the goal of Buddhism. In early Buddhism as well as in the subsequent Theravada tradition, the attainment of Nirvana was theoretically possible for anyone. But Buddhahood itself remained the unique feature of Gautama. The Mahayana Buddhists posited enlightenment and Buddhahood itself as the ultimate goal for all practitioners and regarded Nirvana as a lower attainment for those of a "lesser vehicle" (Hinayana). With this new idea regarding the goal of Buddhism came a radically different understanding of Buddhology. Gautama, for the Mahayana Buddhists, was but one of an innumerable set of Buddhas who populated the cosmos.

Each Buddha ruled a region, or "heaven" or "pure land," which was also populated with highly evolved spiritual beings known as Bodhisattvas. These Buddhas and Bodhisattvas were thought to be filled with compassion and with certain abilities and powers to help those who asked for it. One of the chief features of Mahayana Buddhism is its devotional quality, consisting of the worship of and prayers to these celestial Buddhas and Bodhisattvas. Integral to the new Buddhology that distinguishes the Mahayana is the doctrine of the "three bodies" or "three forms" (*rupas*) of the Buddha. The first is the "transformation body" (*nirmana kaya*), which refers to the physical emanations the Buddha sends out to this and other worlds.

The historical Buddha, Gautama, was one such emanation according to Mahayana Buddhism- a notion that also assumes that Gautama was always and already enlightened, being merely an earthly incarnation of a previously enlightened cosmic Buddha. Under this conception, Buddhas have the capability of sending out virtually infinite numbers of transformation bodies out of their compassion and urge to help all sentient beings everywhere. Each Buddha also has what is called an "enjoyment body" (*sambhoga kaya*), a subtle body of light that appears in that Buddha's heaven or pure land, a paradisiacal world populated with advanced practitioners and Bodhisattvas.

Conditions in such a land are highly conducive for the attainment of Buddhahood; one form of Mahayana Buddhist practice is to pray and perform other devotional activities in the hopes that one or another of the Buddhas will admit the devotee into his or her pure land after death. Finally there is what is called the "dharma body" of the Buddha, which refers to the ultimate nature of the Buddha's mind and to reality itself in its ultimate form. The dharma body includes the omniscience or perfect realization of wisdom in a Buddha's mind. It also includes the ultimate nature of reality itself, its "thusness" or "suchness."

Another innovation in Mahayana Buddhism was the superseding of the Eightfold Path with a new method (leading to a newly reconceived goal). This was what became known as the "Path of the Bodhisattva." The first step on this path was to attain what was termed bodhicitta, the "mind of enlightenment" or the motivating wish to attain Buddhahood out of compassion for all sentient beings. A key ingredient to bodhicitta and, indeed, a virtue that takes center stage in Mahayana Buddhism, is compassion (*karuna*), which, together with "loving kindness" (*maitri*) and wisdom (*prajna*), form a triad of the distinctive virtues characteristic of the *Bodhisattvas* ("beings of enlightenment," the ones who have attained bodhicitta) and the Buddhas as conceived by Mahayana.

Out of this driving wish for enlightenment, impelled by the altruistic intention to help end the suffering of others, the Mahayana practitioner takes various vows, swearing to live a life guided by compassion, and then engages in the "six perfections," each associated with a progressively higher stage of the Bodhisattva path. The first of these "perfections" (*paramitas*) is generosity, including the giving of material things, protection from fear, and the giving of dharma teachings themselves. In its most advanced form, the perfection of giving includes the willingness of the *Bodhisattva* to give up his or her own body if necessary. Also included under this perfection is giving in the form of what is known as "transfer of merit" (*parinamana*), the perpetual turning over to the benefit of others any karmic merit done by any meritorious act.

The second perfection is ethics (*sila*) and consists largely of avoidance of the ten basic misdeeds of body, speech, and mind (killing, stealing, sexual misconduct, lying, divisive speech, harsh speech, idle speech, coveting, ill will, and wrong views). Third is the perfection of patience (*kshanti*), specifically combating anger with compassion and loving kindness. The fourth perfection is joyful effort or "vigor" (*virya*), defined as taking joy in doing meritorious and compassionate acts. Fifth comes meditative concentration (*dhyana*) followed by the sixth perfection, wisdom (*prajna*). The "perfection of wisdom" consists of realizing the truths of the distinctive metaphysics that also defines Mahayana Buddhism. Especially associated with the great philosopher Nagarjuna (c. 150–250 C.E.) is the important doctrine of "emptiness," or shunyata.

Nagarjuna argued that, as a sort of universal extension of the earlier doctrine of "no-self," all phenomena are "empty" of inherent nature or self-existence. Persons and phenomena exist only dependently, not independently. Emptiness is thus not the ultimate ground of being but rather the insistence that there is no such ultimate, irreducible ground. Emptiness is not some thing but the absence of intrinsic existence to all things. But neither, argued Nagarjuna, does this mean that "nothing exists." Things do exist, but only dependently. The philosophical school associated with Nagarjuna's thought was called the "Middle Way" school (Madhyamika), positing neither nihilism nor eternalism but a median between the two.

Another important philosophical tenet of Mahayana Buddhism is the identity of *Samsara* and Nirvana. Liberation is not "outside" or "apart from" a world of suffering; they are not two separate realities. Both are equally "empty" of self-nature and exist, as all things, only dependently. While other traditions and schools of Buddhism also went from India to China, Korea, and Japan, it was Mahayana Buddhism that flourished and was further developed in those regions. Mahayana is thus sometimes called "northern Buddhism" in contrast to the predominantly Theravada traditions of "southern Buddhism."

Mahayana Buddhism in China was heavily influenced by the preexisting religious philosophies of Confucianism and Taoism and by the presuppositions of a culture already ancient, literate, and sophisticated by the time Buddhism was brought to it in the early centuries C.E.

Among the difficulties Buddhism faced in China were monasticism and celibacy, which were understood to be in opposition to the Chinese emphasis on filial piety and ancestor worship. Conversely, the Chinese readily embraced and further elaborated the Mahayana concept of all beings having a "Buddha nature," or the potential to achieve Buddhahood and enlightenment. By the fifth century C.E. different schools of Buddhism arose in China. Some of these were simply Chinese equivalents of Indian Buddhist schools. San-lun, or the "Three Treatises" school, was the Chinese version of Madhyamika, and Fa-hsiang, or "Characteristics of the Dharma" school, was the equivalent of the Indian philosophical tradition known as Yogacara. But also at about this time, distinctively Chinese schools of Buddhism arose that reflected indigenous cultural and religious emphases.

The importance of harmony, for example, produced schools like the T'ien-t'ai ("Heavenly Terrace"; Tendai, in Japan), which placed one text (in this case the Lotus Sutra) above all others and then organized the rest of the diverse Buddhist tradition into a hierarchically ordered synthesis. The T'ien-t'ai philosophy embraced the idea that Buddha nature exists in all things and that the absolute and phenomenal worlds are not ultimately different. Another school that attempted to harmonize the teachings of Buddhism into a syncretistic whole was the Hua-yan (Kegon, in Japan) school, which elevated the Avatamsaka Sutra to the highest place and oriented the rest of Buddhist texts and teachings around it. Of special importance, however, were two other schools that arose in China, spread to neighboring regions from there, and survive to the present.

The first of these was the "Pure Land" school (Ch'ing-t'u), a devotional and faith-based sect centering on the figure of Amitabha Buddha. Pure Land became the most popular form of the religion in China, Korea, and Japan, especially among the laity. Pure Land promises an easy path to salvation in the guise of rebirth into the heaven or pure land of Amitabha, where one will quickly become enlightened. The principal practice of this form of Buddhism has been to call upon the grace of this Buddha through repeating a formula known as nien-fo (nembutsu in Japanese). In its more radical forms, Pure Land has insisted that one must rely totally on the "other-power" of the Buddha and not at all on one's own efforts.

The second of the two most important schools that arose initially in China was that known as Ch'an, or Zen as it was termed in Japan. Deriving from a Sanskrit word for "meditation," the Ch'an/Zen tradition offers a stark contrast to the devotionalism of Pure Land. Traced back to an Indian monk-missionary named Bodhidharma, whose radical and uncompromising meditational techniques become legendary, the Ch'an/Zen tradition developed a simple but disciplined and demanding set of methods for directly intuiting one's own Buddha nature and achieving various levels of awakening (wu, or satori in Japanese). These methods included meditation, the "direct transmission" of wisdom from the mind of the enlightened teacher to that of the student, and the contemplation of riddles known as 'koans'.

10

Emergence of Buddhism and Basic Buddhist Teachings

Buddhism, founded in the late 6th century B.C.E. by Siddhartha Gautama (the "Buddha"), is an important religion in most of the countries of Asia. Buddhism has assumed many different forms, but in each case there has been an attempt to draw from the life experiences of the Buddha, his teachings, and the "spirit" or "essence" of his teachings (called dhamma or dharma) as models for the religious life. However, not until the writing of the Buddha Charita (life of the Buddha) by Ashvaghosa in the 1st or 2nd century C.E. do we have a comprehensive account of his life.

The Buddha was born in North India (ca. 563 B.C.E.) at a place called Lumbini near the Himalayan foothills, and he began teaching around Benares (at Sarnath). His era in general was one of spiritual, intellectual. and social ferment. This was the age when the Hindu ideal of renunciation of family and social life by holy persons seeking Truth first became widespread, and when the Upanishads were written. Both can be seen as moves away from the centrality of the Vedic fire sacrifice. Siddhartha Gautama was the warrior son of a king and queen. According to legend, at his birth a soothsayer predicted that he might become a renouncer (withdrawing from the temporal life).

To prevent this, his father provided him with many luxuries and pleasures. But, as a young man, he once went on a series of four chariot rides where he first saw the more severe forms of human suffering: old age, illness, and death (a corpse), as well as an ascetic renouncer. The contrast between his life and this human suffering made him realize that all the pleasures on earth where in fact transitory, and could only mask human suffering. Leaving his wife - and new son (Rahula or fetter) he took on several teachers and tried severe renunciation in the forest until the point of near-starvation. Finally, realizing that this too was only adding more suffering, he ate food and sat down beneath a tree to meditate. By morning (or some say six months later!) he had attained Nirvana (Enlightenment), which provided both the true answers to the causes of suffering and permanent release from it.

Now the Buddha ("the Enlightened or Awakened One") began to teach others these truths out of compassion for their suffering. The most important doctrines he taught included the Four Noble Truths and the Eight-Fold Path. His first Noble Truth is that life is suffering (dukkha). Life as we normally live it is full of the pleasures and pains of the body and mind; pleasures, he said, do not represent lasting happiness. They are inevitably tied in with suffering since we suffer from wanting them, wanting them to continue, and wanting pain to go so pleasure can come.

The second Noble Truth is that suffering is caused by craving - for sense pleasures and for things to be as they are not. We refuse to accept life as it is. The third Noble Truth, however, states that suffering has an end, and the fourth offers the means to that end: the Eight-Fold Path and the Middle Way. If one follows this combined path he or she will Attain Nirvana, an indescribable state of all-knowing lucid awareness in which there is only peace and joy. The Eight-Fold Path - often pictorially represented by an eight-spoked wheel (the Wheel of Dhamma) includes: Right Views (the Four Noble Truths), Right Intention, Right Speech, Right Action, Right Livelihood/Occupation, Right Endeavor, Right Mindfulness (total concentration in activity), and Right Concentration (meditation).

The Eight-Fold Path is pervaded by the principle of the Middle Way, which characterizes the Buddha's life. The Middle Way represents a rejection of all extremes of thought, emotion, action, and lifestyle. Rather than either severe mortification of the body or a life of indulgence in sense pleasures the Buddha advocated a moderate or "balanced" wandering life-style and the cultivation of mental and emotional equanimity through meditation and morality. After the Buddha's death, his celibate wandering followers gradually settled down into monasteries that were provided by the married laity as merit-producing gifts.

The laity was in turn taught by the monks some of the Buddha's teachings. They also engaged in such practices as visiting the Buddha's birthplace; and worshipping the tree under which he became enlightened (bodhi tree), Buddha images in temples, and the relics of his body housed in various stupas or funeral mounds. A famous king, named Ashoka, and his son helped to spread Buddhism throughout South India and into Sri Lanka (Ceylon) (3rd century B.C.E.). Many monastic schools developed among the Buddha's followers. This is partly because his practical teachings were enigmatic on several points; for instance, he refused to give an unequivocal answer about whether humans have a soul (*Atta/Atman*) or not. Another reason for the development of different schools was that he refused to appoint a successor to follow him as leader of the Sangha (monastic order). He told the monks to be lamps unto themselves and make the Dhamma their guide.

About the first century C.E. a major split occurred within the Buddhist fold-that between the Mahayana and Hinayana branches. Of the Hinayana ("the Lesser Vehicle") branch of schools, only the Theravada school (founded 4th century B.C.E.) remains; it is currently found in Sri Lanka and all Southeast Asian countries. This school stresses the historical figure of Gautama Buddha, and the centrality of the monk's life-style and practice (meditation). Theravada monks hold that the Buddha taught a doctrine of *Anatta* (no-soul) when he spoke of the impermanence of the human body/form, perception, sensations/feelings, consciousness, and volition. They believe, however, that human beings continue to be "reformed" and reborn, and to collect karma until they reach Nirvana. The Theravada school has compiled a sacred canon of early Buddhist teachings and regulations that is called the Tripitaka.

The Mahayana ("Greater Vehicle") branch of schools began about the 1st century C.E.; Mahayanists are found today especially in Korea, China, Japan, and Tibet. The three most prominent schools are Pure Land, Chan or Zen, and Tantra. Mahayana schools in general utilize texts called sutras, stressing that lay people can also be good Buddhists, and that there are other effective paths to Nirvana in addition to meditation - for instance the chanting and good works utilized in Pure Land. They believe that the Buddha and all human beings have their origin in what is variously called Buddha Nature, Buddha Mind, or Emptiness. This is not "nothing," but is the completely indescribable Source of all Existence; it is at the same time Enlightenment potential.

The form of the historical Buddha was, they say, only one manifestation of Buddha Nature. Mahayana thus speaks of many past and also future Buddhas, some of whom are "god-like" and preside over Buddha-worlds or heavenly paradises. Especially important are *bodhisattvas* - who are persons who have reached the point of Enlightenment, but turn back and take a vow to use their Enlightenment-compassion, -wisdom, and -power to help release others from their suffering. Mahayana canon says that finally there is no distinction between "self and other," or between *Samsara* (transmigration, rebirth) and Nirvana! Because of this the bodhisattva is capable of taking on the suffering of others in *Samsara* and of transferring his own merit to them.

Although Buddhism became virtually extinct in India (ca. 12th century C.E.) - perhaps because of the all-embracing nature of Hinduism, Muslim invasions, or too great a stress on the monk's way of life - as a religion it has more than proved its viability and practical spirituality in the countries of Asia to which it has been carried. The many forms and practices that have been developed within the Buddhist fold have also allowed many different types of people to satisfy their spiritual needs through this great religion. Buddhism is a set of practice and spiritual development believed to lead a person towards the final realization of the true nature of life. Since it is devoid of the idea of worshipping a God, some people do not consider it as a religion.

However, like all religions, it does have the idea of "transcendence" (that is "going beyond" the ordinary consciousness) which is central to its teaching. Buddhism which was founded by Gautama Buddha (formerly known as Prince Siddhãrtha before his enlightenment) about 2500 years ago with about five followers in the beginning, has grown to about 350 million Buddhists around the world today. The tradition is characterized by non-violence, tolerance of differences, lack of dogma and the practice of meditation to experience inner peace. Indeed, these features have become relevant and has an appeal to the masses in the world we live today - the ever increasing dilemma and materialistic outlook and the growing insecurities around the world.

THE EMERGENCE OF BUDDHISM

Similar to this modern day scenario, these dilemmas and insecurities were also characteristic features way back in the 6th century BCE. Interestingly, the 6th century BCE is marked by religious upheavals in various parts of the world that saw the emergence of its contemporaries like Zoroastrianism in Iran, Taoism in China, and the subsequent emergence of heterodox religions like Buddhism, Jainism, Charvakas and the Ajavikas in the Indian subcontinent.

Historians have pointed out that in many parts of the world; the 6th century BCE was marked by the emergence and growth of urban centers. In the Indian context, many historians have contended that, apart from the conventional explanations that the masses were under the monopoly of the propagators of Brahmanism, the era also experienced the second urbanization. Indeed, the emergence trading centres and the subsequent emergence of urban centres, business guilds and commerce that were replacing pastoral life and placing individuals in wholly new situations might have brought about complications in their lives.

Earlier, their lives were governed by the Brahmanic beliefs and practices. However with the growing insecurities and the meaning of life and of being a person becoming a matter of renewed interest, Brahmanic religion could not provide much answer to the questions in everyday life. Hence, with people beginning to look for other means in solving their questions on life, this situation paved way for the emergence of many Shamanic (heterodox) religions of which Buddhism was one.

The founder, Gautama Buddha (Siddhãrtha Gautama) was a prince in a powerful Sakya Clan. And unlike many other nobles who were more focused towards governance, Prince Siddhãrtha was more concerned about the problems in life and the futility of the mortal soul. He believed that there is a way to end human suffering. His quest in pragmatically answering these fundamental questions of human life and death finally culminated in his renouncement of the world becoming a wandering ascetic at the age of twenty nine. After observing that his associations with learned holy men, his severe asceticism and his extreme self mortifications for six years were leading him nowhere near his intended goal, Siddhãrtha is said to have sat under a Bodhi tree with a resolve not to stop meditating until he found an answer to end suffering. It is under the Bodhi tree that Siddhãrtha attained "enlightenment" upon which he took up the title "Buddha" (one who is awake).

SERMONS OF BUDDHA

He shared his first sermon at a Deer Park near Benares with five holy men. This sermon embodies his four fundamental findings which he came to realize while struggling to attain enlightenment. They are the "Four Noble Truths" - There is suffering (Dukkha); the cause of suffering is desire/Attachment (*Trsna*); cessation of suffering is possible

(Nirvana); and the end to suffering can be attained by following the Noble Eightfold Paths (*Ariyo atthangiko maggo*). Under three percepts (morality, concentration and wisdom or insights), the Buddha prescribed the Noble Eightfold Paths as a "middle path" which was neither of the two extremes of suffering and pleasure.

They are the instructions to observe the right speech (*Samma Vaca*), right action (*Samma Kammo*), right livelihood (*Samma Ajivo*), right exertion or right effort (*Samma Vayamo*), right awareness (*Samma Sati*), right concentration (*Samma Samadhi*), right aspiration (*Samma Sankappo*), and right understanding (*Samma Ditthi*). The five holy men understood this immediately and became his disciples. This marked the beginning of the Buddhist community.

THE TENETS OF BUDDHISM

Buddhism's basic tenets are straightforward and pragmatic: there is no permanence; actions come with consequences; and there is possibility of change. Thus the addresses of Buddhism have a universal appeal irrespective of race, gender or nationality. It approaches life pragmatically enabling people to realize and utilize its teachings in order to be fully accountable for their lives and at the same time develop qualities of Wisdom. This development within the Buddhist tradition over centuries has created an alternative resource for all those wishing to follow a path which would ultimately culminate in Enlightenment or Buddha-hood.

Buddhism considers life as a constantly changing process. Unlike many religions which underline the fixation of fate by the divine authorities, Buddhists believe that one can always strive towards a change for the better. A practical approach to this is "meditation" which helps in developing a more positive state of mind. This is characterized by calmness, a more focused concentration, awareness, and a soothing emotion. Lay-followers of Buddhism abide by the five rules: do not kill, do not steal, do not indulge oneself in sexual misconduct, do not lie and do not take intoxicants.

Indeed, with these high ideals, Buddhism has significantly become a major World religion.

In 1991, the Thai Buddhist monk Phrakhru Pitak Nanthakhun sponsored a tree ordination in Nan Province. The ritual- conducted by twenty northern Thai monks and attended by close to 200 villagers, district officials, and journalists- formally established and sanctified a protected community forest for ten adjoining villages. The hour-long ceremony included chanting, sanctification of water, and wrapping a monk's orange robes around the largest remaining tree in the forest. The ten village headmen drank the holy water to seal their pledge to protect the forest. This ritual was one of numerous tree ordinations conducted by Buddhist monks in the 1990s in an effort to preserve the nation's rapidly depleting forest and protect people's livelihoods within it.

"Environmentalist monks" (phra nak anuraksa in Thai) form a small percentage of the total number of monks in Thailand. Nevertheless, their actions are visible in Thai society. They tackle urgent and controversial issues, such as deforestation and the construction of large dams, using modified Buddhist rituals and an ecological interpretation of Buddhist teachings. The effectiveness of environmentalist monks' projects remains unclear. Because these monks have only been active in Thailand over the past decade, not enough time has passed to assess projects aimed at stopping deforestation or cleaning polluted rivers. Their projects do not have sufficient scope to change what most environmentalists perceive as the destructive patterns of deforestation and growth-oriented economic and industrial development that have been dominant in Thailand since the 1960s.

Despite their small numbers and limited effectiveness, this group represents a case of people within a specific cultural setting who are implementing their own environmental concepts. They reinvent human relationships with nature in the face of what Arturo Escobar (1996) criticizes as the capitalization of nature worldwide. Their environmental seminars and their relations with local people illustrate the processes through which this small group of monks challenges the dominant trend of "ecological capital" (Escobar 1996). Despite a historical link between the Buddhist Sangha (the community of monks) and the Siamese state, these monks reject the state's definition of development and how it is implemented.

A high degree of environmental degradation has accompanied the government's growth and export-oriented development policies. The Thai forest has been cut down at one of the fastest rates in Asia. (According to official figures, forest cover in Thailand decreased from 72 percent of the total land in 1938 to 53 percent in 1961 and 29 percent in 1985 [England 1996:60]. Most environmental non-government organizations [NGOs] estimate that less than 15 percent of the country's total land area can be considered forest today.) Activist monks join a growing, popular environmental movement that questions the government's priorities and policies.

The contemporary development concept was first formulated in the mid-1800s when King Mongkut brought his kingdom into the global economy and restructured the Buddhist Sangha to legitimize the central government. Changing Thai governments have continued to use Buddhism to support their development agendas, especially since the 1960s. This process resulted in the rise of independent "development monks" in the 1970s and "environmental monks" in the late 1980s who challenged the government's concept of development, Buddhism's legitimation of it, and the suffering that they believed it caused the Thai people. Ironically, engaged Buddhism in Thailand emerged out of the same political-economic situation and close relationship with the state that it seeks to change.

Engaged Buddhism and Buddhist environmentalism are significant less because of their use of Buddhist principles than because they incorporate people's culture, values, and concerns for their livelihood and an understanding of historical, social, and political context into a creative approach to dealing with social problems.

DEVELOPMENT IN THAILAND

Siam, as Thailand was formerly known, remained a small, relatively isolated kingdom until 1855 when the Bowring Treaty with Great Britain formally brought it into the emerging global economy. Even as the Siamese attempted to limit foreign access to their markets, the colonial economies being developed in neighboring countries forced them to rethink their relations with the international community and begin to modernize. Initiated by King Mongkut (Rama IV, reigned 1851–1868), Siam introduced modern scientific concepts, economic practices, and education.

Mongkut also instituted religious reform in the 1830s and 1840s, and established the Thammayut Order of the Sangha. Similar to the modernization of other aspects of Thai society that Mongkut initiated, he rationalized the religion, aiming to eliminate practices that he felt were too ritualistic, metaphysical, or overly influenced by local or regional culture. Mongkut attempted to develop an interpretation of Buddhism consistent with Western science and learning, and this attempt marked the beginning of a fundamental epistemological shift in doctrinal Thai Buddhism.

The theoretical shift, which continues to have significant religious implications today, involved the rejection of the layered or hierarchical notion of truth which underlay traditional Buddhist teachings and its replacement with the notion of a single, universal, and all-encompassing truth. Mongkut linked the Sangha hierarchy with the absolute monarchy based in Bangkok, using it to legitimize the central government and weaken the influence of regional forms of religion and the power of regional political leaders. The legitimizing role that the Sangha played toward the state was strengthened as Bangkok expanded its control to the peripheral regions, using wandering forest monks to forge relations with remote rural peoples.

During the modernization period, Siam- renamed Thailand in 1932 established the three-fold concept of religion, monarchy, and nation, formalizing the connection between religion and state even further. Three Sangha Acts enacted by the Thai government in 1902, 1941 and 1962 brought the Sangha formally under the government's control. Each of these Acts created a state-imposed organizational structure for the Sangha that paralleled the current forms of government: in 1902, Siam was still a monarchy, and the hierarchical, centralized Sangha was headed by a Supreme Patriarch; in 1941, a decentralized Sangha structure was established that paralleled the democratic, constitutional monarchy in place at the time; in 1962, a top-down structure was reintroduced to match the autocratic government of Field Marshall Sarit Thanarat. Underlying the Acts, especially that of 1962, was an effort to garner support not only for the current government, but to legitimize its development policies as well.

The 1962 Act, in particular, aimed to use the Sangha to foster Prime Minister Sarit Thanarat's development agenda. After coming to power through a coup in 1958, Sarit aggressively pushed Thailand into an intensive development policy. Based on a Western model, Sarit promoted agricultural intensification and expansion toward an export-oriented, industrial economy. He encouraged a shift toward cash-cropping, bringing more forest land under cultivation, thus "civilizing" the wild forest and making it useful for humans. He also drew on traditional cultural values to promote his development agenda. Yoneo Ishi comments that Sarit thought that national integration must be strengthened to realise national development. To attain this goal he planned to start with fostering the people's sentiment for national integration through the enhancement of traditional values as represented by. the monarchy and Buddhism.

Using the concept of a single, absolute truth and a centralized Sangha organization, Sarit incorporated Buddhism into his development campaign through community development and missionary programs involving monks. These programs included thammathud, which sent monks to missionize in politically sensitive and economically poor border provinces, thammacarik, through which monks worked with the Department of Public Welfare among minority hill peoples to convert them from animism and to develop them, as well as community development programs sponsored by the two national Buddhist universities. Their aim was to strengthen the sense of national identity of peripheral peoples through Buddhism. These programs were- and are still today- supported and overseen by the government rather than the Sangha.

Governments following Sarit's have continued his aggressive industrial and export-oriented development and agricultural intensification policies. The results have been mixed: Thailand's growth until the economic crisis of 1997 was phenomenal, but the rate of environmental degradation, especially forest loss and pollution levels were among the highest in Asia. The gap between rich and poor widened and consumerism spread symbolizing by the growth of malls and McDonald's restaurants. Rural people's quality of life deteriorated as they moved from subsistence to market farming or left the countryside to seek work in urban factories. Through the use of a national, centralized concept of Buddhism, local culture and regional diversity were devalued.

DEVELOPMENT MONKS

Not all members of the Sangha agreed with either the government's development agenda or the involvement of monks in it. Beginning in the early 1970s, a handful of monks began independent rural development projects based on their interpretations of Buddhist teachings and in opposition to the capitalism promoted by the government. Of particular concern was the impact of the government's rapid development program on rural people's lives, and because of the government's emphasis on Buddhism as a form of nationalism, the erosion of traditional local Buddhist values. These monks feared the effects of growing consumerism and the dependence of farmers on outside markets.

Working in specific villages and addressing localized concerns and problems, these self-proclaimed "development monks" (phra nak phatthana) began conducting alternative development projects. One of the first development monks,

Phra Dhammadilok, (formerly Phra Thepkavi) formed his own NGO, the Foundation for Education and Development of Rural Areas (FEDRA), in 1974 just outside of Chiang Mai city in Northern Thailand (Darlington 1990). He realized that if people are hungry, cold, and sick, they will not and cannot devote their energy toward religious ends. Similarly, without spiritual development and commitment, they cannot overcome material suffering. FEDRA was established with the goal of developing spirituality and economics simultaneously.

The organization has four major objectives: 1) to support agriculture; 2) to encourage education (specifically that which is appropriate for the rural occupation of the farmers); 3) to promote religion; and 4) to develop local areas. "Local areas" means the people, land, institutions, traditions, and cultures of the rural Northern Thai. FEDRA's projects, located in over thirty-five villages today, include rice banks, buffalo banks (which provide buffaloes for poor farmers to plow their fields), credit unions, small revolving funds for agricultural development initiatives, integrated agriculture projects, and training for rural women in traditional handicrafts and sewing to enable them to supplement their agricultural incomes.

Unlike most government programs, the projects of Phra Dhammadilok and other development monks are aimed at local, rather than national or regional, development. They respond to immediate needs identified by the rural peoples themselves. Most of the development monks are from the areas in which they work, making them aware of the problems that rapid economic change has brought to rural people. They initiate projects designed for a specific location and problem using local cultural concepts and beliefs rather than pulling people into a national agenda that often ignores their needs and wants.

The emergence and growth of development monks paralleled and accompanied the rise of NGOs engaged in alternative development. NGOs since the 1970s have become a major social opposition movement within Thai society. Both secular NGOs and development monks emerged because of concern over the negative impacts of government development policies toward Thai society, culture, and environment. Together they have fostered the rise of a national environmental movement.

RISE OF THE ENVIRONMENTAL MOVEMENT

While development monks worked on a local level, the environmental movement grew on a national level in response to the government's economic development agenda. Many of the NGOs that were engaged in a search for alternative forms of development moved into environmental activism because of their concerns about the rate of environmental destruction and degradation caused by the policies of the central government. The causes for environmental degradation in Thailand are numerous, multifaceted, and virtually impossible to verify, but the coincidence of the nation's rapid economic growth from the 1960s until the mid-1990s and its high rate of forest loss and environmental problems during the same period fuel fierce debate.

The government, supported by international organizations such as the World Bank, argues that environmental destruction is primarily due to poverty, making economic growth imperative to solving environmental problems. Environmentalists, on the other hand, point to the inequalities underlying the government's development agenda as the root of much of the country's poverty. The government's policies, they argue, further promote destruction of the forest by encouraging agricultural intensification and capital growth through the exploitation of natural resources. The arguments are complex and beyond the scope of this chapter, but it are critical to note the range of positions surrounding environmental issues, even within the environmental movement.

The case of forest reserves and national parks illustrates the complexity of environmentalism in Thailand. Forests represent a major natural resource for the nation. Thailand invested heavily in logging until a ban was passed in 1989 after

300 people died in floods caused by deforestation and erosion. Debates still rage concerning the best way to manage the country's forests and the role of local people. The creation of national parks and forest reserves points to an environmental sensitivity on the part of the government. However, Few of the parks have been well managed.

No one agrees, even within the environmental movement, on the best way to manage the forest reserves and parks. On one side, local peoples living within the forests are blamed for destructive agricultural practices such as the silash-and-burn method. Advocates of this perspective argue that to preserve the remaining forest land these people should be moved out of the forest and trained in more environmentally-friendly methods. Others argue that it is the local people who can best look after the forest because their livelihoods depend on the natural resources that they contain. Therefore, rather than moving them out and allowing illegal loggers, hunters, and developers to take advantage of the changes, forest dwellers should be granted titles to the land that they have used for generations.

Environmentalist monks are also caught up in this debate. The majority takes the position that local forest dwellers will best protect the forest. A few others argue strongly that people must be removed from forests, especially watersheds, if there is to be any chance of protecting the remaining forested land. Thai environmentalism cannot be simplified into a two-sided debate. It entails multiple perspectives that are grounded, according to Philip Hirsch (1996), in a variety of material and ideological bases. As seen in the debate over forests, "environmentalism in Thailand needs to be seen as a multi-faceted discourse that deals with key social, economic, and political issues, including questions of control over resources by empowered and disempowered groups".

The environmental movement is composed of both a growing middle class with the time, resources, and influences to engage in environmental debates and rural farmers whose livelihoods depend on a healthy environment. Many middle-class Thais were educated abroad and therefore tend to approach these issues informed by a Northern concept of environmentalism. They see the need to protect and preserve nature from human impact. Most farmers see themselves as caretakers intimately familiar with and dependent upon a natural environment that includes people as part of a whole ecological system. Activist monks often use the latter argument as an example of the Buddhist concept of dependent origination, showing the interdependence of all things.

Even within the environmental movement, with its diverse interpretations supporting a wide range of economic and ideological interests, the influence of the concept of environmentalism in Thai society cannot be denied. NGOs carry significant weight within environmental discourse and influence government policy. Crucial environmental legisilation was enacted due to NGO activism and its popular support. For example, environmentalists won a major case in 1988 when the government decided to shelve the Nam Choen Dam in Kanchanaburi Province in response to protests by a diverse "coalition of local groups, farmers, journalists, Buddhist monks, students[,] and foreign environmentalists". This event, early in the environmental movement, demonstrated its potential, even though several other controversial dams have since been built.

EMERGENCE OF ENVIRONMENTALIST MONKS

It is within the context of debates over development and the rise of a diverse yet influential environmental movement that the self-proclaimed environmentalist monks emerged. Just as the environmental movement in Thailand grew out of the concerns of the NGOs about the ecological impact of government development policies and global ecological capitalism, the work of environmentalist monks evolved from that of independent development monks with concerns about local people's lives and spirituality. The first case in which Buddhist monks took an environmental position as monks involved the 1985 proposal to build a cable car up Doi Suthep Mountain and through Doi Suthep-Pui National Park in Chiang

Mai to promote tourism and economic development. Chayant describes the importance of the site for Northern Thai Buddhists:

> Doi Suthep is a mountain lying at the outskirts of the town of Chiang Mai, named for a seventh-century Lawa chieftain who converted to Buddhism, became a monk, and retreated from the world to the mountain which now bears his name. It is the location of an important Buddhist monastery, Wat Pra That, which houses a relic of the Buddha. Local people revere the mountain temple as a destination of spiritual significance for Buddhists. Since the construction of the temple in the fourteenth century, Doi Suthep has been an important pilgrimage site.

Reflecting the emerging environmental movement as a whole, opposition to the cable car project included students, people's organizations, social action groups, local media, and the general public of the city. Buddhist monks joined the protests as the cause gained publicity, and the full ecological and cultural impacts of building the cable car became apparent. Concerns were raised over the deforestation of the mountainside, especially in a national park that contained diverse plant, bird, and animal species. Arguments focused on environmental conservation versus economic development, but the motivation of the monks involved was mostly framed in terms of concepts of sanctity and the threat to a sacred Buddhist heritage site.

One monk in particular, Phra Phothirangsi, district head of the Sangha for the city of Chiang Mai, took a leading role in the fight against the cable car. He articulated a link between Buddhism and preserving trees and the forest beyond the immediate religious concern for a pilgrimage site. He argued that Buddhism and the forest cannot be separated. The cable-car case was the first time that Buddhist monks concerned about development incorporated environmental concerns in their actions. It is not typical of the kinds of actions in which environmentalist monks engage, however, because their fears involved the threat to a sacred Buddhist site as much as to Doi Suthep's ecosystem.

Nevertheless, it was the first time that Thai monks articulated the relationship between Buddhism and the natural environment as a motivation for social and political activism. They responded to a local social and historical situation as much as to an ecological issue; the threat to the sacred sites of Doi Suthep and Wat Pra That should not be underestimated as a powerful motivation for monks to move into political activism. As a result of this initial action, the Thai public was less surprised by other monks' more explicit environmental actions that followed.

Environmentalist monks cannot be described as forming a coherent social movement, although the potential for effecting social change clearly exists within their actions. Many of the monks engaged in environmental projects participate in an informal network that periodically brings them together to share their activities, concerns, obstacles, and successes and generate new ideas. It is through these Buddhist environmental seminars, sponsored by NGOs from five to ten times a year and involving from twenty to two hundred monk participants at a time that a new concept of human relations with nature and human responsibility toward nature is being constructed.

Despite the importance of the dialogue and exchange of ideas that take place at these seminars, the real construction of knowledge occurs through the interaction between monks and villagers as they implement their ecological projects within local environments and informed by local histories. The new social relations forged between monks and villagers, local officials and businessmen are as important as the localized ecological conservation efforts enacted. The work of two monks in Nan Province, northern Thailand, illustrates the process and the potential of the knowledge created by environmentalist monks. The first monk is Phrakhru Pitak Nanthakhun. He was born and raised in the village of Giew Muang, deep in the mountainous forest north of Nan City. His introduction to both environmental concerns and Buddhism arose out of an incident that occurred when he was a child.

Phrakhru Pitak witnessed his father shoot a mother monkey while hunting. Its baby clung to the mother's body, allowing itself to be captured. For three days, it cried from its cage, and when the boy finally released it, it went, still crying, straight to the skin of its mother hanging out to dry. This experience contributed not only to Phrakhru Pitak's later conservation work, but also was part of the reason that he ordained as a novice and has remained in the Sangha for almost 30 years. He realized that the teachings of the Buddha could help prevent such human-induced suffering. Growing out of his childhood experience with the baby monkey, Phrakhru Pitak incorporated a message of the environmental responsibility of humans into his teachings.

The urgency of preaching an environmental ethic became clearer to him as he witnessed the continual deforestation of the mountainous province. This was caused by logging concessions, illegal logging, silash-and-burn agriculture, overuse of the land by villagers, and the introduction of cash cropping. In the late 1980s, Phrakhru Pitak realized that preaching alone was not enough, that he needed to become actively engaged in conservation work. He visited Phrakhru Manas of Phayao Province, the monk generally credited with first performing tree ordinations to raise awareness of the value of the forests. Symbolically ordaining large trees in an endangered forest by wrapping monks' orange robes around them serves several purposes.

First, the action draws attention to the threat of deforestation. Second, the ritual provides the opportunity for the ecology monks and the laity who work with them (predominantly non-government environmentalists and development agents) to teach about the impact of environmental destruction and the value and means of conserving nature. Finally, the monks use the ritual to teach the Dhamma and to stress its relevance in a rapidly changing world. After visiting Phrakhru Manas, Phrakhru Pitak returned to Nan and began actively teaching villagers about environmental conservation, presenting slide shows, and holding discussions with people about the problems that they face due to deforestation. In 1990, he helped his home village formally establish a community forest encompassing about 400 acres of land.

The community forest was officially consecrated, and the villagers' commitment to preserving it was marked by the ordination of the largest remaining tree. Letters were sent to the surrounding villages announcing the creation of the protected area and making clear that it was forbidden to cut trees or hunt within it. The villagers also performed a ceremony requesting the local tutelary spirit to help them protect the forest and its wildlife. Phrakhru Pitak's work is not limited to his home village, but instead is constantly being expanded. Since 1990, he has sponsored several tree ordinations and phâ pâ ceremonies, which are traditionally used to give "forest robes" to monks, but in these cases they include giving seedlings for reforestation.

Lay people make religious merit through their donations and participation. In May 1993, an adapted traditional ceremony was held to preserve and lengthen the life of the Nan River in conjunction with a seminar to highlight the problems of desiccation and pollution that the province faces. A fish sanctuary was established at the site of the ceremony as well. By 1999, over thirty-nine community forests and 100 fish sanctuaries had been established by Phrakhru Pitak's NGO, the We Love Nan Province Foundation.

Phrakhru Pitak emphasizes basic Buddhist principles such as dependent origination and an interpretation of the Buddha's life that highlights a close relationship with the forest. His work is significant less because it incorporates Buddhism with ecological conservation principles than because he works closely with local villagers to identify and develop ways of dealing with the problems that they face. Phrakhru Pitak also encourages sustainable development practices such as integrated agriculture and growing food for subsistence rather than for sale.

Villagers are willing to try his approaches because of their respect for him as a monk and their awareness of his concern for their well-being. He is outspoken in his criticism of government-sponsored economic development promoting cash crops and the use of chemical fertilizers. Although Phrakhru Pitak has become famous and his NGO has grown to work in several villages and on multiple conservation projects, his work is still based in the specific environmental context of Nan Province. He has also inspired several other environmental projects, some sponsored by monks, others by lay people in their own villages. The case of Phra Somkit represents the second example of an environmentalist monk engaged in the construction of new knowledge.

Phra Somkit, unlike Phrakhru Pitak, only works in his home village. Similarly concerned with deforestation around his village, Phra Somkit began in the early 1990s to protect the village's forest. He went bindabat for forest, which is traditionally the practice of going on alms rounds providing lay people with the opportunity to make merit through giving food to monks. Phra Somkit's innovation entailed offering villagers the opportunity to make merit by donating land to the village temple. His father was the first to make an offering, presenting approximately an acre of hilly land that had been denuded through intensive cultivation of corn as a cash crop.

As a means to protect the forest, Phra Somkit began a model integrated-agriculture farm on land belonging to his temple. With the help of his younger brother, he maintains two fish ponds, raises free range chickens, and plants natural rice plots behind the temple. In the chaotic garden, pigs feed among numerous varieties of fruit trees. (Phra Somkit does not kill the fish, chickens, or pigs, raising them only to show villagers integrated agricultural methods.) He uses no chemical fertilizers, pesticides, or herbicides to demonstrate the benefits of natural farming to the villagers. On the land donated by his father, Phra Somkit has allowed the forest to regenerate naturally. In the almost ten years since the original gift, the forest has again grown dense. When I visited him in October 1999, Phra Somkit told me that he had counted close to 100 separate species of plants in the area.

A steady train of visitors come to see Phra Somkit's natural farm. In 1999, he received more than 1000 people from both Thailand and abroad. In September, ten British students spent one week volunteering on the farm to learn about integrated agriculture and sustainable development. Even more important is Phra Somkit's claim that all but about ten of the more than 100 families in the village have begun to implement some form of integrated agriculture. Phra Somkit strongly believes in the importance of education in the protection of the natural environment.

Using the mountainous terrain surrounding the village, he regularly takes children on ecology meditation walks. He works with them to consider the value of the plants and wildlife with which they share their environment. His belief is that through teaching children about human responsibility toward nature, they will take their lessons home and teach their parents. Phra Somkit undertakes all this work as part of what he perceives as his own responsibility as a Buddhist monk. Both Phra Somkit and Phrakhru Pitak illustrate ways in which environmentalist monks respond to changing national, regional, and global agendas concerning development and the environment within local contexts. Their motivation comes from witnessing environmental degradation and the suffering that it creates.

Actively seeking out the causes of this suffering has led them to redefine the underlying concepts of development and progress. Their awareness has led them to reexamine Buddhist teachings to support their work rather than follow any inherent ecological principles within the scriptures. As Buddhists have done since the Buddha's time, they adapt their interpretations and practices of the religion to fit a changing sociopolitical- and natural- environment, in this case, a result of modernization. Their work is an example of the concept of environmental imaginary formulated by Peet and Watts (1996), which they describe as follows:

There is environmental imaginary, or rather whole complexes of imaginaries, with which people think, discuss, and contend threats to their livelihoods. Notions like 'environmental imaginary,' which draw on the Marxist conception of consciousness, poststructural ideas about imagination and discourse, and, dare we add, environmental determinism from early-modern geography, open political ecology to considerations so different that we propose a new term to describe them- liberation ecology. The intention is... to raise the emancipatory potential of environmental ideas and to engage directly with the larger landscape of debates over modernity, its institutions, and its knowledges.

While environmentalist monks do not form a united, coherent movement, the collective implication of their work illustrates the concept of liberation ecology described by Peet and Watts. Their emergence within a particular historical, political, economic, and environmental context enables them to reassess Buddhism to fit that context and engage in debates over modernity and one of its primary institutions: development. They demonstrate a willingness to confront the traditional mutual support of the Sangha hierarchy and the state- a relationship that was itself a product of modernization. The impact of their individual projects may be impossible to assess, but the potential of their activism to challenge Thai Buddhists to rethink their religion, their society, and their place in both the political and the natural world cannot be denied.

Bibliography

Akira, Hirakawa, The *Formation of the Panca-Sila in Early Buddhism,* World Fellowship of Buddhists Review 32 (3): 8-23, 1995.

Aung, S.Z., *Introduction to the Compendium of Philosophy,* W.C.I.: Luzac and Company Ltd., 1956.

Aung, S.Z. & Davids, Rhys, *The Compendium of Philosophy,* London: Pali Text Society, 1910.

Bahm, A.J., *Philosophy of the Buddha,* New Delhi : Vikas Publishing House Pvt. Ltd., 1982.

Bapat, P.V., *2500 Years of Buddhism,* New Delhi : Publication Division, 1987.

Barua, Dipak Kumar, *Viharas in Ancient India: A Survey of Buddhist Monasteries,* Calcutta: Indian Publications, 1969.

Conze, Edward, *Thirty Years of Buddhist Studies,* Oxford: Cassirer, 1967.

David-Neel, Alexander, *Buddhism : Its Doctorine and its Methods,* London : B.I. Publications, 1977.

Dutt, Nalinaksh, Ed., *The Early Monastic Buddhism,* Calcutta : Firma K.L. Mukhopadhyaya, 1958.

Dutt, Nalinaksha, *Buddhist Sects in India,* Calcutta: Firma KLM, 1977.

Frauwallner, E., *The Earliest Vinaya and the Beginnings of Buddhist Literature,* Rome: Istituto Italiano per il Medio ed Estremo Oriente, 1956.

Guenther, Herbert V., *Philosophy and Psychology in the Abhidharma,* Berkeley, Calif.: Shambhala, 1976.

Horner, I. B., trans., *The Book of Discipline,* 6 volumes. London: Pali Text Society, 1938-1966.

Horner, I. B., *Women Under Primitive Buddhism,* Delhi: Motilal Banarsidass, 1975 (reprint).

Jacobson, Nolan Pliny, *Buddhism, the Religion of Analysis,* London: Feffer & Simons, 1974.

Kashyap, Bhikkhu J., *The Abhidhamma Philosophy,* Vol. I & II, Delhi and Varanasi : Bhartiya Vidya Prakashan, 1982.

Keith, A.B., *Buddhist Philosophy in India and Ceylon,* Delhi : Delhi Publishing Company, 1993.

Law, Bimala Churn, *A History of Pali Literature* (2 vols.), London: Kegan Paul, Trench, Trubner & Co., 1933.

Ling, Trevor, *The Buddha: Buddhist Civilization in India and Ceylon,* Baltimore: Penguin, 1976.

Mahathera, Narada, *A Manual of Abhidhamma,* Kandy : Sri Lanka, 1980.

Murti, T.R., *The Central Philosophy of Buddhism,* London : George Allen and Unwin Ltd., 1955.

Nyanaponika, Thera, *Abhidamma Studies,* Kandy, Sri Lanka: Buddhist Publication Society, 1965.

Nyanatiloka, *A Guide through the Abhidhamma Pitaka,* Kandy: Buddhist Publication Society, 1971.

Pande, G. C., *Studies in the Origins of Buddhism,* Allahabad, India: University of Allahabad, 1957.

Pardue, Peter, *Buddhism: A Brief Account,* New York: Macmillan, 1971.

Prebish, Charles S., *Buddhist Monastic Discipline: The Sanskrit Pratimoksa Sutras of the Mahasamghikas and Mulasarvastivadins,* University Park: Pennsylvania State University Press, 1975.

Thanissaro Bhikkhu, *The Buddhist Monastic Code: The Patimokkha Training Rules Translated and Explained,* Valley Center, CA: Metta Forest Monastery, 1994.

Varma, Vishvanath Prasad, *Early Buddhism and Its Origins,* Delhi: Munshiram Monaharlal, 1973.

Wagle, Narendra, *Society at the Time of Buddha,* New York: Humanities Press, 1967.

Watanabe, Fumimaro, *Philosophy and its Development in the Nikayas and Abhidhamma,* Delhi: Motilal Banarsidass, 1983.

Willemen, C., et., al., *Sarvastivada Buddhist Scholasticism,* Leiden: E.J. Brill, 1997.

Index